Active

Boundaries

Selected Essays and Talks

ALSO BY MICHAEL PALMER

BOOKS AND CHAPBOOKS

The Company of Moths
Codes Appearing
The Promises of Glass
The Danish Notebook
The Lion Bridge: Selected Poems 1972–1995
At Passages
An Alphabet Underground
For a Reading
Sun
Songs for Sarah
First Figure
Notes for Echo Lake
Alogon
Transparency of the Mirror
Without Music
The Circular Gates
C's Songs
Blake's Newton
Plan of the City of O

SELECTED TRANSLATIONS

Voyelles by Arthur Rimbaud
Jonah Who Will Be 25 in the Year 2000 (Film by Alain Tanner)
The Surrealists Look at Art (with Norma Cole)
Blue Vitriol by Alexei Parshchikov (with John High and Michael Molnar)
Theory of Tables by Emmanuel Hocquard
Three Moral Tales by Emmanuel Hocquard
in *The Selected Poetry of Vicente Huidobro*
in *The Random House Book of Twentieth-Century French Poetry*
in *Nothing the Sun Could Not Explain: 20 Contemporary Brazilian Poets*
in *Twenty-two New French Writers*

OTHER

Code of Signals: Recent Writings in Poetics, ed. Michael Palmer

Active Boundaries

Selected Essays and Talks

Michael Palmer

A NEW DIRECTIONS BOOK

Manufactured in the United States of America
New Directions Books are printed on acid-free paper
First published as a New Directions Paperbook 1111 (NDP1111) in 2008
Published simultaneously in Canada by Penguin Books Canada Limited

Library of Congress Cataloging-in-Publication Data

Palmer, Michael, 1943–
    Active boundaries : selected essays and talks / by Michael Palmer.
        p. cm.
    ISBN 978-0-8112-1754-5 (alk. paper)
    I. Title.
    AC8.P255 2008
    081—dc22

                                            2008008745

New Directions Books are published for James Laughlin
by New Directions Publishing Corporation
80 Eighth Avenue, New York, NY 10011

CONTENTS

Preface

WHAT

What to make of them now, these reflections and speculations over many years? Some certainly present an earlier perspective on the possibilities and achievements of the art, one that I have chosen not to modify to meet my current, equally partial, and partisan, understanding of things. So, let them stand as early evidence of insights, blind spots and prejudices. Many of the later texts speak to the struggle to seize the meaning of poetic making in light of the recent dark history of our criminal misgovernance, a period of corrosive, even murderous mendacity in international affairs, and cultural oblivion, cynicism and repression on the domestic front. Like Tu Fu, "I brood on the uselessness of letters," while remaining deeply convinced otherwise. Perhaps these essays and improvisations represent simply (simply!) an effort to articulate the necessity of the art in its most challenging manifestations, its truths in the eternal confrontation with the lies and the cynical indifference of power. That, in the face of a quite relentlessly materialistic culture which, nonetheless, remains rich in poetic activity, almost despite its hierarchy of values. (This morning, for example, I read the stunningly cursory obituary in the *New York Times* for Aimé Césaire, a Martinique-born poet and anticolonial activist of the profoundest international significance across a very long life.)

What determined and indeterminate gestures we fashion in pursuit of this art of difficult pleasures, fugitive perceptions and resistant meanings, an art that is in many respects essentially unknowable, its silences articulate, its freedoms perversely demanding. I once was certain that the famous wolfhound at Osip Mandelstam's back was Stalin. It was that of course, but was it not also poetry itself, hounding him toward a necessary resistance, a fated, oppositional stance? Was it not also a hound that he in turn pursued, up to the very moment of his extinction?

What is to be said of such necessity? It certainly expresses a need well beyond the secure gratifications and comforts of well-fashioned verse, and the praise such may elicit, well beyond any desire for fame or reward in the literary world, even well beyond, at its most dire, any promise of publication. It insists upon the efficacy of an imaginative power at language's limit, a power that perhaps only poetry, only some poetry, can claim, one that throughout history, by its harmonies and disharmonies, has caused even illiterate tyrants to pause and, at those moments just before sleep, to tremble.

I have sought in these pieces an active form that reflects a sometimes peripatetic (sometimes comically inert) life and mode of thought. Obviously they do not, and are not meant to, conform to academic models of style or presentation, though indeed a number have been produced at the invitation of academic institutions. It may be true that all writings *in* poetics by poets are most revealing in their contradictions and inconsistencies, as are all societies, and as are the writings of many philosophers and theorists. I have not attempted to impose an artificial consistency after the fact but instead have tried to allow the errancies, the impasses, the turns and returns of the process to reveal themselves, mirroring the ever-evolving, ever-elusive nature of the subject itself, our delusive recasting of the words of the street and the sea.

The subject? At the heart of the various influences, concerns and interests addressed here lies, quite obviously, the problematic of the lyric voice in turbulent times. The lyric: at once a singular voice and a multi-voiced part-song, replete with echoes; at moments, of necessity, anti-lyrical in the extreme. What?

A few pieces may appear anomalous, at least at first glance. "The Danish Notebook" was commissioned by the Danish fiction writer and editor Iselin Hermann, with no restrictions as to form. I chose to keep a sort of travel journal as a mode of exploration. As the work's seemingly chance economy began to cohere, I came to understand that it was in fact another essay—or assay—in the poetics of memory and experience. "Poetic Obligations" came together during a particularly fraught time in my life, a period of wandering and loss, and its shape was meant to reflect precisely those circumstances. "Counter-Poetics and Current Practice" is an edited transcription of a series of lectures improvised from a few pages of notes and delivered to a graduate seminar at the University of Iowa Writers' Workshop many years ago. Its rambling syntax and occasional disjunctiveness are the unavoidable result. I thought to include it because over the years it has circulated in one form or another and copies have frequently been requested. Whatever its failings, it seems a useful window into one kind of oral presentation, usually unrecorded, that I've made many times. Much has been left for some later collection—interviews, reviews, most occasional pieces, other reflections on dance, et al. Scholarly apparatus has been kept to a minimum.

✶

The debts I owe to others across this lifetime's conversation are innumerable. Most will be immediately evident in the texts themselves. I want particularly to offer my gratitude to Lauri Ramey for her selfless efforts on behalf of an earlier version of this collection. Eliot Weinberger's advice has been crucial during the editing process. Whatever may be good here is in great measure due to the exchange over the years with friends and co-conspirators such as Norma Cole, Robert Kaufman, Michael Davidson, Ann Lauterbach, Nathaniel Mackey, Rosmarie and Keith Waldrop, Fanny Howe, Susan Howe and Bei Dao, to cite only a very small number. Finally, this book would not exist without the extraordinary editorial efforts of Jeffrey Yang at New Directions. His patience in the face of my endless dithering and occasional despair has been exemplary. I am of course solely responsible for all errors of fact and judgment.

TAKE THE X TRAIN:
A DISCRETE SERIES: FOR OPPEN

write he sd, for
christ's sake, look
out where yr going

   So the voice in a dream recently, as I worried the question of
this talk. Creeley's voice, most obviously and most appropriately,
since it was in part through Bob's urging that, as a twenty-year-old
in 1963, I was reading what little work of the so-called Objectivist
poets I could then find. Nothing at once so simple and so complex
as that injunction—*write*—as Creeley's own, early agonistic lyrics
and Oppen's lifetime of gaps, fissures, parings, cuttings and past-
ings attest. Something like what Valéry, as Giorgio Agamben notes,
would call a necessary "hesitancy." And how indeed do you "look/
out where yr going," while waiting for the words to propose a des-
tination, or at least a course? A double message, then: as in poetry,
let it come as it needs to, but don't go completely off the rails. Yet,
how clear, finally, is this voice, and whose is it? We'd best go back to
the poem itself, as a whole, to witness the turns that occur:

   I Know a Man

   As I said to my
   friend, because I am
   always talking,—John, I

> sd, which was not his
> name, the darkness sur-
> rounds us, what
>
> can we do against
> it, or else, shall we &
> why not, buy a goddamn big car,
>
> drive, he sd, for
> christ's sake, look
> out where yr going.

The poem arrives in the form of a seemingly casual and abbre-
viated conversation with listener or reader, the telling of a mo-
ment. Within that telling resides a conversation retold, that with
a friend, John, which was not his name. The friend renamed: Is it
for reasons of discretion? Is it for reasons of erasure? Displace-
ment? Is it because naming, within the framework and under
the pressure of lyric condensation, is in itself unstable? For the
most part, the language could hardly be simpler or less self-
consciously literary, yet through the use of radical enjambment
and abbreviated orthography, defamiliarization occurs, of a
sort not common to the generally passive lyric voice of Ameri-
can poetry at that time. Who indeed is Bob (let's call the name-
less speaker "Bob") exchanging words with, within the poem,
and whom is he addressing "beyond" that conversation within?
And what nameless or misnamed other is addressing him? And
what of you, nameless reader, what have you to say in response?
Within the "simple" lyric occasion, then, the enigmatic vortex of
consciousness. We will come back, later, to this question of con-
versation, of multiple conversations, at the core of the poetics
of certain lyric poets after World War II, and indeed throughout
the history of poetry.

(Many a hell-ride had I shared with Bob in his Volkswagon
during those years, by the way, too callow and intimidated to tell

him, for Christ's sake, to watch out, but that's neither here nor there at this moment.)

I first heard Creeley read that poem live at the University of British Columbia in the summer of 1963. Near the midpoint of the poem ("the darkness . . ."), there was a power failure in the auditorium, and the reading was completed by candlelight. That's for any skeptics among us. Recall that Baudelaire, in the dedication to *Les Fleurs du Mal*, conferred upon Théophile Gautier the honorary graduate degree of *Magicien ès Lettres*. Anyway, returning to the voice in the dream, let's see where it takes us.

Part of my title, and something like the form of this work, if indeed it is to have a form, derives obviously from the first of Oppen's books, *Discrete Series*, published by the Objectivist Press in New York in 1934. I recall an interview where Oppen spoke of a discrete series as something like the stops along a subway line: 8, 14, 23, 28. . . . In other words, it is a series empirically verifiable but not mathematically derived. As a subway rider myself, from the years of my childhood in New York, to other cities around the world, this seemed as good a formal trope as any, and an excuse to meander as I might. Of course, I am also thereby invoking Oppen's vaunted discretion in discussing poetics, politics, the details of a life, the purposes of poetry. It is an intimidating discretion. What is the effect of this *leaving out*, of these gaps both in syntax and narrative, these silences, these gaps between the stations? How easy, in the face of such gestures, to say too little or too much. How easy, following the various meanings of the word, to betray the freedom to act or decide on one's own and to settle for received opinion or settled effects. Nothing simpler, in fact, than to write an essay or poem that the culture, be it of the left or the right, tacitly or openly calls for to support its central predispositions regarding the role and the limits of the various arts.

Beneath the ground, not far from where my daughter now lives in Brooklyn, runs the A train, Coney Island to Harlem, Coney Island (actual or of the mind) to the Cotton Club, immortalized in the Billy Strayhorn composition for Ellington's band.

That seemed an appropriately resonant cultural voyage or loop, with its own discrete series of stops and starts, to propose. So I thought, Well, yes, that's my title. Then I thought, Well, no, watch out, not quite; the "A" carries with it far too much of a Zukofskyan echo, one which would not at all have amused George, however much he honored the echoic, and however much he admired certain parts of "A." Hence the X train, with no predefined starting point, no stations listed and an as yet undiscoverable destination, much like any poems of real interest. I would imagine it existing on an asymptotic curve with the path of the A train, resembling the frequently asymptotic relationship of poetry and philosophy. I would imagine us en route, underway, among the company of others, in a zone of translation and, with apologies to H.G. Wells and Robert Zemeckis, of time travel. Have I tortured the metaphor enough? Not quite yet, since "metaphor" itself from its Greek origin is in itself a form of travel, of bearing across: metaphor, which Oppen finds suspect when manipulated as a device; and the exploratory journey of the poem, which he does not.

I want to speak not so much about Oppen alone, but about the figures that constellate as I think of him across time, poets and others caught in the dilemma of poetic speech as posited by the times then and now. Yet as I do so, an uneasy feeling arises. Last April, while in Tokyo for a festival of poetry and dance, I was asked to speak about American poetry at Waseda University, that is, American poetry as I had experienced it from the time of coming into that world in the late fifties and early sixties. As I nervously prepared to speak (I always prepare nervously, filled with doubt and hesitation), I asked myself, Who am I to speak in the place of who I was? In fact, do I have any idea, in retrospect, of who I was or how the events and poetries I encountered moved me and others here to there? It was certainly not the thirties, the decade Oppen always identified with. The Depression, the rural Dust Bowl catastrophes and the urban proletarian struggles were little more than echoes to those of us who had not directly experienced them, in part due to our remarkable American capacity for amnesia. McCarthyism had reminded us of the fascist tendencies always beneath the surface, waiting for their moment. And Vietnam was building, in what seemed increasingly like a discrete series of contiguous, lethal military adventures. I suppose I and most of my company knew nothing, simply enough. A rather grimly myopic and sedating orthodoxy dominated the field of accepted American verse, the closed field, the exploratory discoveries of Modernism and the various world vanguardisms having been effectively repressed. Perry Como crooning in the background . . . that train was, quite contentedly it seemed, going resolutely nowhere.

We were looking, it seems in retrospect, for an opening, a way out of the stultification then predominant, looking at once to dismantle and reconstruct, or maybe for a while, only to dismantle. Fumbling toward a poetic agency, and in particular a lyric agency that would interrogate the compromised means of expression themselves and the formal values supporting them. Against closure; against the static poetic edifice; and for what? For a desperately necessary form? For the conscience, as well as consciousness, of lyric address? Perhaps, now speaking much too grandly, for the restoration of some sort of truth-function in making. Not for Truth itself, wherever, if anywhere, that was to be found. *Lichtung* might be another way to put it, a forest clearing, a patch of light, via Celan, drawn in turn, and with painful irony, from the poisoned well of Heidegger. Oppen put it best, "that truthfulness / Which illumines speech."

I count sixteen other passengers in the subway car, as we rise from underground in Brooklyn and pass the Brooklyn Bridge to the south of us, before descending beneath the streets of lower Manhattan. I'm the only one gazing out at the bridge. I suppose the others see it every day, and so it has become invisible. Seven people are listening to MP3 players and iPods, plugs in their ears, wires dangling down. Three others are checking the screens of their cell phones. Two more are reading the tabloids ("Wounded Vets Demand Inquiry"). A student is reading what looks like a technical textbook and highlighting passages in yellow. The remaining three are simply sitting, two of them nodding off. (Would the sort of faceless descriptive prose I'm writing now be considered baseline "realism"?) My first reaction is to mourn for the monadic life of the MP3 crowd, carrying their isolation booths around with them. Then I wonder what they might be listening to, whether in fact entire sonic land-scapes may be opening up to them through these headphones. I understand too that it is not impossible, it is not mathemati-cally inconceivable, that one or another has downloaded po-etry readings from various sites and is listening to them as we travel: readings by Oppen and Reznikoff, for example, available through the San Francisco State Poetry Archives. In fact I have a young friend living in Brooklyn, call him Eddie (which is not his name), who regularly does just that. I make a mental note to purchase such a device.

Yes, As A Look Springs To Its Face

a life colors the meadow.
"This is the place," Abraham said.
The field and the cave therein arose,

even that lies hid in everything,
where nothing was, comes before his eyes
so that he sees and sings
central threnodies, as if a life had

but one joyous thread, one wife, one
meeting ground, and fibre of that thread
a sadness from that moment
into that moment led.

Poems come up from a ground so
to illustrate the ground, approximate

> a lingering of eternal image, a need
> known only in its being found ready.
>
> The force that words obey in song
> the rose and artichoke obey
> in their unfolding towards their form.
> —But he wept, and what grief?
>
> had that flowering of a face touchd
> that may be after struggle
> a song as natural as a glance
> that came so upon joy as if this were the place?
>
> It returns. He cannot return. He sends
> a line out, of yearning, that might be
> in movement of music seen once in a face
> reference to a melody heard in passing.

That poem from *The Opening of the Field* is for Hilda Burton tonight, who asked some weeks ago, rather plaintively, whether I would be reading some poetry at this talk. It seems representative, albeit from a singularly high Romantic perspective, of the aspiration of the time—the field of convergence, the site, as drawn from the words of Abraham in the Zohar, at once hidden and revealed, both hidden and revealed. Characteristic of Duncan's lyric work during that period, it revels in paradox, logical impasse and undecidability, as if offering the music of poetic logic, music's call, as defiant alternative to the instrumentalist and materially oriented ideology of the society at large. A song arising from the ground, at once the source of its being and the staging point for the dance in the field's opening.

Station: Place de la Résistance. Most of us, that is, most of the few of my generation who were aware then, first came to Oppen not through the earlier *Discrete Series* of 1934, hard if not impossible to find, but through *The Materials*, issued in 1962 by New Directions in collaboration with the *San Francisco Review*. It would mark not only the breaking of a long silence, but also a reaffirmation of that originary, prosodic silence or ground from which the poem springs, and to which, in Oppen's case, it continues to pay homage as enduring source and repository of a transient presence among the materials, among things. We might find it in a love song, the vein of desire that pulses quietly throughout Oppen's work, which he would call Mary's work as well, and daughter Linda's. A love song that invokes one of the earliest extant lyrics in the language, one that would continue to re-sound as late as *Myth of the Blaze* and *Primitive*:

> O Western Wind
>
> A world around her like a shadow
> She moves a chair
> Something is being made—
> Prepared
> Clear in front of her as open air
>
> The space a woman makes and fills
> After these years
> I write again
> Naturally, about your face
>
> Beautiful and wide
> Blue eyes
> Across all my vision but the glint of flesh
> Blue eyes
> In the subway routes, in the small rains
> The profiles.

As I think of *Discrete Series*, I remember a time in Paris in 1982, visiting Le Corbusier's 1923 Maison La Roche with Cathy and Sarah, my wife and daughter. An arrondissement of solid and stolid, apparently Beaux Arts, apartment buildings for the upper-middle class, and in their midst, this open-plan creation of Corbusier, all unadorned space and ramps and acoustical resonance. Sarah saw it right away for what it was, a playhouse rather than a place for domestic sequestration. Upon departing, we began to look at the surrounding buildings, all signed by their architects and dated, and all from the same time as the Maison La Roche, not decades earlier as I had assumed. Then we took the metro back to our hotel.

So in distant parallel perhaps, the adamant and austere reserve and refusals of *Discrete Series*, as against the pentametric porticoes and fluted columns of the academic-formalist verse of those very same thirties. Difficult to reimagine the shock and disdain or simple disregard for the work of Oppen, Zukofsky, Williams, Reznikoff and others at the thought that they were writing about "nothing," which is to say nothing poetic, which is to say nothing that registered to the refined and tested poetic sensibility—subways, girders, wheelbarrows, chickens, the glass of windows, perhaps at times the lyric "nothing" itself, and to say further that moral edification was lacking or that, from another, rather different, though equally conventional perspective, that of the lock-step left, the proletarian message was not being narratized. It could be said that the space of the poem and the things of the poem had taken on their own authority, and that the standard guideposts for poetic delectation had been effaced. This all would sound rather Savonarola-like, were it not for the *ars nova* that was being tested in these new measures, were it not for the spaces opening to the active reader, and the music.

2

Thus
Hides the

Parts—the prudery
Of Frigidaire, of
Soda-jerking

> Thus
>
> Above the
>
> Plane of lunch, of wives
> Removes itself
> (As soda-jerking from
> the private act
>
> Of
> Cracking eggs);
>
> big-Business

Untitled #2, within a sequence of series that constitutes *Discrete Series*. The head, if you will, the pronominal subject is missing, opening a characteristic space of both speculation and indeterminacy. The scene before us, like the poem itself, presents a drama of withholding and disclosure. Conventional description is absent, replaced by a kind of fragmented encounter, a probing of the truths and mysteries of appearances. By way of the small drama, the small actions, of the soda counter, we experience the oblique critique of "big-Business," the hiddenness of its workings, its "obscene," that is off-scene, workings. All to be found in the interstices, in the unspoken, of the poem. (We confront here, in microcosm, what Walter Benjamin called "the promises of glass," of glass architecture that is, the great modernist towers that at one moment appear open and another closed, depending on the light.) A certain irony, re: Objectivism itself, one that will persist, is that the poem-as-object has been destabilized, almost dematerialized, to be replaced by a sort of ceaseless inquiry or searching, along the way. All of Oppen's work will be characterized, to greater or lesser degree, by this dynamic of exploratory process, of "thinking toward," a concept expressed and implemented by poets as wildly divergent as Oppen and Stevens. The model is one of discovery rather than invention. We are reminded of Steven's objection, however arguable, to the Surrealists, that anyone (as I roughly recall it) could propose a crab playing an accordion, but that this was merely invention.

Oppen declared himself an antinomian, thus placing himself within a rich American tradition of resistance and refusal. Only by reading through the endless loop, the endlessly filtering and refining loop of the daybooks, the letters, the poems and their variants, does one begin to become fully aware of the multiplicity of Oppen's refusals. He rejects, of course, literary careerism, though he is quick to state that he would very much like to see the work published and read. He avoids the creative writing industry. He reads in public rarely, having neither the voice nor the temperament for it. He is not given to reviewing. Interviews produce a modest, if articulate, diffidence. His statements on poetics might be characterized as understatements, abjuring grand claims. It is, however, at the level of the writing practice itself that the degree of negative determination or alterity becomes most evident. He operates within a dramatically reduced lexicon, among his famously "small nouns"; he avoids complex metaphors and simile as a device, and most literary conceits; he moves in and out of normative grammar; he refuses consistency in his orthography and line breaks, the latter of which respond not so much to breath or voice, and certainly not to metrical patterning, but to the turns of thought in process. In short, he takes pains to eliminate most artifices and the kinds of rhetorical staging that would signify the "literary." Yet he is, quite paradoxically, ever alert to the aesthetic dimension, as apart from aestheticism. The poems are structured within a framework of rhythmic recurrences and junctures, considered, and often reconsidered, turns along a path of discovery. I am reminded of Mandelstam's remark that Dante's measures are those of the pace of a person out walking, that they take form at that point "where *la diritta via*, the straight way, was lost."

Anyone who has read Oppen's letters will be familiar with the ruptures and discontinuities, the lacunae, the quasi-randomness of grammatical markers, etc. They in fact come to represent the "distinctive features," to misuse a term from linguistics, of his procedure, and are to be found throughout the daybooks, letters and finally the poems. Since Marjorie Welish's Oppen lecture last year, I've thought often of the ungraspable poem, perhaps the true Oppen poem, without opening or closure, that exists only in circulation, constantly in formation, *en route* among these three different mediums. Perhaps it is a process of distillation that, in an alternative world, might be allowed to continue indefinitely, articulating the shipwreck of the singular, resisting what cannot be evaded, that in the act of making we are both singular and isolate, even before the counterfact "of being numerous." Thus, in a letter:

> "The shipwreck of the singular" I wrote. We cannot live without the concept of humanity, the end of one's own life is by no means equivalent to the end of the world, we would not bother to live out our lives if it were. . . .

> and yet we cannot escape this: that we are single. And face, therefore, shipwreck.

> And yet this, this tragic fact, is the brilliance of one's life, it is 'the bright light of shipwreck' which discloses—'all.'

If we are to speak of a style here, as we must, it is useful to remember the distinction Umberto Eco makes in one of his collections of intellectual entertainments, translated into English as *On Literature*, between style as surface and style as necessity. I think it is to the latter that Charles Olson points when he declares, "Style is soul." That the style is a carefully considered one, ceaselessly undergoing adjustment as it passes out of the frequent, relative rawness of the daybooks, then back and forth between the poems and the correspondence, seems also beyond argument. Style, possibly, as relentless purpose. In a letter of 1971 to Dan Gerber, Oppen comments:

> . . . if I were not now self-conscious about the epistolary style you praise and which I considered merely high wide and possibly handsome, I would say something about breaking the words, the sentences, the locutions *open* to make some room for ourselves   Here among the subatomic fragments

It is perhaps something as simple (and not simple) as reconfiguring the space of reflection, there on the page but also in the air, such that it might become both responsive to and indicative of the actual turns or tropes of thought, rather than representing completed and codified, therefore ossified, thought. Leaving closure to the simple fact of mortality, apart then from our being present in the world, if inevitably a part of it. A part and apart, the bright light.

Station: Place du Rêve: a second dream (26 nov 2007). This time, I—definitely a younger version of me—am passing in the subway tunnel under, rather than over, the East River, somewhere near the Brooklyn Bridge nonetheless. But the subway car itself is filled to the ceiling with water, and it is strange indeed, dream-strange, to be thus submerged yet still breathing in a realm of ripples and bubbles and aqueous light. There is one other passenger, halfway up the car on the other side, an older man, slightly slumped in his seat. He is wearing Buddhist garb, and I notice that it is Allen Ginsberg. After some hesitation, I approach him. "Allen," I say, "did you notice the mantis clinging to the roof? It must be Zukofsky's." He looks up into my face, but his eyes are clouded and distant and seem not to register anything. I wonder whether he knows the great Zukofsky subway poem in which the mantis appears. I wonder too whether the mantis has been riding this same car throughout the many decades since Zukofsky wrote the poem. I am about to make a second attempt at

conversation when the scene shifts, and I am driving a car some-
where in the vicinity of Boston. One of the passengers suddenly
exclaims, "Look, a mantis!" I turn to look and there, clinging to
the fabric inside the car roof is indeed a mantis, hitching a ride to
town. The dream ends.

As I'm preparing this talk over time, why this dream of
Ginsberg and Zukofsky (and perhaps too, even more spectrally,
of Whitman and Hart Crane)? Why my desire to include it in
the talk? Regarding the first question, I have no idea. Regard-
ing the second, why not? Further questions: What subway line
is this, the C? The Z? The A? And what is it we are drowning, or
not drowning, in? The alphabet? The ink? *Fly, mantis, on the poor,
arise like leaves . . .*

Station: Place du Silence. I wrote above of the figures that
constellate around my picture of Oppen, and here, very briefly,
I'd like to introduce (there's no time for more) the question of
lyric, and lyric silence, and the lyric conversation in the interest-
ing convergences among three quite different poets: Oppen, Paul
Celan and the Chuvash poet Gennady Aygi. A brief stop along
the way, for a topic that is much larger than our space here. For
Celan and Oppen, of course, the problematic figure of Heidegger
plays a role, a very large one for Celan, a smaller and less well-
documented one for Oppen. He is an undeniable presence in
their "thinking-toward" and "thinking through" questions of
poetry and being-in-the-world, and the origins of language and
poetic speech, and the function of the lyric voice.

Silence in poetry and experience, and in "poetry as experi-
ence" (as Philippe Lacoue-Labarthe usefully titles his work on
Celan), takes myriad forms. There is the silence of complicity and
complacency, and the imposed silence of tyranny. There is the
alternation of silence and stress in our measures, from which po-
etic rhythms of recurrence and difference emerge. There is the
silence of the act of listening, so central to the poetics of each
of these writers. There is as well the silence of the ellipse, within
whose invisible boundaries meanings gather, and which plays

an equally central role in the work of these poets. Then too, and closely related, is the originary silence out of which some would say language arises, and to which poetic speech returns, in its effort to rescue meaning from the rhetorical degradation of commerce and power. Whether we entirely accept this model or not, and I hesitate to say that we should, it can be seen to speak to the role of the lyric voice in history—and not beyond history. It seems clear that the actual, human conversation of the poem, with an other who is present and real, not some fetishized category of the Other, preserves this model, in much altered form, from Heideggerean metaphysics and mystification. In the face of Stalinism, Hitler, endless slaughter and failed utopias, thinking toward if not exactly truth, but a poetic relationship to what remains true, or truly possible, in language . . . an unfinished sentence. And the necessary, necessarily shipwrecked, singular, of the making . . . ? And "the meaning of being numerous," and the shipwrecked many . . . ?

What has been little noted critically, is that in each instance, such poetic thought involves stepping away from vanguardist experiment per se. That question of invention versus discovery, the crab and the accordion, a cream soda and an astrolabe on an operating table. It is just such invention, though not that alone, that Oppen mistrusts and firmly rejects. Though his early work, particularly the youthful poems written in Romanian, bear a distinct stamp of Surrealist influence, Celan very quickly moves beyond such forms of image making and construction, beyond in a sense what the literary imagination thus makes available as composition. Aygi once remarked, "I have never *experimented*—I simply have no time for it." In all three poets, listening and attending take primacy over systematized artistic construction. However resistant it may appear, and may be, poetry becomes a form of encounter, or conversation, a way of being with others. A goal then: to project lyric interiority itself into a shared world, a world of exchange between the singular, the singularity of the poem, and the plural.

Aygi's poetry deploys the active memory of the Chuvash land-scapes and rituals of his childhood, as well as echoes of ancient Chuvash pagan mythologies. The "childhood" he invokes is not a sentimental one, but one of entering into awareness and into speech with full openness. His fields, and the poetic field of his verse, the "open field" of his uncanny measures, echo the actual landscape of that moment of coming into language. It is a radically, that is to say deeply, innovative poetry, yet one which also speaks to the recovery of what the forces of history have attempted to efface. Shadowed through much of his life if not by Stalin, then by Stalinism's shadow and the dictates of socialist realism, Aygi learned to invoke silence and "sleep" as a ground of resistance, and thereby affirm the still possible and the still to be said. Here, from an interview given in 1985:

> The Noise-World sometimes begins to seem like a Lie-World—who can purify it to the point of *quietness?*—perhaps only art. One has to do more than simply "converse with quietness." In poetry it seems that one also must be able to *create quietness*.
>
> And this is the paradox: In poetry, alongside speaking, there is also silence, but it too can only be created through the Word: the poetry of silence speaks, but in a different way. . . .

It is easy to see why the poetry of Celan, with its mute chorus of buried voices, would resonate so deeply for Aygi (and why, in turn, a silenced Mandelstam would speak directly to Celan).

"Message delivery has failed," my computer now announces, and why should it not, since no message is intended, only a greet-ing, and a question or two to be placed in the spaces in between, no pretense to conclusion or destination.

Final stop, for now: Utopia Parkway. Language is a constantly evolving, hybridizing and self-renewing entity. Language, we might also say, is always forgetting itself, becoming lost, in its daily efforts to deliver a message, to convince and control, make the sale, arrive at a destination. There is no clearer instance of this than the relentlessly murderous misrule to which we in this republic, and the greater world, have been subjected, to which this nation has been subjected and has in some very significant degree acquiesced, during the years of a present administration that I will not name here, since it is not, if we honor the name and naming, deserving of any name. Perhaps its principle players will take star turns in the updated edition of the *Inferno* (or as Hollywood might call it, "the remake").

As to Dante, his measures and his journey, the endless Hell of war, mass slaughter, injustice, mendacity, the corruption of speech, remains obvious and immediate enough. Against that, if we are to glimpse from time to time a Paradiso in Oppen's work, it is perhaps to be found in those moments of clarity, *claritas*, the poems discover along the way through a fractured Noise-World, the sublime of the ordinary or quotidian, the finite, a shopping cart abandoned in the dunes, a brick in a brick wall, "the things we live among." "A limited, limiting clarity," as Oppen puts it in *Of Being Numerous*. An almost wordless space, where:

> The small nouns
> Crying faith
> In this in which the wild deer
> Startle, and stare out.

This place, where "dark / truths and blazing / truths are the same . . ." It is and is not of our making, Oppen would undoubtedly say.

[*Talk given for the 22nd annual George Oppen Memorial Lecture at the San Francisco Poetry Center, December 2007.*]

ON ROBERT DUNCAN'S *GROUND WORK*

The story is well-known in poetry circles: around 1968, disgusted by his difficulties with publishers and by what he perceived as the careerist strategies of many poets, Duncan vowed not to publish a new collection for fifteen years. (There would be chapbooks along the way.) He felt that this decision would free him to listen to the demands of his (supremely demanding) poetics and would liberate the architecture of his work from all compromised considerations. He would allow the grand design ("grand collage") to emerge in its own time from the agonistic dance of Eros and Thanatos, chaos and form, darkness and light, permission and obligation. It was not until 1984 that Ground Work I: *Before the War* appeared, to be followed in February 1988, the month of his death, by Ground Work II: *In the Dark*.

Together, the volumes offer a complex record of Duncan's intellectual, aesthetic and emotional concerns during those often turbulent years, even as they trace his effort to conjoin the personal with the political, the immediate with the eternal, and to make a space capacious enough for the myriad contending presences within his art. Much of the drama of these two volumes lies in this quest to discover an "open form" sufficiently responsive to what is, essentially, an ungovernable vision. On the face of it, the task is impossible, as with any quest, or with any poem that chooses to manifest, perhaps even celebrate, the incommunicability at the heart of things. During these two decades, Duncan would commit himself to a vatic, daedal opposition to the Vietnam War, resulting eventually in the break-up of his deep and prolonged friendship with Denise Levertov, whose opposition was of a different order; he would discover the surviving members of his birth family; and he would receive news of his ultimately fatal illness.

Duncan was a legendary talker or word-spinner. Any given conversation might weave its way through Freud and the *Zohar*, Nietzsche and the Gnostics, the Albigenses, the *Mabinogion*, anarchism, the *Tibetan Book of the Dead*, Dante, Pound, Stein and H.D., Helen Adam, Piaget and Melanie Klein, Alfred North Whitehead, *Dark Shadows* (the campy afternoon gothic television soap he and Jess enjoyed), the *Oz* books, Renoir's late, fleshy nudes, George Herriman, George Herms, George MacDonald, Homeric prosody, Zukofsky and Creeley, Stravinsky, Mahler's *lieder*, Mahler's correspondence with Freud, those recent recordings of the Bach cantatas, independent film (Brakhage, Kenneth Anger, Maya Deren, et al.), new dance, the latest generation of poets, new painting, new music, and that sale on halibut fillets over in the East Bay (frozen, but anyhow). Such conversation was often joyous, always intensely vital, yet often also marked by an undercurrent of unquiet desperation. Electric connections would occur or fail to occur. The process was strikingly heuristic, resistant to closure, the goal a mapping of attention and a form of comprehension. It could be argued that a not dissimilar associative mechanism is frequently operative in the poems, but ruled there by what Duncan referred to as the Laws of Form, that obligation to attend to the harmonies and disharmonies of specifically *poetic* thought, thought engaged in a process of discovery, guided by measures both historically resonant and immediate to speech. Twin lenses: the eternal and the instant, each in Duncan's mind focused upon, and focusing, the other, a (perhaps unobtainable) gnosis, or understanding, the desired end. Yet the end is elusive, even acknowledged at many points as illusionary.

Before the War: the various meanings of this phrase are crucial to an initial comprehension of Volume I. Readers were naturally perplexed by the title, as Duncan meant them to be. Why "before" when this work was appearing *during* the war and was so evidently immersed in its issues? In Duncan's order of things, as citizens we are placed as witnesses *before* the war itself, in this case Vietnam, with its attendant lies, deceptions, profiteering, massive, murderous violence and tragic miscalculations. Dantean polysemy ("Letter to Can Grande") is at work however. The war, all war, also always implies for Duncan the eternal, dialectical contention between creation and decreation, light and dark, form and void, being and non-being. Within the poet's psyche, the creative imagination struggles endlessly to manifest itself, and by that, paradoxically, to transcend the limits of self, to obliterate self, to become other. To Duncan then, work of the imagination involves a form of *psych-osis*, a standing outside the boundaries, and a sort of madness. *Ec-stasis* would offer the brighter image of this state, and for Duncan both terms are operative. Forces formed within the Ego (that is the "*Ich*," the "I") must be channeled toward the obliteration (or else positive overcoming) of that "I" or self. In addition, this "before" implies that war is an eternal condition of human nature. War will follow war, within and without. Any opposition to the immediate war must acknowledge its various meanings, the forms of contention that for Duncan are also the source of *poesis*, poetic making and meaning. The poet is everywhere implicated in such human and metaphysical circumstances. He or she cannot stand apart or above. The poem itself cannot preach without betraying its nature; it must enact. Here we come to the painful rupture between Duncan and Levertov. For Duncan, the poet and the poem have no grounds for self-righteousness. Political engagement must not deny the complex and contradictory forces of the poem's voice as it comes into being and voices the multiple aspects of human desire. The poem's "message" as such must not be manipulated or predetermined, which for Duncan would imply an essential betrayal of the poetic act, of poetic listening. Yet this demand leads to a classic quandary. How make a space for both personal poetic intention and that of the poem? Duncan's solution lies in part in an ever-greater openness of form, in the hope that all vectors of poetic thought may find their place in the poem's field. His *Passages* sequence, taken up again in these two volumes, offers perhaps the most radical example of this poetics. It certainly contains his most Poundian verses. Poetic form is stretched almost to the point of dissolution. The poem-as-object yields to the exigencies of process. Such a potential impasse, between the immediate and the eternal, also reminds us of Duncan's concept of myth as "the story that cannot be told."

Homages, derivations, imitations: Ground Work I: *Before the War* forms a kind of echo chamber, where song circulates across time, as Duncan pays tribute to the many voices that constitute his own and which, assembled, fashion the "other voice" of poetry, the antinomian stream beneath the tides of history. In the "Dante Études," Duncan's poetry occurs in counterpoint to passages from such works as Dante's *De Vulgari Eloquentia, De Monarchia,* and the *Convivio.* As outlined in his preface, Duncan hopes to celebrate the immediacy of Dante to his own poetics and, through the lens of his work, to reflect—musically—on the poetic and political orders of our troubled times, and at the same time "to unfold the secrets of the heart." The outer and the inner worlds are not to be distinguished; the truths of one enfold and amplify those of the other:

> My whole life
> needs to be here
> to come alive
> in this consideration.

There is an intimate and, as Nathaniel Mackey notes in "Uro-boros: Robert Duncan's *Dante* and *A Seventeenth Century Suite*," almost confessional character to much of this work. Duncan's

"Homage to the Metaphysical Genius in English Poetry," quoting and invoking Ralegh, Southwell, Herbert, Jonson, and the Neoplatonist John Norris of Bemerton couldn't be farther from T. S. Eliot's coolly authoritative and seemingly detached examination of writings from the same period. Even as the exploratory forms of modernism deeply inflect these works, an intimate, romantic immediacy has been reintroduced. It is an immediacy both fervent and desperate in its effort to capture a moment of atemporal transmission, exchange, circulation. What we arrive at is an ardent contact between voices across time, a conversation about life experience, artistic imagination, eternal bafflement, in which each text is altered by the presence of the other. I doubt whether many of my generation, for example, could experience Duncan's invocation of Southwell's Burning Babe without conjuring the horrifying photograph of the young Vietnamese girl, Kim Phúc Phan Thi, burned by napalm and fleeing naked down a road. Yet caution is necessary here. The poem is in fact a response to Levertov's "Advent 1966," which Duncan first received by mail from Levertov in December of 1966. There, the parallel with the napalmed children is explicitly and directly asserted. For Duncan, inevitably, the image is multidimensional, acquiring an eternal, existential and spiritualist resonance. It is not so much a rebuke, at this point, of Levertov's poem, as a commentary and response from another perspective. In hindsight, though, it is instructive in regard to the unbridgeable gulf that would eventually open between them:

> This is not a baby on fire but a babe of fire,
> flesh burning with its own flame,   not toward death
>   but alive with flame,   suffering its *self*
> the heat of the heart the rose was hearth of;

Duncan will identify with this image as mirror of the drama of the self's necessary struggle and undoing in pursuit of the imagination's Art, its end. It is a theme powerfully voiced in Volume

I, one that will be taken toward its limit in Volume II. Present in some form from the time of Duncan's earliest works, it now reaches full resonance with his premonitions of approaching death. The "nothing" of dissolution, of course, is a necessary part of the mythic cycle that the poet, in Duncan's syncretic cosmology, is obligated to embrace and enact.

In that regard, let me briefly draw attention to what seems to me one of the finest achievements in Volume I, a masterpiece of elegy, circularity and negative lyricism, "A Song from the Structures of Rime Ringing As the Poet Paul Celan Sings." The "I" singing is at once Duncan/Celan, if not some First Person beyond them both. A wrecked world has brought him to wreckage, to nothing; from his wreckage, the world "returns / to restore me . . ." The nothing the poet comes to, the grief of necessary knowledge, is also what causes him to be in the fullest sense. The movement is cyclical and unending, without closure or resolution, and the poem mirrors this in its irresolvability, its dwelling (much like one of Duncan's most frequently cited poems, "Often I Am Permitted to Return to a Meadow") in paradox. I hasten to add that the "likeness" Duncan discovers is by no means a presumptive identification with Celan's actual life-experience, its origins in the horrors of Shoah. The likeness or sympathy is realized in the ground of poetry itself and its recognitions or acknowledgments.

Before the War opens with the solitary voice of Achilles, lost in the vastness of the sea and its voices calling upon him to return to himself. What "vehicle" will be sufficient for this? Troy (and his death) long past, he has returned home to homelessness, among "the mothering tides." Thetis, then, and the sea, what guidance can they offer in the face "of an old longing" whose spell still consumes him? Is it the enchantment of the spell itself, or the remembered rhythms of war (and "the deeper unsatisfied war beneath / and behind the declared war"), or some unquiet memory, unresolved desire? With its specific mythic imagery and irresolvable questions, the poem clearly represents a deeply felt acknowledgement of Duncan's debt to H.D., in particular her *Helen in Egypt*.

The volume closes, by contrast, with the sometimes ecstatic, devotional "Circulations of the Song," in homage to Rumi. "Song" is found in the titles at the start and finish of the book, reminding us that whatever the necessary fractures, dislocations and violent, declamatory upswellings, the lyric impulse drives the vision of the whole. Against the earthly tyrannies and the "cloud of lies," there is the realized experience of poetic company and domestic companionship, and there is the confirmation of a poetics of desire through the mystical ghazals of Rumi. The poem celebrates the long partnership with Duncan's companion, the painter and collagist Jess, even as it speaks, once again, of "falling into an emptiness of Me . . ." The something and nothing conjoined alone render the entire truth of experience. The metaphor of the title stands as central to Duncan's poetics of call and response, of a responding to the actual beyond the limits of the single, isolate voice. The poem is always in circulation among the poems, coming to life there.

In the fall of 1984, I believe it was, I received an excited phone call from Duncan. He had completed a new poem, the first fully achieved in the time since his kidneys had failed and he had been forced to submit to a debilitating regimen of dialysis, medication and dietary restrictions. Might he come by and read it aloud, to see whether it was the real thing? Of course. The poem, "After a Long Illness," was indeed "the real thing" in its quiet rehearsal of what had come to pass during the years the toxins had incrementally altered Duncan's internal and external life. It contains both a greeting to Jess, after Duncan's hospitalization and near-death experience, and a tacit farewell. There is a measured calm, a reflectiveness about it as he looks back at the turbulent moods of recent years, the uncontrollable surgings of the blood, the upswellings of rage at many of those most close to him. A voice says, "I have given you a cat in the dark." As Norman Finkelstein notes in his excellent, detailed study of *Ground Work* ("Late Duncan: From Poetry to Scripture"), this is a *familiar*, a presiding daemonic spirit attendant upon the work of the mage, a conduit between the various realms of image-gathering and understanding, and between the light and the dark. Its "magnetic purr" speaks and soothes. The poem would signal the completion of *Ground Work II*.

The volume ends with Thanatos presiding. It begins, by contrast, under the sign of Eros, "this dark of the sexual moon." The sequence "An Alternate Life" tells of an affair with a younger man, undertaken during a trip to Australia, an affair that compels Duncan to acknowledge old age coming upon him. "New age" and "old youth" whirl together within him as he contemplates "the matter of Love" with "my own particular death in it." It leads him, as so often in his work, back to an affirmation of his life's enduring center in Jess's domestic company, and of life's brevity. The final stanzas, in their characteristic, tortuous syntax, fill with a certain foreboding, even as they celebrate "Love / that overtakes me and pervades the falling of the light." We are reminded of the phrase, "in the dark."

Like Volume I, Volume II is constructed, with a few exceptions, of sequences and summonings. There are the open sequences of *Passages* and the "Structures of Rime" that extend across the body of Duncan's work, and the closed sequences, such as "To Master Baudelaire" and "Veil, Turbine, Cord & Bird," the latter the fortuitous result of an exercise conducted while giving a workshop at the Naropa Institute. Baudelaire, Yeats, Rilke, Swift, Nietzsche, Mallarmé, Pound and Carlyle all appear as dark familiars in the work of poetry. "To Master Baudelaire" establishes the tone of malaise and infection that will prevail in much of what follows. "When I come to death's customs, / to the surrender of my nativities . . ." He peers into the Baudelairean mirror to acknowledge that "Hatreds / as well as loves flowd thru as the / sap of me." He summons the "Muse of Man's Stupidities" and acknowledges "the endlessness / of a relentless distaste." We are in the full atmosphere of Baudelaire's "spleen." He will reappear in one of the darkest and strangest of the *Passages*, "In Blood's Domaine," where the "Angel Syphilis" and the "Angel Cancer" preside over "the undoing of Mind's rule in the brain" and where "cells of lives within life conspire." We have arrived at the heart of darkness, where Form has been infected by "scarlet eruptions," and where another language prevails.

Among the "exceptions" noted above is "The Sentinels," a poem of intense, visionary lyricism that reminds us of the great dream songs in collections such as *The Opening of the Field* and *Roots and Branches*. It echoes an earlier, more self-contained mode, mostly submerged in *Ground Work* beneath the violent, polar forces at play. Elsewhere, I have said of it, "The poem represents a descent into a crepuscular, wordless, near indiscernible world over which earth owls preside, as sentinels. It is a world of 'after-light,' a zone where waking and dream, conscious and unconscious uneasily meet, mingle and intertwine; a world of mute memory ('silent as a family photograph'), ghosts and traces, through which the poet, himself wraithlike, passes, interrupting the silence with the scratching of his pen. The owl (should we think of Minerva's owl?) is always the 'bird of poetry' in Duncan's work, yet here, in this sequence of fragments or dream recollections, we have owls 'clumpt' 'in ancient burrows' in the earth, 'so near to death,' as if buried but not quite. Chthonic beings, they preside over an Orphic world the poet must enter to find the 'secrets of the earth,' that 'owl-thought . . . hidden in all things.' It is a placeless place, prior to language, from which the measures of the poem arise. From there the poet returns to the upper, waking world, harboring the figures and forms he has been given." Its complex coherence reminds us of such epiphanic moments in Duncan's work as "My Mother Would Be a Falconress," and "A Dream of the End of the World," where the different realms of imagined being, for all their psychic contention and violence, offer "counselings . . . hidden in all things."

To work "in the dark," to proceed by errancy in a dark wood, to allow the forces of reason and unreason to fully contend, runs against the grain of a serviceable poetic practice, too often content to offer up hors d'oeuvres of the scenic and sentimental. Duncan was prominent among a generation of poets who sought to recover poetry's exploratory capacity from the strictures of orthodox critical propriety. Perhaps no one among his peers committed himself more profoundly to the magical, Orphic dimension of the poetic voice, and to the dynamic tension between the flowing currents of a restlessly associative mind and the demands of construction. To proceed in such a manner is to give yourself over to the poem, to be at the mercy of its figures. Both the costs and the rewards are evident here.

[*Introduction for the new compilation of Robert Duncan's* Ground Work, *New Directions Publishing, 2006. First published in the online journal* Jacket.]

ON THE SUSTAINING OF CULTURE IN DARK TIMES

"When I hear the word 'culture' I reach for my gun."
—Joseph Goebbels (attributed)

I haven't been asked to give a keynote address before, nor do I think poets are often invited to do so, at least outside a strictly literary context. Perhaps our "notes" and "keys" seem a little too aberrant, too "off," too "blue" for most occasions. It's equally possible that our modes of thought would appear too given to errancy and vagabondage, too committed to non-reason, to be entirely trustworthy in most contexts, and there may well be some justification for that assumption. I trust, at the very least, that I'm not entirely trustworthy. In any case, as a novice in this area, I'd like to begin by examining some relevant terms. Let's see after that where "poetic reason," however oxymoronic, may take us regarding the sustaining of culture at a fraught and contentious and corrupted moment in our history. And please allow me to speak with you from a certain muteness and impossibility, since words certainly don't come easily, or why else would there be poetry?

"Synergy" seems a rather blowsy word these days, with its implications of corporate merger for profit-enhancing capacity right alongside those that should most concern us here. I would like to define it for our purposes in its early sense as simply a kind of "working with," an interaction, from the Greek *sunergia*, "cooperation," in turn derived from *sunergos*, "working together." Its opposite then would be "working against," or less negatively, "working apart." All of us in our lives at one time undoubtedly have worked with, have worked against, and have worked apart. "Keynote" in musical terms is the tonic of a musical key, the first note of a diatonic scale. It is this for which we are searching, hoping the notes will ascend from there in a play of harmonies and disharmonies, freeing the measure. (As a gesture toward synergy, by the way, I'll be occasionally interlarding my paragraphs with quotations from my friend Eliot Weinberger's article, "What I Heard about Iraq," just published this month in the *London Review of Books*.

In February 2001, I heard Colin Powell say that Saddam Hussein "has not developed any significant capability with respect to weapons of mass destruction. He is unable to project conventional power against his neighbors."

In July 2001, I heard Condoleezza Rice say: "We are able to keep his arms from him. His military forces have not been rebuilt."

For the word "culture," I turn to Raymond Williams' important book *Keywords*. Williams first confirms our suspicion that it "is one of the two or three most complicated words in the English language." Interestingly, its root Latin word is *colere*, which "had a range of meanings: inhabit, cultivate, protect, honor with worship." From *colere* derives *cultura*, hence our "culture," a noun of process "for the tending of something, basically crops or animals." Around the eighteenth century, its multiple modern meanings begin to emerge and evolve, but the ancient resonances, I would suggest, never entirely disappear. They linger as faint echoes in our contemporary word "culture," reminding us that "culture" must be mindful of the earth and of husbandry, and that without a spiritual dimension, a dimension of reverence if you will, it is empty. (We should note, too, the parallel that has often been drawn between the ploughing or cultivating of a plot of land and the movement of lines of verse across the field of the page, a field that may be open or closed, regular or irregular. The word "verse" of course comes from the Latin *versus,* a turn.)

On September 11, 2001, six hours after the attacks, I heard that Donald Rumsfeld said that it might be an opportunity to "hit" Iraq. I heard that he said, "Go massive. Sweep it all up. Things related and not."

The sustaining of culture is an issue of particular urgency in these times that I have called dark, when language itself seems under daily assault, and when the living arts are declared suspect or more frequently simply ignored by those in power. The assault on language, its communicative and truth functions and its acknowledgment of the other, is a necessary prerequisite to the assaults on the environment, civil rights, women's rights, the Constitutional separation of church and state, social programs, education, science, international treaties and, quite explicitly, reason itself, post-Enlightenment culture itself. The list goes on. The war, and the systematic propagation of fear in the populace can certainly be viewed as both emblematic of, and bogus rationale for, all or many of these things. It represents the triumph of a kind of phantasmatic medievalism, a hubristic turning away from the actual lessons of the past, from cultural memory, from the founding values of the Republic, toward a fevered and one-dimensional pseudo-messianism, a relentless "working against" the many for the few, the other for the same. It has about it an air of nihilistic fantasy, a fever-dream of empire founded on air by those awaiting the Rapture, when the Elect will be assumed into the eternal, celestial Reich of the pure of blood and spirit, while the rest of us experience Armageddon here below. What need to preserve resources or suffer questions or acknowledge others when fired by such visions of time's end?

Demagoguery, deceit, and denial of the other, such crimes against language are the grounds of despotism. And all in the trusted name of "liberty," "freedom" and "democracy," repeated mantra-like as death and mutilation reign down on untold (and unacknowledged) numbers. Yet, for brazen and blatant lies to work, there must be people to believe them, or choose to believe them, or simply be indifferent. Recently, my attention was drawn to a passage in Hannah Arendt's *The Origins of Totalitarianism*, published in 1951, which reads:

> In an ever-changing, incomprehensible world the masses had reached the point where they would, at the same time, believe everything and nothing, think that everything was possible and that nothing was true.... Mass propaganda discovered that its audience was ready at all times to believe the worst, no matter how absurd, and did not particularly object to being deceived because it held every statement to be a lie anyhow. The totalitarian mass leaders based their propaganda on the correct assumption that, under such conditions, one could make people believe the most fantastic statements one day, and trust that if the next day they were given irrefutable proof of their falsehood, they would take refuge in cynicism; instead of deserting the leaders who had lied to them, they would protest that they had known all along that the statement was a lie and would admire the leaders for their superior tactical cleverness.

I don't mean in the least to suggest precise historical parallels here, merely to raise questions that must be asked in time and then asked again, lest we reach a point where questions may not be raised.

I heard the president say that "Iraq has a growing fleet of manned and unmanned aerial vehicles that could be used to disperse chemical and biological weapons across broad areas." I heard him say that Iraq "could launch a biological or chemical attack in as little as 45 minutes after the order is given."

Early in the last century, the poet Guillaume Apollinaire, born Wilhelm Apollinaris de Kostrowsky in Italy, composed a poem entitled "Zone." It was one among several founding gestures of a new, global poetic sensibility, a vision of flight and unboundedness, an erasure of borders. Colored by a Whitmanic rhetorical exuberance and excess, it would challenge the limits of the real and the everyday, while being simultaneously filled with the movements of the streets and of cosmopolitan life. It would, in effect, attempt to create an alternative space within the actual. And this, while Apollinaire worked in intimate collaboration with the Cubist painters and others attempting to embody the "new spirit." The poem is at play both with state power and religious authority, one foot still in the rhythms of the late nineteenth century, one in the twentieth. It is a bridge under construction. Some lines from the beginning, translated by Ron Padgett:

> You're tired of this old world at last
>
> The flock of bridges is bleating this morning O shepherdess Eiffel Tower
>
> You've had enough of living in the Greek and Roman past
>
> Even the cars look ancient here
> Only religion has stayed new religion
> Has stayed simple like the hangars at Port-Aviation
>
> O Christianity you alone in Europe are not ancient
> The most modern European is you Pope Pius X
> And you whom the windows observe shame forbids this morning
> Your going into a church and confessing
> You read the handbills the catalogs the posters that really sing

That's poetry and there are newspapers if you want prose
this morning
There are dime serials filled with detective stories
Portraits of great men and a thousand other categories

This morning I saw a pretty street whose name I have
forgotten
Clean and new it was the bugle of the sun
The managers the workers and the beautiful secretaries
From Monday morning to Saturday afternoon go by
four times a day
Each morning the whistle wails three times
About noon a clock barks out twelve angry chimes
The words written on signs and walls
Like squawking parrots the plaques and Post No Bills
I love the charm of this industrial street
Located in Paris between the rue Aumont-Thiéville and
the avenue des Ternes

In the coming years, Blaise Cendrars would ride his Trans-Siberian Express all the way to São Paolo, where the seeds of a new and distinctly Brazilian vanguardism would be planted, which would in turn leave its mark on the new poetry cultures of Europe. Vicente Huidobro, the "poet of air," would make his round-trip journey from Chile to Buenos Aires to Paris to Barcelona to Chile, eventually creating his *Altazor*, perhaps the ultimate twentieth-century poem of global flight. Aimé Césaire and Léopold Sédar Senghor would appropriate and transfigure the rhetoric of Surrealism to found the Negritude movement in Africa and the Caribbean, and spur anticolonialist expression among their peoples. Influenced as well by the Harlem Renaissance, they would add their tones to African-American poetries of the sixties and seventies in the United States, just as the example of Apollinaire would resurface in the activities, ironies and interactions of Frank O'Hara and the New York School of painters, poets, dancers and composers.

The Russian Formalists and Futurists would dream of a truly revolutionary art and, even after their suppression by Stalin, would go on to influence countless political and artistic formations around the world. The stories of these pockets of cultural renewal, resistance and circulation are, of course, far too numerous to elaborate here. (You can follow the tale in its full flowering in the capacious two volumes of *Poems for the Millennium*, edited by Jerome Rothenberg and Pierre Joris, from the University of California Press, though even there the full story can't possibly be told.) In our moment, the Internet has already dramatically enhanced and altered this form of global interaction and exchange. Its virtual space has fostered the notion of virtual place, the gathering point that is-not, somewhere in between. It is easy to speculate on both the positive (no boundaries) and negative (no *there* there) aspects of this development for the future of artistic cooperation and collaboration. (I do not speak here for our indigenous and tribal arts, our "technicians of the sacred," who would present a different, if no less complex, tale of transmission and exchange.)

I heard the Vice President say that the war would be over in "weeks rather than months."

I heard Donald Rumsfeld say: "It could last six days, six weeks. I doubt six months."

I heard Donald Rumsfeld say there was "no question" that American troops would be "welcomed": "Go back to Afghanistan, the people were in the streets playing music, cheering, flying kites, and doing all the things that the Taliban and al-Qaeda would not let them do."

There are several points relevant to our topic. First, though poetry is often considered a solitary art, and it may well contain an element of isolate making, it is always, from its inception, *in conversation*. ("Conversation is thought," says Jean-Luc Godard.) Poetry does not exist without a recipient, who must complete the circuit in his or her own manner and read among its various meanings. This never occurs without some degree of transfiguration, mind to mind, body to body, culture to culture. Second, what some may see as a purely aesthetic gesture is never in fact without its imbedded, social dimension. Third, though new artistic movements may begin as relatively small and isolated events, they will often conjoin with larger social forces and alternative disciplines to create an enduring effect upon our cultures, to insist upon the "other view" and to maintain, as Octavio Paz phrases it, the "other voice," between religion and revolution. With much justification, the poet Robert Hass traces some of the impetus for contemporary ecological movements to the Romantic poets, as they confronted a world of nature and craft suddenly imperiled by the Industrial Revolution and the capitalist (not only, of course, capitalist) urge for endless expansion and endless exploitation of resources. This conjoining of energies will often occur more or less in the moment, but just as frequently it will constitute the unpredictable, contingent afterlife of the work. However anti-modernist, at their most direct certain of the Georgian poets of World War I bear first-hand witness to the psychological and physical costs of war, and above all to its folly and wasting of the spirit (echoing Greek tragic drama in this regard). The great post-Holocaust poet, Paul Celan, writes from the silence of ruined time. As another great poet Andrea Zanzotto puts it, "[Celan] represents the realization of something that seemed impossible: not only to write poetry after Auschwitz but to 'write' within those ashes, to arrive at another poetry by bending that absolute annihilation while remaining in a certain way inside it." He goes on: "language knows that it cannot substitute itself for the drift of a destructuration that will transform it into something other, that will change its sign. Yet at the same time, language has to 'overthrow' history and something more than history; while remaining subjected to this world, it has to 'transcend' it and at least point toward its horrible deficits." So it is that the smothered tongue of Celan outlasts the thousand-year Reich, and Anna Akhmatova's intimate lyric voice survives the depravities of Stalinism by means of a poetry both in-side and outside of time. It is her contemporary, Osip Mandelstam, who wrote in "The Word and Culture" that "Poetry is a plough, turning up time so that its deep layers, its black earth, appear on top." There's a closely related poem in the first of his *Voronezh Note-books* (translated by Richard and Elizabeth McKane), written during his internal banishment at the hands of Stalin. Mandelstam would die within a couple of years, but the poems of the *Notebooks* seem already to emerge from an afterlife, where all of life has been denied by the State, where nothing but the poem and the earth remain as counters to the dictatorial word:

Black Earth

The damp clods of earth of my land and liberty
are all overworked, extra black and well-groomed.
They are all in airy little well-tended ridges,
crumbling, and forming a chorus.

In the early spring the earth is bluish black,
and ploughing is pacifist work.
The rumour is ploughed open revealing a thousand
mounds.
Know this, there is something boundless within these
boundaries.

The earth is a mistake and a rifle butt,
immovable, however often you implore her on bended
knee.
She sharpens our hearing with a decaying flute.
She freezes our ears with a morning clarinet.

The fat crust of earth is so pleasant against the
ploughshare
as the steppe lies in the April upheaval.

> Salutations, black earth, be strong and alert,
> there's a fertile black silence in work.

Here the different meanings of "culture" discussed above merge in a thinly veiled plea for memory, for renewal and for what must be sustained in the face of catastrophe and cultural annihilation.

I heard an official from the Red Crescent say: "On one stretch of highway alone, there were more than fifty civilian cars, each with four or five people incinerated inside, that sat in the sun for ten or fifteen days before they were buried nearby by volunteers. That is what there will be for relatives to come and find. War is bad, but its remnants are worse."

There is one more instance I feel obliged to mention here, which has to do with the much discussed, and too often vaguely elaborated, notion of poetry-as-witness. Like great reporting and profound research, witness in its many forms renews memory and uncovers or ploughs up the truths that lie beyond the rhetoric of forgetting and denial. It is unavoidable to mention the example of Miklos Radnóti, one of the great Hungarian poets of the twentieth century. As a Jew, he was frequently conscripted into forced-labor battalions. In 1944, the Nazis transported him to work in the Bor mines of Serbia. Toward the war's end, he was taken on a forced march toward Germany. Exhausted and ill, he was shot by guards in western Hungary and interred in a mass grave. After the war, the grave was opened and a notebook with his last and some of his greatest poems was found in his pocket, poems that speak up to the moment of death and then live on, beyond their own assassination and burial. Here are the opening lines of his "Forced March," written roughly two months before his death, in my very provisional revision of an existing translation:

> Crazed, you sink to the ground, rise up and walk again,
> your knees and ankles move

but you begin again as if with wings.
The ditch calls to you, no good, you're afraid to stay
and if someone asks why, maybe you'll turn and say
that a woman and a sane death, a better death, await
you.

A conversation, one might say, with madness, his own near madness and the insanity of the times, where the only "other" is the poet himself, falling and rising up. What hope, that these words would ever enter the world? There must have been just enough, perhaps spurred in part by the woman mentioned, the absent other.

From this near-death solitude, this stark reminder of history, I'd like to move to some actual, personal instances of artistic practices that may serve as models for "working with," for transcending the isolate self and the isolate discipline.

I'll make no attempt to define or delimit the notion of "collaboration" itself. It is at once too vast and too slippery for that. It must also be evident that everything I do seems a form of collaboration, across time, with the voices of poets and others that pass through me as I work. Suffice it to say that another, an other, becomes present in a way that is both like and unlike the dialogic work of the poem. My ideal of pure collaboration, never fully realized, produces a work that belongs neither to one maker nor to the other or others. It escapes or surpasses the kind of intentionality we associate with the product of an individual. It is a work, in the words of one of my poems, "that is neither you nor I." If we consider the topic of this conference then, "working with" is a means of overcoming what the poet George Oppen referred to as "the shipwreck of the singular," in an attempt to arrive at the experience (in Oppen's words again) "of being numerous."

I heard an old man say, after 11 members of his family—children and grandchildren—were killed when a tank blew up their minivan: "Our home is an empty place. We who are left are like wild animals. All we can do is cry out."

I heard that 100,000 Iraqi civilians were dead. . . . I heard that 1,400 American soldiers had been killed and that the true casualty figure was approximately 25,000.

For over thirty years now, I've worked with composers, painters, other writers and one particular choreographer, Margaret Jenkins and her dance company in San Francisco. It was never my particular intent to do so, though I've never considered the arts as isolate entities, either from one another or from other pursuits in this life. They are part of a vision of creative labor, of the imagined life, no different in principle from the aspirations of others participating in this conference. We can, I think, not glibly speak of a shared cultural ecology that conserves as well as innovates, that resists habits of thought and action when necessary and builds a non-nostalgic vision of pasts and possible futures, and of a less predatory present. When George W. Bush claims that he doesn't think about his place in the future "because we'll all be dead," the remark provides singular insight into a certain mode of thought (if it can be called thought) that has no presence, since the future is not some vague abstraction but fact and consequence of present action. It inheres and defines us *as we are.* As present, it articulates notions of community and exchange, of making and unmaking, but here I'm wandering a bit from the topic sentence.

We began many years ago with an examination of those elements common to poetry and dance, such as rhythm, duration, concepts of measure and space (space of the page, space of the stage), and the performative. We thought a great deal about certain crossings, where language becomes gesture and gesture language. We thought about story and abstraction, narrative, anti-narrative and fragmentation. We thought about the given and the possible, convention and invention, and the difference between closed and open forms. In short, we considered how we view and represent the world and time through our arts. I was constantly reminded of body and voice in actual space, and therefore of the body in poetry and the world, circulating among other bodies. In this particular choreographic process, all are collaborators: dancers, lighting and set designers, costume designer, composers, choreographer all engage in a dance to make a dance. The difference from the apparently solitary work of poetry could not at first have seemed more different or more welcome, as a kind of balance—all elements of the whole work to modify all others. Looking at the resulting work, it is often difficult to completely separate one contribution from another, even though we all have our "titles" and supposed roles in the process. So, a certain paradigm for making and a paradigm for community, if a temporary and metamorphosing community, evolved together. I don't mean to offer a utopian model; the process itself can be difficult, contentious and fragile. Differences matter as much as agreements. In fact, one might speak of "a community of differences," not always perfectly resolvable. And then there is the odd business: the day arrives, the lights go up, the work is performed and disappears. The "product," if one can speak of such, is ephemeral. For a moment, time stops and is reconfigured, and then it resumes.

I'm no longer so sure that this is very different from poetry. The great geomorphologist Carl Sauer made the point years ago that to examine any square foot of earth is to examine infinite life and time, infinite intersecting histories. Walking with my wife and daughter and friends north of San Francisco recently, on the trails of Point Reyes, I thought about Sauer and about the "invasion" of nonnative plant and animal and insect species. Grasses from China and elsewhere, French garden snails, fallow deer, native to the Mediterranean and Asia Minor, axis deer from India and Sri Lanka, and so on. Similarly, imbedded in the poem (even the most determinedly "American" of poems) we find strains of linkage going back to the ancient origins of lyric and narrative.

That is, we find infinite elements, native and foreign, but we also find countless other voices that constitute its voice. (Paradoxically, that voice, if it is truly a poem, has also never been heard before.) Viewed this way, the poem is less an isolate cultural artifact than a diachronic and synchronic cultural echo chamber. As for the stage and the curtain, when the reader closes the book, the poem is no more. Will the book ever be reopened? It is impossible to tell, but in most instances it will not. It exists, though, only when it comes to light, by the grace of another or others.

Very briefly, one of many experiences of working with a painter, though not in the most immediate sense of collaboration. Three years ago, along with twelve other poets and the musician/composer Bill Frisell, I was invited by the poet and art critic David Breskin to respond to a sequence of eight abstract paintings by Gerhard Richter, in commemoration of his then forthcoming retrospective at the San Francisco Museum of Modern Art. I studied not only the eight paintings and the "images" sequestered within them, but also Richter's notebooks and interviews, wherein he subverts conventional notions of authorship and genre, abstraction and representation. As his work and voice passed through me, the eight poems of my sequence "Scale" began to take form. The ice that I had been caught in was broken, and the sequence became the "hinge" or turning point between the first and last half of my new book, and also offered momentum for what was to come. A happy result of collaboration: to take you out of yourself, your accumulated habits of making, into a place that is not your own. The various participants become "communicating vessels," opening a space for making that is neither that of one nor the other.

Behind the work, as in the making of a dance described above, there is often an elaborate, silent backstory, a submerged and silent dimension. It is in this silence, beyond intention, that a work often grows. My new book, from which I read last night, is entitled *Company of Moths*. At frequent points it is inspired by a collaboration, a trading back and forth, with the artist

Augusta Talbot. We agreed at one point, for many reasons, to focus
on moths and see what that might generate between us. When a
painter-friend of Augusta's heard about this, she pointed us toward
an astonishing three-page passage in W. G. Sebald's novel *Austerlitz*.
As it happens, I was a great admirer of Sebald's work and had been
hoping to visit him in East Anglia when I heard of his tragic, early
death. I found the passage in question and copied it for Augusta. I
then flew for a summer vacation to the East Coast, carrying along,
among many other books, *Austerlitz* and a mystery novel by the
popular Arturo Perez-Riverte, whose title, significantly, I've forgot-
ten. The contrast, of course, could not have been greater. The Perez-
Riverte was a classic piece of genre fiction, a "page-turner," though
not without a degree of intellectual pretension. A reader speeds
through his book, riding the twists of the narrative, unimpeded
by linguistic nuance or complexity. After three to five pages of the
Sebald, I would have to stop, overwhelmed by its baroque textures,
its folds within folds, memory and the moment impossibly inter-
twined. In the Perez-Riverte, time seems to accelerate and in a sense
"vanish." It is a work for killing time. In the Sebald, time slows as
echoes and enigmas encircle and control it. Completed, the Perez-
Riverte left nothing behind. Its job was done, whereas the depths
and narrative swerves found in *Austerlitz* continue to resonate for
me. There is ample room in a culture for both, of course, but for a
culture to sustain itself in any meaningful way, the latter, the slow
food of Sebald and his interrogations, must find its place against
the pressure of immediate gratification. It is a work "against forget-
ting." Finally, that summer I drew from the *Austerlitz* passage on
moths to write my elegy for Sebald. In a sense, I asked his voice to
pass through mine:

> Arc
>
> There is the above and the below of each.
> "Their wings . . . the lining underneath . . ."

There is our daily speech, so clear
and meaning-free. And meaning itself,

to be erased, almost successfully.
There is the red rose

and its double in the dark
avid to swallow us,

the dancing woman, many-armed,
in folds of cloth and gold,

and below, her silent counterpart,
undisclosed. The tree in full leaf

and the tree ablaze
are one we're told

by the riddling, riparian dream
(a dream I dreamt against the River Wye).

Do you remember how quiet
the skies became, that while,

before the clanging began again?
The wild poppies, their caps,

the sentinel owl,
the crescents and veining,

windrows and slopes?
Below they are tracing

an arc or enlacement
that can't be shown.

"No contrasts, no shading anymore . . ."
They are in the dark.

in memory of W. G. Sebald

We work in the company of others (philosophers and farmers, artists and scientists, as we variously require), and we work in the dark.

The historian Daniel Boorstin has remarked that ignoring the past in making decisions is like trying to plant cut flowers. Likewise, to ignore the future, when "we'll all be dead," is to ignore the present. Here perhaps, at this gathering, we can at least aspire to that alternative space I've been addressing, one that is at once inside and outside, a part and apart, much like the workings of our various arts, a space of circulation and exchange. In opposing the profoundly destructive designs of those presently in power, we might consider the architecture of what the poet Robert Duncan once called the "symposium of the whole," a site where the other is addressed and not demonized, and where reason and imagination conjoin. Maybe that is the tonic from which the scale will arise.

[*Keynote Address, Evergreen State College Synergy Symposium, February 2005. First published in* Golden Handcuffs Review #6, *Summer-Fall 2005.*]

DEAR WALT

Dear Walt,

I must confess that I was thinking of you all last week, as I sat in my daughter's apartment overlooking Fort Greene Park in Brooklyn, across the waters from Mannahatta. Do you still remember how, as editor of the *Brooklyn Daily Eagle*, you entreated the citizens of Brooklyn to build a park worthy of their young metropolis, and fought to save the Fort Greene area from the unbridled greed of developers? Later, there was a movement to honor the bones of the 12,000 or so "martyrs" of the American Revolution, dead of disease and starvation on British prison ships, their bodies interred in shallow graves along the shore of Wallabout Bay. So the Prison Ship Martyrs Monument now stands at the park's highest point.

It's a bit strange to contemplate these things at our present moment in history. I don't know whether you keep abreast of the news, Walt, but it is not good. The current administration, a dungheap of pious hypocrites and liars, has used the pretext of the war against terror to dismantle the founding principles and values of the Republic and to abrogate international treaties. At Guantánamo, foreign prisoners are being held without recourse to legal council and without charges. Have you heard of Abu Ghraib? There and at other locations, prisoners of our illegal war have been tortured, sexually humiliated, beaten and killed. They've been urinated on, shocked with electrical devices, submitted to near drowning, locked hooded and naked in boxes and deprived of food and sleep. All specifically in the name of democracy, freedom, Christian values. Over 100,000 Iraqi civilians have been killed or maimed. Domestically, human and civil rights, gay and women's rights, environmental protections, social programs and freedom of expression are equally under assault. And so, as Paris calls to celebrate you (Paris, Walt—I think you'd have liked it!), I cannot help but reflect on the pall of irony now cast by events over one of your late, if admittedly far from best, poems:

> America
>
> Centre of equal daughters, equal sons,
> All, all alike endear'd, grown, ungrown, young or old,
> Strong, ample, fair, enduring, capable, rich,
> Perennial with the Earth, with Freedom, Law and Love,
> A grand, sane, towering, seated Mother,
> Chair'd in the adamant of Time.

Of course, such a place never was nor could be, as hard as you tried to make it so by means of the poem.

For which we now salute you, Walt, and send love,

Michael Palmer

[*San Francisco, March 23, 2005. First published in* Walt Whitman Hom(m)age 2005/1855, *Turtle Point Press & Editions Joca Seria.*]

POETRY AND CONTINGENCY:
WITHIN A TIMELESS MOMENT
OF BARBARIC THOUGHT

Kant thought he was honoring art when among the predicates of beauty he emphasized and gave prominence to those which established the honor of knowledge: impersonality and universality. This is not the place to inquire whether this was essentially a mistake; all I wish to underline is that Kant, like all philosophers, instead of envisaging the aesthetic problem from the point of view of the artist (the creator), considered art and the beautiful purely from that of the "spectator," and unconsciously introduced the "spectator" into the concept "beautiful." It would not have been so bad if this "spectator" had at least been sufficiently familiar to the philosophers of beauty—namely as a great *personal* fact and experience, as an abundance of vivid authentic experiences, desires, surprises, and delights in the realm of the beautiful! But I fear that the reverse has always been the case; and so they have offered us, from the beginning, definitions in which, as in Kant's famous definition of the beautiful, a lack of any refined first-hand experience reposes in the shape of a fat worm of error. "That is beautiful," said Kant, "which gives us pleasure *without interest*." Without interest! Compare with this definition one framed by a genuine "spectator" and artist—Stendhal, who once called the beautiful *une promesse de bonheur*. At any rate, he *rejected* and repudiated the one point about the aesthetic condition which Kant had stressed: *le désintéressement.* Who is right, Kant or Stendhal?

If our aestheticians never weary of asserting in Kant's favor that, under the spell of beauty, one can *even* view undraped female statues "without interest," one may laugh a little at their expense: the experience of artists on this ticklish point are more "interesting," and Pygmalion was in any event *not* necessarily an "unaesthetic man."

—Friedrich Nietzsche,
On the Genealogy of Morals, third essay, translated by Walter Kaufmann, as quoted by Giorgio Agamben in *The Man Without Content*

*

England in 1819

An old, mad, blind, despised, and dying King;
Princes, the dregs of their dull race, who flow
Through public scorn,—mud from a muddy spring;
Rulers who neither see nor feel nor know,
But leechlike to their fainting country cling
Till they drop, blind in blood, without a blow.
A people starved and stabbed in th'untilled field;
An army, whom liberticide and prey
Makes as a two-edged sword to all who wield;
Golden and sanguine laws which tempt and slay;
Religion Christless, Godless—a book sealed;
A senate, Time's worst statute, unrepealed—
Are graves from which a glorious Phantom may
Burst, to illumine our tempestuous day.

—Percy Bysshe Shelley

*

Phloxes in Town

as if
in the impersonal thinking of the world
quiet and clear
here—as in the center of a clearing—p u r i t y
    t r e m b l e s—and we pass by
not disturbing it
even with the imperceptible
breeze of attention
    13 July 1983

—Gennady Aygi, *Child-And-Rose*

*

So much
depends upon
collateral
damage

invisible
through a night-scope
in the evening
sky

—MP, with WCW

*

Contingency, selected definitions from the *OED*:

Close connexion or affinity of nature; close relationship.

The condition of being liable or not to happen in the future; uncertainty of occurrence or incidence.

The befalling or occurrence of anything without preordination; chance, fortuitousness.

The condition of being free from predetermining necessity in regard to existence or action; hence, the being open to the play of chance, or of free will.

The quality or condition of being subject to chance and change, or of being at the mercy of accidents.

A chance occurrence; an event the occurrence of which could not have been, or was not, foreseen; an accident, a casualty.

A conjuncture of events occurring without design; a juncture.

(et al.)

✳

In April of last year, Bradin Cormack contacted me to ask whether I would be willing to come to the University of Chicago to give a reading and a talk, and I happily agreed. I believe it was in July that I was asked for a title for my talk, and I hastily decided on something about "Poetry and Contingency," though with no clear approach in mind. The events and images of 9/11 were still very preoccupying, along with the administration's ominous rhetoric of crusade-like retribution. The attack upon al Qaeda and the Taliban (and whatever innocents happened to be in the way) in Afghanistan was taking place, our promises of funds for reconstruction to the Afghan people not yet broken. It was already clear from the ultranationalistic rhetorical bombast of Bush, Rumsfeld, Cheney, Wolfowitz and Ashcroft, as well as assorted right-wing ideologues such as Richard Perle, William Kristol and Robert Kagan, that international laws and relationships, and domestic values once considered essential to the moral probity of the Republic, were coming under siege in the very name of that probity. Reason itself, as some shabby remnant of Enlightenment thought, was under siege. The poetry community, if thought of at all, was initially excoriated for not turning its full attention to the production of uplifting, elegiac verse in response to the destruction of the Twin Towers. When our designated public poets did dutifully begin to produce such verse, the results could be charitably described as lamentable and, in some odd way, self-aggrandizing.

And, of course, things had begun, even then, to accelerate in such a manner that it seemed impossible to find any fixed point from which to assess the situation. All statements of fact and purpose were subject to instant revision, as soon as proven untenable. Responsibility to language and memory was henceforth inoperable. Pure flux. We were suddenly at war not only with Terrorism, wherever it lurked, but with the earth and its resources, the Bill of Rights, the poor, the godless and, of course, discourse itself. And acceleration a central fact of culture now: today, our blitzkrieg finds our troops within a few miles of Baghdad. When I actually speak with you, who knows.

I hasten to add that this talk will reflect that flux: an assemblage of fragments, shored perhaps against the ruins. With no theory, no argument to speak of, and only that tentative knowing, that knowing of nothing, that the uncertain yet actual experiencing of poetry offers. Poetry, which includes the unspoken. Within a timeless moment of barbaric thought. Of what is and what returns; of memory and forgetting. Since I think we can agree that we find ourselves in a very strange time, yet also, remembering, a sadly all-too-familiar one. As it happens, poetry has something to say about all of these things, the "strange," the "familiar," and, of course, "time."

As I began to reflect on my title, problems soon emerged,

as seen in the above definitions. "Contingency," as a word, would seem to be both itself and another, or its other. It seems to bind as well as liberate, to conjoin and to fracture, to open to chance or to tether to circumstance. As it yields its meanings, it at once exceeds itself and undermines itself. Like any word in a poem, examined closely it grows more strange rather than more familiar. And it points both forward and backward in time, and toward an unsettled present. Of which, more later. So much depends upon the glance, the gaze, but also upon the chance of what may be there: a red wheelbarrow, a bed of phlox. Contingent, dependent. Two weeks ago, I escaped probable, meaningless death on a highway by a few inches, and my wife the same a week before that.

✳

A man, born into wealth and privilege, finds God in the bottom of a bourbon glass. This is not unusual. It is in fact banal, but not necessarily a good thing or a bad thing. To the man, it appears salvific. His first birthing did not work out. He has, in fact, little recollection of what preceded his being born again; he is said to suffer "drop-outs," abyssal memory events. This is not unusual. Then the God the man found in the glass tells him of his destiny—he at least remembers this and often recounts it—that he is to be President of the most powerful nation on earth. The man can name the heads of state of perhaps two or three foreign nations. His sense, in fact, of world geography is hazy, though he knows about Mexico, since it is adjacent to his state of rebirth. Mexico is to the south, beyond the river. He has great difficulty recalling any books he has read, except of course for the Good Book. This seems more than sufficient. He does not "believe in" evolution, or in reflection. In a laudatory memoir, an epigone reports that he is "suspicious of conspicuous intelligence," as well he might be. Everyone knows the story. (No one knows the story.)

Another man, born into wealth and privilege, dreams of driving the Infidel from the Arab lands and reestablishing the Kingdom of Islam, and he dedicates his fortune to that end. Like the other, he has undergone a kind of conversion. Like the other, he too believes in the fundamental truth of the One Book. Like the other, he converses with God; he receives messages. The one and the other are in touch with the Logos. Their families are friendly and engage in global business practices together. Everyone knows the story. (No one knows the story.)

The first man lives in a zone cleansed of poetry save, perhaps, for certain psalms and hymns. The second is given to reciting traditional religious verse during his speeches, with variations to suit the occasion. It is the kind of devotional poetry swept aside in many cultures by the tides of modernism, the modernism of which Giorgio Agamben writes, where the subject has disappeared. In the culture of fundamentalist Islam, the poetry of the one subject is the only form of poetry permitted. The poet Adonis, and many others, have spoken often of this, at their peril.

Each would destroy, and each instantly authenticates, the other. Good versus evil. As if by magic, each fulfills both roles.

And then there is Saddam, the would-be Saladin, with his meat hooks and his toxins.

Today, I gather, we are entering Baghdad.

And so, of the two possible catastrophes, those of conquest or defeat, it appears the former awaits us.

Poetry and catastrophe: we know it, poetry, makes nothing happen; we also know, or trust, it is something happening among other things happening. We know it is something happening in language, and happening to language. For some its strangeness and estrangement represent catastrophe, and they would cast the poets out of the city. They speak of the Logos besieged, as we speak of language under siege. We have a guided missile called the peace-keeper. And it seems the rhetoric of "freedom," "justice," "democracy," has been turned on its head. *Tutta per nulla, dunque?* asks Montale in his poem "Primavera Hitleriana."

We know it is something happening in language and in silence. We know in its silences a certain excess gathers, an excess, or surplus, of meaning that can cause meaning to tremble. Yet, "No more than a breath between / there and not there," as Celan writes. We know the breath-turn itself is silence, the moment in which the poem gathers itself, the site where the conversation is to begin, and where another is to be found. Whereas, it would seem the voice of God in the bottom of the glass brooks no other, except perhaps a beseeching. We know poetry is a form of listening. Both the making and the receiving are forms of listening. To an unknown language found everywhere among our daily words, in the currents of our common speech, where Jack Spicer's low-ghosts lurk. In the winding streets. We knew as we marched through the winding streets that the powers-that-be were not listening, had not the capacity to listen. Just as the discourse of control annuls conversation and represses all questioning as it erases the other, thereby ultimately erasing itself. Whereas poetry is nothing if not a question, and then a book of questions. To which the answer is, perhaps, no more than another question. Poetry in that sense remains open, and without authority. Its authors, is there anything to say of them?

Is that woman, sitting and drinking coffee, the person who wrote that poem about coffee? Is that man, talking with his daughter, the same one who wrote the poem about the moths? He seems to have misplaced his glasses once again.

✱

Poetry and memory. What does the poem remember, that otherwise the culture hastens to forget? It was no more than a week or so ago, as the bombs, the smart bombs, were first falling in unbelievable profusion, that my copy of *Child-And-Rose*, by the great Chuvash poet Gennady Aygi, arrived. It is a book concerned with childhood, sleep and silence as poetic sources. It is also a book that, as the translator Peter France writes, remembers in its rhythms, riddles and incantations the tribal origins of Chuvash song and choral dance—before the period of enforced christianization, and before Stalin. It remembers, rather than simply being remembering. It is a book not of folkish nostalgia but of the present, a work of fractures, fragments and gaps, in which the missing resides, or into which the missing has been translated. In it too, is that poem I quote at the beginning of this talk, which remembered poetry for me that day while I was forgetting it, in the ashes, and "in the impersonal thinking of the world." Or, one might say, in the noise of the world, the obliterating and deafening roar. Would you agree, that it has become harder to hear these days? Overhead, in New York, as we marched, we counted at least three helicopters. They hovered all day. Here is the opening of Aygi's "Poetry-As-Silence":

> Listening—in place of speaking. Even—more impor-
> tant than vision, any vision (even—in imagination).
> And: rustling-and-murmuring. Rustle—of the ori-
> gin—already—so distant. "Mine," "my own self."
> There "everything" is silence. All—long since—took
> their leave. Buildings are empty. Cold. The former wind,—
> dead. Deserted the lumber-rooms. The wind,—dead scat-
> tering—of dead flour.
> *Not to give way to nostalgia.* For I also am *not* . . . how
> could I! Too much—from spaces interrupted—from
> "powers" long since abolished.

I can't help adding another memory jogged by the book, that of wandering with Aygi through the Paris streets on a wet winter day years ago, while conversing in a third, shared language about Pasternak and Peredelkino, and about the French and their dogs. It was almost certainly then that I first read some of the work included in *Child-And-Rose*, in a volume of translations into French entitled *Le livre de Véronique*.

All poetry is, of course translation, a bearing across from one region to another, a crossing of borders, a conjoining of same with other. It is a voyage out of the self-same or the self-identical or the self-satisfied into a fluid semantic and ontological field. That is, to translate is also to be translated, to commit to an act of becoming . . . what? Human perhaps, in a world where we cannot assume that as a given, but as something to be earned partially and imperfectly. The extensions of voice, beyond that one with which we come into the world. The elsewhere so necessary to any understanding of the here-and-now. Yet the "here-and-now" of our national conversation seems suddenly to have filled with a virulent xenophobia, and a hatred, as well as a fear, as well as a willful ignorance, of the other, the foreign, even of difference itself. The closing of minds is represented as certainty of belief and of righteousness. Outside must be remade to conform with inside, by total force if necessary. We cannot help being reminded of the language of earlier empires, of the "white man's burden," of the "*mission civilisatrice.*" Language under siege from within.

*

Under siege: a man in a half-ruined apartment complex during Sharon's intense bombing of Beirut in 1982 wants his coffee. The man is the poet Mahmoud Darwish. He wants his coffee and his cigarette. He wants to read the newspaper over coffee and a cigarette:

> Gently place one spoonful of the ground coffee, electrified with the aroma of cardamom, on the rippling surface of the hot water, then stir slowly, first clockwise, then up and down. Add the second spoonful and stir up and down, then counterclockwise. Now add the third. Between spoonfuls, take the pot away from the fire and bring it back. Repeat this several times until the water boils again and a small mass of the blond coffee remains on the surface, rippling and ready to sink. Don't let it sink. Turn off the heat, and pay no heed to the rockets. Take the coffee to the narrow corridor and pour it lovingly and with a sure hand into a little white cup: dark-colored cups spoil the freedom of the coffee. Observe the paths of the steam and the tent of ris-

ing aroma. Now light your first cigarette, made for this cup of coffee, the cigarette with the flavor of existence itself, unequaled by the taste of any other except that which follows love, as the woman smokes away the last sweat and the fading voice.

Now I am born. My veins are saturated with their stimulant drugs, in contact with the springs of life, caffeine and nicotine, and the ritual of their coming together as created by my hand. "How can a hand write," I ask myself, "if it doesn't know how to be creative in making coffee!" How often have the heart specialists said, while smoking, "Don't smoke or drink coffee!" And how I've joked with them, "A donkey doesn't smoke or drink coffee. And it doesn't write."

I know my coffee, my mother's coffee, and the coffee of my friends. I can tell them from afar and I know the differences among them. No coffee is like another, and my defense of coffee is a plea for difference itself. . . .

A remarkable photograph appeared in the *New York Times* a few days ago, that kind of organic surrealism so typical of war scenes. A flock of Apache helicopters in close formation is heading in one direction, while below them, on the desert sands, a herd of camels, in equally close array, heads unconcernedly in the other. If I read the orientation of the picture correctly, the Apaches would seem to be heading north, in the direction of Baghdad perhaps, and the animals south.

I've just come across a note I made in early August of last year, while briefly visiting a very beautiful, very tranquil, small island off the coast of Maine. I indicate that it is "for the Chicago talk":

It is only among the less interesting artists that this question of "the aesthetic vs. the political" becomes relevant, since there is no integration, only superposition.

Regarding those such as Dante and Darwish, Beckett, Goya, Salgado, et al., it is laughable . . . the chatter of minds that cannot comprehend the concept of "the work" and its goals, its human urgency, agency. Yet to say this will bring no end to the talk, and no end of false terms. No end of noise. In fact it could be now that the noise is only beginning to rise. (And yet how quiet here.)

*

And now that noise . . . "within a timeless moment of barbaric thought." Timeless because, as Umberto Eco has written, "Bad ideas don't go away." For my generation, the assault upon language, the equation of patriotism with support of violence, the double-speak, the provocation of anxiety and paranoia, the triumphalism, all evoke the Vietnam era, and in certain ways, the Cold War ethos of the fifties. Yet, we are to go about our business, above all fulfilling those material desires represented as desire itself. In that time of growing up for me, the fifties and the sixties, there were several interconnected formative nexuses, or points of resistance, to the "culture-as-such." One was the intensely active and often collaborative world of the arts, as experienced in New York, where the visual arts, music and contemporary dance and performance were undergoing a moment of extraordinary creative ferment. Another was the international modernist and vanguardist tradition, "tradition of the new," still at the time largely unacknowledged in many of our institutions, that seemed to offer forms of resistance to the given which might prove useful to building the alternative life. That in turn led to various theoretical matrices not otherwise readily available. Thus, to cite just one example, the Russian Futurists and Formalists led to Roman

Jakobson, among others, and Jakobson and his peers led to alternative prosodies, alternative perspectives on language, on the social, and much else. Third, the exploratory counter-tradition in American poetry, with its centers in New York and San Francisco and Black Mountain, but with its adherents characteristically also scattered about the States. I think of its challenge to the settled subjectivity and self-absorption of much canonical verse of the time. And finally, the fact of Vietnam itself, that forced us to reconsider not only our own positions as artists or would-be artists in the society, but also the status of the art object itself, which had been represented to us as a kind of Grecian urn, outside of time. And though the urn may well be timeless, the poem about the urn is subject to time, is contingent upon time, its own and many others. (I quoted Shelley's sonnet at the beginning of this talk not only as an instance of scathing political verse, but also to show in an obvious way how the poem is altered by events that it cannot possibly foresee. It does not know what awaits it, any more than Dante could have foreseen Milton and the Romantics awaiting him. Nor could I have known how a particular poem of mine, being used in a dance performance, would be so altered by the events of 9/11. The point is not simply how work responds to current events, but how previous work is altered by and alters those events.) The focus of this necessarily truncated remembering is that these nexuses were not isolated but interconnected, as fact of one's thinking about poetry, the process of poetry, and its critical relation to habits of speech and thought and institutional assumptions about the function of art. Poetry as something happening among other things happening. As something happening in language, and to language under siege. Poetry as memory, sometimes memory of the future. Poetry as both fixed and in process, ever a paradox. Above all, poetry as experience, as Philippe Lacou-Labarthe would put it. (He would add, poetry as interruption of the "poetic," but that's for some other time.)

*

And yet we must acknowledge the poem's not-so-secret dream of an idea of order, a glimpse of a palm at the end of the mind, where contingency would be annihilated, perhaps by a throw of the dice.

*

Last night, as I drove home from teaching, the radio was full of rumors of the death of Saddam and his sons, killed or not killed by "bunker-buster" bombs. So far, however, in the ruins, they've only found the bodies of a twenty-year-old woman and an eight-year-old child. And it seems that the Giants have won seven in a row to start the season.

*

A timeless moment of barbaric thought, at once endlessly strange and endlessly familiar. Under siege, to drink our cup of difference and look for a clearing. To keep the conversation with language alive and open—this makes nothing happen. Yet, does it not somehow, and crucially, contribute to the restoration of Logos as ratio, as measure, and as human bond? And wouldn't that have surprised Plato?

*

And so, uncertainly, in the noise and fog of this moment when some in power would see the conquest of Baghdad as only the first among many such actions, we return to the critical concept of art as participatory if-at-all, and to Stendhal's *promesse de bonheur*, as cited by Nietzsche as quoted by Agamben. Then we trace a question mark.

[*Talk given at the University of Chicago, April 11, 2003. First published in the* Chicago Review 53:2/3, *Summer 2004.*]

ON DANTE'S *VITA NUOVA*

A curious thought, in retrospect: that a medieval Tuscan poet, Dante Alighieri, would emerge as a figure central to early twentieth-century modernism in its broadest reaches and to much of the literature that followed. It seems equally odd that the first complete translation of the *Commedia* into English did not appear until 1802, and that the first of demonstrable value, by the Anglican cleric H. F. Cary, would not arrive until 1814, some five hundred years after Dante's death. The profound appeal of his work to the poets of the Romantic movement would be magnified among the true heirs to that heritage, the innovative practitioners of modernism. While writers such as Yeats, Joyce and Beckett, Eliot and Pound (as well as many African-American writers, such as Tolson, Baraka and Naylor), were to focus centrally on the *Commedia* itself, the quieter influence of the *Vita Nuova* and the lyrics of the *stilnovisti* should not be underestimated at a time when poets were looking to break free from the hothouse of neoromantic ornament that late Victorian poetry was perceived, justly or not, to have become. The *Vita Nuova*'s echoic presence can also be felt in the prose of Joyce's *Portrait of the Artist as a Young Man*. In addition, as Rossetti himself recognized in the modest introduction to his translation, and as Eliot would later emphasize, the *Vita Nuova* represents a key to a larger understanding of the trilogy that would follow and finally be completed late in the long years of exile from Dante's native Florence.

It is generally agreed that the *Vita Nuova* was composed some-where between 1292 and 1295. On the surface, it would appear to be a simple enough work, a selection of thirty-one poems from Dante's early years, along with narrative framing devices and rather scholastic prose commentaries (Rossetti left the latter for his brother, William, to translate). It would be a book of the "new life" engendered by his first revelatory encounter with Beatrice Portinari at the age (symbolic or otherwise) of nine, a book of beginnings, dedicated to his fellow Florentine and erstwhile men-tor, the masterful lyric poet Guido Cavalcanti. Yet, given the con-text of a voracious scholarly curiosity about Dante's life, as well as the work's evident prefiguration of the *Commedia*, the "story" has come to be viewed in many, sometimes conflicting, lights. By juxtaposing prose narrative with lyric, Dante in effect narratizes his lyric impulse, in anticipation of the crossing of lyric, dramatic and narrative voicings in the epochal poem to follow. Further-more, by adding an element of poetic obliquity to the prose, he lends the commentaries a nonlinear dimension that leaves them open to multiple interpretations. Mention must also be made of the striking and strategic discrepancies, at points, between poem and commentary. To put it simply, Dante very characteristically complicates the plot while attempting to fashion a poetics more capacious than the lyric impulse of his youth, a poetics that would eventually engage fully with medieval and classical philosophy, and that would include history. So it is that his *libello*, his little "book of my memory," can be seen to open in many directions and to be open to many possible readings. This "polysemy," to use a term favored by Dante, is evident in the lyrics themselves, of course, but it is further multiplied by the interspersed prose. It is as if the rather ephemeral body of Beatrice, of the living Beatrice and the dead and the dreamed, were enfolded within layers of text of varying hues and degrees of opacity.

Is the *Vita Nuova* the book of Beatrice, the book of love, the book of memory, an allegorical autobiography, an occulted, theo-logical conversion tale, a treatise on poetics, even a kabbalistic inscription of the revealed truth in life's orders? The arguments would seem to miss the central point of Dante's evolving vision of *harmonia* and grace. The gradual overcoming of a Cavalcantian poetics of agonistic personal psychology is synchronous with a new comprehension of self and other, and of the material and the metaphysical. The new poetics *is* the new life. It is precisely within the body of the poem, a poem metamorphosing from the struggles of youthful erotic fantasy and disappointment toward an evolved, spiritualized sense of desire, that the vision is realized, and that the concepts both of memory and of the biographical self are recast. Here dream and waking interpenetrate to create a new mode of understanding, and here too the play of intuition and judgment, moment and duration, reveal the strangeness of lyric to itself, as well as its hidden, dialogic nature. The *Vita Nuova* then can be seen as the first book in Dante's lifelong project of self-commentary and self-overcoming, a beginning. Yet as such it also represents an ending to the very poetics of his youth that first gave him the possibility of the "new life." Dante announces that, after the final sonnet, "una mirabile visione" appeared to him. He resolved to say no more of Beatrice until he learned to write of her in a worthier manner.

What Rossetti might have thought of all the scholarly *combattimenti*, it is difficult to say. By explicitly disclaiming any personal scholarship in his introduction, he allows himself to focus on the mainly poetic issues the act of translating this "book of youth" evokes. The *Vita Nuova* translation appears in 1861 in a very particular context, that of Rossetti's *Early Italian Poets*. The book, Rossetti's first, is divided into two parts, "Poets Chiefly Before Dante," and "Dante and His Circle." *The New Life* was originally printed in the latter. Amid such company, Rossetti's version of the *Vita Nuova* can be seen as part of an act of transhistorical aesthetic redemption, one that would draw an implicit parallel with the artistic aspirations of the Pre-Raphaelite Brotherhood.

The work would have a profound effect on Ezra Pound and, indirectly through Pound (even as Rossetti's reputation went into partial eclipse), on twentieth-century translation theory and practice. The influence on Pound, and on modernism, had two dimensions. The first of these consisted of the attention drawn to the Tuscan poets themselves, and through them to the early vernacular tradition of Europe, the Sicilian School at the court of Frederick II in Palermo (where the sonnet is said to have been born), as well as, crucially, the troubadours and *trobairitz* of Provence, from whom the Sicilian School derived. Understanding of what constituted the lyric tradition, and cultural transmission, was thus significantly, if gradually, altered and enhanced. The second determinative influence on Pound concerned the approach to translation itself. Rossetti's skilled deployment of metrical equivalents to evoke, rather than mimic, the Italian, and his unforced handling of those meters, would forever mark Pound's Italian translations. Particularly in his early efforts, Pound would also borrow heavily from what we might call Rossetti's personal style of translation, including the, to our ears, somewhat precious use of archaisms and occasional other mannered effects. It is Rossetti's philosophy of translation, however, that would most affect not only Pound but through him countless others in the succeeding century. He summarizes this philosophy in the preface to *Early Italian Poets*:

> The life-blood of rhymed translation is this,—that a good poem shall not be turned into a bad one. The only true motive for putting poetry into a fresh language must be to endow a fresh nation, as far as possible, with one more possession of beauty. Poetry not being an exact science, literality of rendering is altogether secondary to his chief aim. I say literality,—not fidelity, which is by no means the same thing. When literality can be combined with what is thus the primary condition of success, the translator is fortunate, and must strive his utmost to unite them; when such object can only be attained by paraphrase, that is his only path.

For Rossetti, in other words, translation is an essentially poetic activity bound to a program of cultural renewal.

We have at our disposal several highly useful and skilled versions of the *Vita Nuova* in English. Some certainly take fewer liberties with Dante's text. None, however, bear the historical and poetic resonance of Rossetti's, which must qualify, in itself, as a significant literary document of its time.

With the *Vita Nuova*, Dante offers us his particular, invaluable *gradus ad Parnassum*, a journey from the circumscribed consciousness of the early lyrics, still heavily inflected by the voices of Cavalcanti, Guido Guinizzelli and others, to the great poems of first, full maturity (such as the canzone "Donne ch'avete intelleto d'amore" in the nineteenth section, which will be recalled in *Purgatorio* 24 as the definitive source of the "new rhymes"). Inseparable from this poetic journey is the altered sense of person and of calling that the death of Beatrice will occasion. The lyric will no longer be predominantly the medium of familiar, confessional complaint about personal despair and the pains of longing and unfulfillment, but rather the site for a radical transfiguration of both self and other, as well as a transformed conception of love and its language.

[*Preface for Dante Alighieri's* The New Life, *translated and with an introduction by Dante Gabriel Rossetti, New York Review of Books, 2002.*]

ON BEI DAO

Would that it were possible, right at the outset, to consign the "Misty Poets" rubric to those cultural bureaucrats' file cabinets from which it first emerged. However accurate a rendering of the Chinese (*menglong*), in English it inevitably suggests a stale, neo-romantic impressionism that has nothing to do with the work of Bei Dao or of other poets captured by the term. Nothing to do with the complex interweaving of inner and outer worlds, the private and the public, the personal and the official, the oneiric and the quotidian, the classical and the contemporary. Nothing to do with the act of resistance to cultural orthodoxy their work represents, and nothing to do with their critical deconstruction of the language of power and oppression. Nothing to do with the quest for a radical and responsive subjectivity, a lyric instrument of discovery and disclosure.

It can be a mixed blessing when a poet's work acquires sudden notoriety and immediate historical and political pertinence. Certainly it is fortunate when, due to particular historical and social conditions, poetry is attended to beyond the narrow confines of a strictly literary community. In such circumstances, the territory of its conversation expands dramatically, and poetry can seem to make things happen in ways Mayakovsky briefly thought possible, and Auden notoriously denied. Yet poetry must also always *be* "something happening"—to language, to consciousness, to time and memory. Lacking that dimension, it is no more than

verse, cultural décor, reflecting modes of representation and af-
fect already habitual. The temptation of early fame is to abandon
the work to a delusional and self-glorifying instrumentality. We
saw this happen all too often among the public poets of the six-
ties and seventies, whose voices grew hollow as they basked in
their celebrity status, and their need for immediate response be-
came akin to an addiction. The ironic result was that, instead of
critiquing the materialism, prevarications and repression of their
cultures, the poetry too often came to seem a pure product of
those same cultures, exhibiting the same desires and the same
emptiness. The terrible trap of sloganeering is that poetry can
end up echoing that very discourse of power and control it sets
out to resist.

Anointed as an icon on the Democracy Wall and as the voice
of a generation by the events of Tiananmen Square in 1989, and
thereby also fated to exile, Bei Dao has followed a path of re-
sistance that abjures overt political rhetoric while simultane-
ously keeping faith with his passionate belief in social reform
and freedom of the creative imagination. Under the guidance of
such determinedly resistant poetic intelligences as Mandelstam,
Celan and Vallejo, he has continued to develop and deepen his
own poetics, even as the conditions of exilic displacement have
exacted such enormous tolls on his personal life. In fact, it seems
to me that it is the very condition of exile that has helped Bei
Dao come to more intimate terms with that displacement at the
core of all significant, exploratory lyric poetry. I do not mean by
this to invoke some hoary, romantic cliché of poetic alienation.
Rather, I am speaking of the displacement *into* alternative tem-
poral and spatial organizations that we tend to repress in order
to configure or project a more or less linear narrative of every-
day life. (Our culture is littered with verse designed to reinforce
that same, annealing or consolatory version, as if that were true
realism.) The poet disappears—almost disappears—into this
deterritorialized, lyric space while becoming, to borrow a term
from Pessoa, the *resonateur* of various forces and tones of the

mind and the world. What results is a poetry of complex enfold-ings and crossings, of sudden juxtapositions and fractures, of pattern in a dance with randomness. It is a perilous negotiation, dependent for its coherence on a depth of attention, of listen-ing, and a commitment to that which is not yet known, rather than to the given.

We are not speaking of "pure poetry," whatever that might be, but of one that is as open to the noise of the world, and to the inhumanity and mendacious bleatings of authority, as it is to the information of dream, the immediacy of memory and the knowl-edge that arrives with loss. The "I-do-not-believe!" (from his early poem "The Answer") that became a rallying cry for the Democ-racy Movement continues to resonate through Bei Dao's later poetry. The commitment to a radical reenvisioning of experience, however, has grown progressively bolder and more assured. The conjuring of the uncanny and the indeterminate within the folds of the actual now seems less a literary debt to Surrealism than an existential acknowledgement of continuous passage through different landscapes and codes, the randomness of circumstance brought to a pitch by the poem's intense, echoic compression: "dust of the private / litter of the public." The work, in its rapid transitions, abrupt juxtapositions and frequent recurrence to open syntax evokes the un-speakability of the exile's condition. It offers us, as perhaps poetry most precisely can, the paradox of un-controllable and/or aleatory forces—of history, memory, dream, the subconscious—being brought to form within the poem. Yet what Bei Dao constructs is a form faithful to the flux itself, to the vortex of experience, and to the constant reconfiguring of time and space within that vortex. It is a poetry of explosive convergen-ces, of submersions and unfixed boundaries, "amid languages." Seeds are sown on marble floors, seasons break loose from their sequence. The subject multiplies, divides, disappears into the "wound of narration." We hear a voice at once out of time and caught in streaming time. The poem projects both the "fire of the venture" and the "ash of the unknown." First, for Bei Dao, the rescue of subjectivity, followed by the deepening knowledge of what that subjectivity can be.

I recently attended a literary festival in Berlin. Bei Dao, Eliot Weinberger, Charles Simic and I were invited to speak on a panel about "Writing from a Distance." We discussed the multiple meanings of nearness and distance in our work and lives, and the far-away-near of writing itself. The following day, Bei Dao left for Rotterdam, after which would come Berlin again, then Vienna, Oslo, Paris and New York, to be followed by a brief teaching residency in Wisconsin. He travels without a passport.

[*Preface for Bei Dao's* At the Sky's Edge: Poems 1991–1996, *translated by David Hinton, New Directions Publishing, 1996.*]

FORM'S MIND (SOME THOUGHTS ALONG THE WAY)

I think I'd better begin this little talk with a double *caveat*: the subject of this talk, strictly speaking, is-not, and the Laws of Form, to which I will at times refer, are unknowable. And, of course, "the times." It is in the nature of our time and of recent, often tragic, history that all questions of form have become decentered, fractured and factionalized. (What could better illustrate our recent century's ambivalence toward concepts of form than that icon of early modernism, *The Waste Land* itself, handed over for radical surgery from writer to editor, Eliot to Pound?)

The topic, which I rather rashly suggested some time ago, has led me at moments into a wilderness of abstraction as I've tried to consider it during the intervening period. Notebooks have filled with possible approaches, sources have been consulted, thoughts jotted down and crossed out. Late at night, things would suddenly seem quite clear, only to disappear from view upon awakening. I thought of abandoning the topic entirely for something more manageable, but the very elusiveness of it seemed to argue for continuing. I'm also aware that it's summer, and we are surrounded by some very well-known wooded landscapes, and it's no time to mistake the forest for the trees.

Since we will be discussing a few aspects of form, aspects that derive in some measure from looking back at the practices and contentions of the century just past, I should probably speak first about the form of this talk and its origins. It is, first of all, a *talk*, partly written, partly improvised. It is listed as a lecture, but this is deceptive. A lecture implies "an exposition of a given topic before an audience or class . . ." A talk, I think, implies a talking with, the beginnings of a discussion. It implies the possibility of digressions and interruptions, of folds rather than lines, all things of formal importance to me and my work. "Some Thoughts along the Way" is meant in the same spirit. It echoes Paul Celan's sense of the poem as a "conversation along the way," which in its way has implications about the fluidity and dialogic nature of active form, and about the reader's role in bringing-to-form, or bringing the poem to the present, and to its present form. I hope it will also suggest an echo of the Dante of the *Commedia*, wandering (lost) along a path and encountering souls. (More of Dante later.) Maybe we could think of it, formally, as a paratactical, partial improvisation, or, in closer to human language, a kind of exploratory ramble, mosquitoes and moths included. It comes at a time in history when there is no consensus on form, no cultural agreement as to the parameters of form and the functions of form, a time when the very invocation of the term can lead to multiple accusations, often ideological in nature, of one or another kind of formalism. (As a poet often qualified, and sometimes patronized, as "experimental," I have become accustomed to accusations of formalism from neomarxist academics and formlessness from mainstream practitioners and critics.) Yet, at the same time, we are looking back at a century of work, whether vanguardist or modernist or oriented toward some notion of tradition, where the creative impulse has been driven, at least in a particular sense, by notions of formal agency, of coming-to-form as inseparable from the informing particular to a poem. Looking backward, of course, we are implicitly looking forward, and trying to read the wildly diverse picture of the present, that present of what Robert Creeley has referred to as "American *poetries*." And conversation, of course, implies *listening*, something crucial both to the making of the poem and to its reception.

I am, by the way, while writing much of this, sitting at my desk in a barn on an island off the coast of Massachusetts. It is a structure whose foundations date to the early eighteenth century, but whose function has altered many times over the years. At some point in the nineteen fifties, by the look of the applied materials (the formica, the knotty pine, and so on), the barn was converted into a summer cottage. The hay loft above is partly filled with cast-off furniture and boxes of summer clothing and gear. The horse stalls below are now a painter's studio. There are two boxes on the makeshift desk. One announces that "The RCN Revolution has begun." Inside, there is a "certificate of authenticity," stating that "This piece of the Berlin Wall was removed in November of 1989 during the initial demolition." Beneath that, glued into its cardboard niche, is a fragment of concrete, a little over an inch long and half an inch wide. In a second box, there is a clear pane of glass. An accompanying text announces it as issue #7 of a little magazine, and gives a list of contributors to this clear pane of glass, my name among them. I can say without hesitation that this issue, this object of pure transparency, has given me great pleasure, has presented no disappointments, and has never failed to transmit light. As for the other box, and its revolution, I still have no idea what "RCN" is, though I suspect it has something to do with "communications," if not communication.

The point being an obvious one, that we live in astonishingly slippery times, where metamorphic flows predominate and where change itself may come to seem the only constant. The age of revolutions has been corporatized even as the once familiar cry to "make it new" in the arts and society recedes into history. One response to this fluidity has been to embrace chance, accident, fragmented form, oneiric imagery, and fractured or multiplied subjectivities. Yet, as Brodsky reminds us in speaking of the Renaissance, and of baroque form, such destabilizations are by no means limited to our age.

In retrospect, I can imagine the personal origins of this subject in several ways. Some years ago, I was invited by the editor of a small Danish publishing house, along with several other writers from around the world, to undertake a project, to attempt "to connect the dots" in my life in whatever form that might imply. I accepted, and then spent some time considering what form suggested itself. I finally decided on no form, or rather, an exploration of what the French call, mainly in the world of plastic arts, *l'informe*, which is usually translated as "formless," though I think "unformed" might be closer to its meaning. I would keep a journal as I traveled around the country and the world either on my own or with the contemporary dance company with which I have often collaborated and toured. As I wrote in the text:

> I once thought I should find a form for this little book you have asked for, but now it seems that unformed would be better, a book at fault. Displaced. I accepted your invitation because it seems an impossible thing for me to do, against my nature as a writer. Of course one should never have such a nature. If you discover that you do, you must erase it, as violently as possible. *Coup de torchon.* Clean slate. One of our cats, the apricot-colored one, is sleeping on the computer as I write this. He doesn't give a shit one way or the other. As long as the machine stays warm.

Den Danske Notesbog was eventually published in Copenhagen in 1998 and an American edition, *The Danish Notebook*, by Avec Books in the fall of 1999. The work is open-ended and notational, but as it evolved, and as areas of memory were jogged by travel and circumstance and what the Surrealists would call "objective chance," it became clear that a rather complex form, of unperceived linkages and tales within tales, was asserting itself within this little book. I was experiencing the quiet persistence of form and its life-revelations, beyond conscious intent or design. Rather than no form, I was facing a new form, one that exposed hidden memories and patterns, and brought to light aspects of a life otherwise undepicted, and largely unacknowledged. The result might best be described as an unforeseen work in poetics. And I began to reconsider the role of dynamic form beyond initial questions of shape and structure as we find them in the encyclopedias of poetics and academic disquisitions. To consider, in short, the Laws of Form as opposed to the Rules of Form or formal rules, the latter being relatively easy to quantify, given sufficient instruction, the former not quantifiable at all.

A second spur to these ruminations occurred during a conversation with a young Russian-born poet about Brodsky's observations on the baroque and its relation to cultural resistance and destabilized subjectivity. (See, for example, Solomon Volkov's *Conversations with Joseph Brodsky*.) What came immediately to mind was my first encounter, in high school, with the (then little discussed) poetry of Gerard Manley Hopkins. And the first of those encounters was with the now very familiar and widely analyzed "Spring and Fall." I'll try to read it to you:

Spring and Fall:

to a young child

Márgarét, are you gríeving
Over Goldengrove unleaving?
Leáves, líke the things of man, you
With your fresh thoughts care for, can you?
Áh! ás the heart grows older
It will come to such sights colder
By and by, nor spare a sigh
Though worlds of wanwood leafmeal lie;
And yet you wíll weep and know why.
Now no matter, child, the name:
Sórrow's spríngs áre the same.
Nor mouth had, no nor mind, expressed
What heart heard of, ghost guessed:
It ís the blight man was born for,
It is Margaret you mourn for.

As has been often noted, the poem offers an uncanny blend of the ancient, balladic folk tradition, marked by alliteration and "latent accents" (plus "outriders") with contemporary measures stretched to the virtual breaking point. It is at once old-new, the "other voice" to which Octavio Paz so usefully refers. Returning to this poem, I experienced the realization that I had first read it in the late spring of my life, at a time of intense spiritual crisis, and was now encountering it again in something like my early fall. Valéry spoke of the "universe opening," what I would simply call the larger world disclosing itself. Of course, we see too that the poem is not a fixed point; it changes with the reader, the times, the context. It is not immutable, a monument, but something fluid in itself, and it is this fluidity that allows it to endure.

At the same time by way, as I remember, of Pound, I had found my way to the poets of the *Dolce Stil Novo*, the Sweet New Style, who opened my eyes to the greater lyric tradition, but just as importantly, to the conversation among poets and poetry that transcends cultural, political and temporal boundaries by means of works faithful to the *Nomoi*, the Laws of Form, and the obligations of poetry, but subject to diverse and ever-changing rules of composition. As illustration, I'd like to read a poem from Dante's *Rime*, translated by Patrick Diehl, followed by an overwriting of same by the West Coast poet Robert Duncan from his collection *Roots and Branches*:

from Dante's *Rime*

Guido, I wish that Lapo, you, and I
Were taken up by strong ensorcelment
And set in ship, wherever winds were sent,
Who'd go the way we chose (no matter why),

And no misfortune, no untimely sky
Might ever make an hour's impediment,
And our minds being always of one bent,
Desire of more increase in every eye.

And mistress Vanna and mistress Lagia then,
With her whose number's thirty of three score,
Merlin would bring us, he who brought us there,

And talk of love would be our only care,
And each would be content to ask no more,
Just as I'm certain we would be, we men.

. . .

Sonnet 3

from Dante's Sixth Sonnet

Robin, it would be a great thing if you, me, and Jack
    Spicer
Were taken up in a sorcery with our mortal heads so
    turnd
That life dimmd in the light of that fairy ship
The Golden Vanity or *The Revolving Lure*,

Whose sails ride before music as if it were our will,
Having no memory of ourselves but the poets we were
In certain verses that had such a semblance or charm
Our lusts and loves confused in one

Lord or Magician of Amor's likeness.
And that we might have ever at our call
Those youths we have celebrated to play Eros
And erased to lament in the passing of things.

And to weave themes ever of Love.
And that each might be glad
To be so far abroad from what he was.

The great poets of the Sweet New Style, Guido Cavalcanti, the young Dante, Cino da Pistoia and others are inheritors of the lyric discoveries of the twelfth-century Sicilian School, where the sonnet is said to have evolved, and they in turn seemed to derive in part from the Judaeo-Arabic singers of the Iberian Peninsula (with their extraordinary access to classical texts), the land known as Sepharad among the Jews. Dante himself of course acknowledges close kinship with and pays homage to the Troubadour poets of Provence. I think we are all to greater or lesser degree aware of the future history of the sonnet and lyric poetry in general to which these examples will lead throughout Europe and beyond, the future history that is of an evolving subjectivity and historical/ cultural and linguistic consciousness. Like Rossetti and his Pre-Raphaelite circle, Duncan and the poets of the Berkeley Renaissance will consciously mirror earlier coteries while forging a new poetics and exploring a new forthrightness in the expression of erotic feeling. Here, even as Duncan offers homage to the sonnet form, he explores a more open, perhaps even broken, variation on it, sounding us back to the age of Wyatt, before the forms of the English sonnet had become standardized. He posits thereby a concept of transmission, of *Traditio*, that is perhaps more welcoming, and certainly more various and fluid, than Eliot's conception of it. It is the shared vision of the poem as beyond the singular, a thing never known as such before, yet also in harmony with the "ancient magickers." That same "ancientness" marks such radical, early vanguardist poets as Khlebnikov, as well as the revelatory contemporary poet of the Chuvash Republic east of Moscow, Gennady Aygi (hardly known here as yet), to say nothing of Akhmatova herself, or the still much underestimated Mikhail Kusmin. Or we might simply experience it in a resonant refrain, such as "I've known rivers." As to this spirit of transmission, we could just as well note Catullus's *carmina* 51 ("Ille me par esse deo videtur . . ."), in relation to the poem of Sappho it derives from, which only survives because the somewhat mysterious scholar we have commonly called Longinus chose to quote from it in the treatise we most often refer to as "On the Sublime."

Here, too, it might be useful to speak briefly of the bodily source of our means. The great Russian poet Osip Mandelstam writes of Dante's measures, "The step, linked to the breathing and saturated with thought: this Dante understands as the beginning of prosody." And, "In Dante philosophy and poetry are forever on the move, forever on their feet. . . . The metrical foot of his poetry is the inhalation; the exhalation is the step." Form's mind, form's body. One can't help being reminded of Paul Celan's sense of the *Atemwende*, the turn of the breath, that point between inhalation, the bringing in of the outside, and exhalation, where, as all singers must learn, the song begins, as well as the poem, as it fashions us. And from that same "Conversation about Dante," "In poetry only the executory understanding has any importance, and not the passive, the reproducing, the paraphrasing understanding. Semantic satisfaction is equivalent to the feeling of having carried out a command." Little wonder that this uncompromised, diasporic spirit would be identified and extinguished as an enemy of the people.

As the Slavics scholar Sidney Monas has noted, Mandelstam's Dante, breathing, embodied, peripatetic, could hardly be more different from the formidable and distant figure in Eliot's essays on Dante, which "are permeated by a nostalgia for a remote, more integral, more spiritually grounded age."

A third box on my desk: matches from the Paradiso e Inferno Restaurant, 389 Strand, London, (opp. Savoy Hotel).

With the poem, we stand, we walk, toward something not visible, something that will come to form in the crossing of intention (what the philosopher might call "judgment") and intuition (or what the musician might call "improvisation"). A place-yet-to-be. As the poet Barbara Guest has noted, form occurs in "conditions of freedom." Yet the word here resonates with paradox. One is never simply at liberty, at play, for the poem occurs, always, within certain governing contingencies, within a culture, and

that culture brings with it complex desires and often conflict-
ing obligations. Even the vanguardist impulse to clear the decks
derives from an observed need to cleanse and restore the power
of the imaginative word. Even the poem of traditional measures
(though here we must always ask which tradition) bears its ob-
ligation toward the never-before. Even the sociological or politi-
cally motivated poem will reveal an aesthetic dimension (which
comprises as well the anti-aesthetic). And of course "freedom"
here must be read as inner freedom, as the history of the world's
poetries all too evidently shows.

In each successful instance, a certain surplus of meaning
will occur, a dimension of semantic inexhaustibility beyond the
strictly communicative function, that will allow the poem to
return, will allow it to converse with an *other*, an unknown ad-
dressee, will allow it to flow and submit to alternative readings,
alteration, othering. Here it is that form's mind insists, beyond
whatever practical or aesthetic intent, on the *more*. This is not
an argument for riddling complexity, but for the echoic rich-
ness and referential breadth of even the simplest poetic speech
in a particular framework of desire, that point where "the po-
etic, world-disclosing function of language" (Habermas) escapes
the constraints of its daily obligations. As all poetry escapes or
overrides what the poet means to say to arrive at what the poem
means. Informing form vs. conforming form. Without this last
step into the dark, so to speak, into a kind of trust or acknowl-
edgment, the poem—and the poet—will never fully come to be.

If I say that the Laws of Form, of active form, are unknowable,
as opposed to formal rules, it is not meant as an act of mystifi-
cation. I mean instead to invoke something like the difference
between a code of ethics and a code of morality. Ethics is largely
determined by circumstances, custom, shifting beliefs, even
though we have an ethical tradition that extends back to earliest
philosophy. Whereas a moral code—and this is not the place of
poetry—tends to be fixed, absolute, and frequently unethical. We
cannot "know" the Laws of Form except as they enact language

across, but not outside of, time. Form, as understood here, includes but transcends the aesthetic, and includes its own particular ethical determinants. We observe this most graphically in the varied goals and desires and understandings of active form among our various poetic subcultures. I shouldn't need to add, as well, that the Laws of Form have nothing to do with so-called "ideal form," but rather with the poem's being-in-the-world, its stance toward systems of control, societal and aesthetic preconceptions and received ideas. One might say, the poem's eternal stance against passive subjectivity, against the given, on behalf of the unspeakable and the unheard. (I like Nathaniel Mackey's term, "discrepant engagement.") Whenever poetry moves too close to power, or is seduced by authority (its own or someone else's), it begins to emit a curious, though recognizable, odor, signaling its demise. So, we might also conjecture that the Laws of Form include something like an ethics of representation, varying from community to community. I leave it for the moment at that. As for the Rules of Form, they will apply as long as and wherever they remain generative, which is to say, as long as they remain capable of renewal and fresh modulation, and wherever they maintain credibility. Wherever, that is, they can still engage and incite form's mind.

We live in a fascinating and intensely vital, if deeply paradoxical, moment for poetry, or for our host of *poetries*. For even as consumer culture and materialism continue to expand exponentially, and even as the marginalization of the noncommercial arts becomes increasingly alarming, the practice of poetry itself manifests a breadth and diversity of undeniable significance. Notions of canonicity, and poetic and social agency, are undergoing a process of rearticulation. Paradise and Inferno occupy the same restaurant, for your dining pleasure. (About the Purgatorial, we can only guess.)

At the same time, we have allowed our debates to wander into a number of areas of seemingly irresolvable contention. Traditional formalists (neo- and otherwise) contend that only a return to narrative linearity and metrical orthodoxy will save us from the flood of nondescript nonmetrical verse. Vanguardists (neo- and otherwise) maintain that the master narratives have collapsed, that a fractured or multiple subjectivity is the only vital reflection of, or commentary upon, the swirling moment, the only viable response to the culture of control. Both, interestingly, rail against the institutional workshop, not without some justification, as producer of the McPoet and McPoem, of relentlessly normal, disempowered verse. Both have adherents who attended those workshops. While others dismiss the two as sides of one, predominantly white, coin, and others set stage against page. In our institutions of learning, meanwhile, many cultural theorists and others reflect antiquated and largely unexamined assumptions about the aesthetic dimension and about poetry's significance within society. This represents an uninspired and superficial reaction to an older mandarinism, which secured poetry's place as a timeless phenomenon of high culture.

I think, for the most part, these debates are to be welcomed and joined. Certainly they may be seen to come with the particular, heterogeneous territory that is the American cultural landscape. At the same time, they risk leaving the poem, once again, homeless or, at least, exiled from the debate itself and without a voice. The prescriptions of the New Formalists tend frequently, in certain hands, toward the formulaic, producing work of a dreary familiarity and transparency and a reader-friendly blandness. Much recent vanguardist activity (often itself now a product of workshops) displays an overdependence on the "device" (collage, fragmentation, the aleatoric, displacement, borrowed Oulipean operations and so on), ironically engendering another version of the overly familiar or formulaic, the "same" as sign of "difference." Maybe I'm saying nothing more than that any poetics can calcify into an evasion, an evasion of listening and attendance to that *other* information, that *othering* voice that arises along the way. It has perhaps something to do with the elusive nature of the poem, its uncanniness, its mindedness, its insistence, its necessary heresies, that it not be welcomed to the debate itself, though I think we can say that the poem will be there once the hall has cleared.

If I am arguing for anything, it is for acknowledgment of a certain formal agency and engagement that does not stand outside or aside but is in fact determined by, and in some measure determinative of, its place and its time; and, perhaps implicitly, I am invoking an alternative model of form that is fluid, shifting, communicative, an unfolding and enfolding, and a mutuality. Form's mind, that figment we have been entertaining here, is a fashioner of time.

[*Talk given at Breadloaf Writers Conference, August 2000; revised 2008.*]

POETIC OBLIGATIONS (TALKING ABOUT NOTHING AT TEMPLE)

for Robert Creeley and in memory of my mother

The Snow Man

One must have a mind of winter
To regard the frost and the boughs
Of the pine-trees crusted with snow;

And have been cold a long time
To behold the junipers shagged with ice,
The spruces rough in the distant glitter

Of the January sun; and not to think
Of any misery in the sound of the wind,
In the sound of a few leaves,

Which is the sound of the land
Full of the same wind
That is blowing in the same bare place

For the listener, who listens in the snow,
And, nothing himself, beholds
Nothing that is not there and the nothing that is.

I am quoting this poem by Wallace Stevens not from page 8 of
The Library of America edition of his *Collected Poetry and Prose*, but
from page 107 of Robert Creeley's recently published *Day Book of
a Virtual Poet*. Stevens' poem might initially be considered famil-
iar, even overly familiar, yet I'm happily informed by the way it
finally resists any easy assimilation. At some point later, I will cite
two more poems from Creeley's book, from this self-designated
virtual poet's virtual day book, to serve in a sense as emblems for
this talk. I am reminded of something entirely obvious, that it is
not only the text that counts, but also the context in which it is
met, even if it has been met elsewhere, and often, before. Thus I
can never think of that consummately wintry book, *Anna Kar-
enina*, without being called back to my initial reading of it, at the
age of seventeen, in the heat of a distant Paris summer. A friend
and I would often go to the somewhat notorious and comical and
now disappeared Piscine Deligny, with its filtered water (I *hope* it
was filtered) from the Seine. We went there to escape the heat, but
more so to listen to the extraordinary conversations of the pimps
and their women who gathered there to relax during those July
and August afternoons. I would bring along my rapidly deliquesc-
ing Modern Library paperback of *Anna K* and read it while lying
on a towel over the rough boards at poolside. So, into those pages
has been inserted forever the slang-laced give and take of the *ma-
quereaux* and their companions. This may inadvertently reveal at
least one of the reasons why becoming a literary critic was never a
personal option. As for Stevens, I must have first read *Harmonium*
during the preceding high school year, though it would be several
more years before I came to a full appreciation of his work.

   I had at one point a particular and somewhat circumscribed
subject for this talk, but the life of someone very close to me was
thrust not long ago into a series of crises and ruptures that ren-
dered such a method both unworkable and, I think finally, in-
appropriate. For weeks, between visits to emergency rooms and
all-night vigils, I struggled to proceed "as normal," but a screen
seemed to be placed between me and those texts with which I

otherwise felt intimate. In my exhaustion, both mental and phys-
ical, reflection and reading itself became virtually impossible. I
came to realize that something more raggedly episodic was neces-
sary, something more proximate to my actual state. The result is this
form, one of dispersal, perhaps a map of my nervous system.

What more, as preface? There are classic texts on poetics,
most famously Aristotle's. They have a subject that is more or
less determined, and they proceed to articulate that subject by
means of discursive reasoning. Then there are the writings *in* po-
etics. These tend to be the work of the poets and makers. There
is no fixed subject, in either sense of that term, and they usually
proceed by a kind of paratactic errancy and urgency. It is writ-
ing that is *unterwegs*, on the way, forward and backward like the
poem itself. Such works might include the letters of Emily Dick-
inson, Rimbaud, Keats and Van Gogh; certain experimental prose
works of Gertrude Stein, such as *How to Write*; the dialogues of
Marcel Duchamp; various personal notebooks and journals; the
writings of John Cage, Toru Takemitsu, Robert Smithson, Anto-
nin Artaud, and Dziga Vertov, to cite an arbitrary handful. Osip
Mandelstam, Louis Zukofsky, Georges Perec, Susan Howe, H.D.,
Kamau Brathwaite, another handful. The Chuvash poet Gennady
Aygi's "Sleep-And-Poetry," Moscow, 1975. Aygi, heir to Maya-
kovsky and Khlebnikov and, like Khlebnikov, steeped in a partic-
ular ancientness. Closer in time and to home, Norma Cole's talk
a few months back, "The Poetics of Vertigo," for the George Op-
pen Memorial Lecture Series in San Francisco. Ann Lauterbach's
recent series of engagements with poetics titled "The Night Sky."
The term "disorderd devotions," from Robert Duncan, comes to
mind. Several years ago, the poet Emmanuel Hocquard invited
me to the University of Bordeaux to give a series of lectures to a
group of Beaux Arts students there and to collaborate with them
on number of works in the visual arts deriving from a sequence
of mine, "Seven Poems Within a Matrix for War," that had been
given to them in translation. The evening before my first class,
Emmanuel showed me a video of the great French philosopher

Gilles Deleuze talking about film near the end of his life. What most struck me, beyond the imaginative character of his thought, was that here at the end, in an extraordinary calm, Deleuze had at last escaped philosophy and had escaped himself. He was in "the open"—to use a term frequently employed by Paul Celan—with nothing before him.

So we will begin, and perhaps even end, this talk with nothing. With "nothing himself." With "Nothing that is not there." With "the nothing that is." I hope we will somehow be on the way.

Another invitation. A couple of years ago I was invited to Paris to be interviewed at the Centre Pompidou on the odd topic of the writer and his tools. At roughly the same time, François Ditesheim of the Gallerie Jan Krugier, Ditesheim & Cie in Geneva asked if I would be willing to write the catalogue essay for a show of pastels by the painter Irving Petlin, who was living in Paris at the time. I could then visit Petlin's studio and view the pastels while there. The show was to be entitled "The World of Edmond Jabès," and would derive from Petlin's reading of the first three volumes of *The Book of Questions*, in Rosmarie Waldrop's superb translation. The catalogue was eventually published, and I received my first copies in the late fall of 1997. I had titled my piece "A Bonfire in the Starry Night." The reproductions of the pastels were of a high order, and the text was well presented. As I leafed through the catalogue, however, I began to realize that I had made a crucial error of judgment, that I had somehow missed what lay at the heart of Petlin's working with Jabès. I had found Petlin following Jabès through the routes of the fifth arrondissement, their shared neighborhood of streets and alleyways and shops, had found him imaging the crossings that occurred there of the living and the dead, of silence and the spoken, and had found as well the rhymes between the whiteness of the city and the desert's whiteness, the whiteness of linen and of page, between the screams of the city and the desert's silence, and had thought I had clearly heard the silence of the screams themselves:

He was seventeen. An age with wide margins.

And then one night, a little before day. And then one day, and then one night, and then nights, and days which were nights, the confrontation with death, the confrontation with the dawn and the dusk of death, the confrontation with himself, with no one.

In the catalogue, I came to a pair of pastels on paper. These, "The soil shifted (for a long time)" (I & II), are as close to pure abstraction as Petlin is ever likely to come. In the catalogue I had written, "Petlin has stated that both works 'almost made themselves,' and that 'certain things can't be drawn, instead they are materialized.'" It is the paper itself, the defining shapes in it, which Petlin allows to model his patterns. In each, what is described is a surface; the unspeakable, beneath, is both implied and screened. Their title is drawn from a passage in *The Book of Yukel* and reads:

And Yukel said:
"In a village in Central Europe, the Nazis one day buried some of our brothers alive. The soil shifted with them for a long time. That night, one and the same rhythm bound Israelites to the world."

The drawings themselves do little more than follow the grain of the paper's surface and highlight its shallow folds. There is barely more than touch. It could be said, in fact, that here it is the paper itself which has become the shaping hand. There are no figures, and the artist/onlooker has withdrawn. They thus offer the ground from which all the rest of the work in the series will arise and to which it will in some sense return. Might they not also be seen as cognates with that phrase of Paul Celan, "Niemandes Stimme, wieder," "No one's voice, again" (which I used as epigraph to my collection of poems *First Figure* in 1984)? In both instances, do we not confront the paradoxical limit-case of representation, as well as something that touches on the central obligations of poetry to itself and the world, something that much poetry, speaking of this and that, all too easily sets aside? I have a little entry in my notebook from July 5, 1998: "That point where the poem, *qua* poem, disappears . . ." Nothing of course to do with linguistic transparency, rather the opposite.

I have another note, only a few days later, "How discuss the other language of poetry, a language that is at once other and the same? The various ways of going 'there' (nowhere/now here)? The poem itself, the boat, its sail a tongue (*Egyptian Book of the Dead*)." I think, in this, what I'm very much fumbling or stumbling toward is some distinction between an art of the given and an art of the actual. (Strangely it is the former that in our culture is most frequently celebrated, but that's for another day.) Not some dim reflection, or reflexive confession, but the actual as it respires, hidden in plain sight. Placement of words as the place meant. For the moment, anyway, let's propose that poetry is translation from a lost, or forgotten, language, that is, one spoken everywhere in the streets and yet unheard or else unlistened to. It comes to us in both its familiarity and its foreignness. Maybe that's not so far from Valéry's sense of "a language within a language," though I hope it takes us in a different direction, closer, let's say, to Williams' beautiful formulation in *Kora in Hell*:

> That which is heard from the lips of those to whom we are talking in our day's-affairs mingles with what we see in the streets and everywhere about us as it mingles also with our imaginations. By this chemistry is fabricated a language of the day which shifts and reveals its meaning as clouds shift and turn in the sky and sometimes send down rain or snow or hail. This is the language to which few ears are tuned so that it is said by poets that few men are ever in their full senses since they have no way to use their imaginations. . . . of old poets would translate this hidden language into a kind of replica of the speech of the world with certain distinctions of rhyme and meter to show

that it was not really that speech. Nowadays the elements of that language are set down as heard and the imagination of the listener and of the poet are left free to mingle in the dance.

Once again, I am quoting not directly from *Kora in Hell*, Section XV, but from Gerald Bruns' "The Remembrance of Language: An Introduction to Gadamer's Poetics," in the volume *Gadamer on Celan*. As I write the title of Bruns' piece down, I hear the ancient Orphic and Egyptian play on the re-membering of language's body, of gathering up the scattered limbs. Orpheus/Osiris.

In his essay, "Who Am I and Who Are You?," Gadamer himself explores the endless shifting of the shifters in Celan's work:

> Readers of lyric poetry always already understand in a certain sense who I is. Not just in the trivial sense of knowing that it is always the poet who speaks, rather than a speaking person introduced by him. Beyond that, readers also know what the poet-I actually is. For the I pronounced in a lyric poem cannot be conclusively limited to the I of the poet, which would be different from that of the I-pronouncing reader. Even when the poet is "cradled in his characters," expressly separating himself from the "instantly mocking" crowd, it is as if he no longer means himself, but rather includes the reader in his I-character, separating him or her from the crowd in the same way he knows himself to be. This is especially true with Celan, where "I," "you," and "we" are pronounced in an utterly direct, shadowy uncertain and constantly changing way. This I is not only the poet, but even more so "that individual" [*jener Einzelne*], as Kierkegaard named the one who is each of us.

Gadamer goes on to note the readerly obligation, parallel to the poetic one I refer to above, of allowing him- or herself to be "equally implicated." It is within this agreement, this pact if you will, that the conversation of the poem begins and its social nature is affirmed. In focusing on this point, Celan distances himself from any "object-nature" of the poem, in favor of an idea of process, "the unforgetting of language," as Bruns puts it, "*living* language: language whose mode of existence is the event, a language of *Erfahrung* that lives through and undergoes the experiences of all those who speak it and hear it, and which is therefore never self-identical, but always on the way. . . ."

In their parallel exiles then, Celan and Jabès explore the dismembered body of language (Celan's German) and dismembered memory, where identities constantly metamorphose, in search perhaps of a vanished *I-thou*. Yet this play of absence and presence, this shifting among shifters, temporal and pronominal, as Gadamer notes, this disappearing, is central to the lyric experience. I would suggest as well that it is part of the unsounded nature of all linguistic experience, part of that world of the destabilized and the relational we choose to cover over, to leave unheard, the shifting, or destabilized, ground. A ground, in Celan, often blanketed with snow:

Deine Frage—deine Antwort.   Your question—your answer.
Dein Gesang, was weiß er?   Your song, what does it know?

Tiefimschnee,   Deepinsnow,

Snowshroud, sometimes snowfield, it is no one thing in Celan's work. At times it is perhaps no more than the everyday, what is before you, returned to itself here on a page. But what of snow on a page? If it is also the hidden, so too it may be an open and silent field of unforgetting; or the linen, at once surface and winding sheet; or the inversion of sky and ground; "the inverted flower." Is it the stillness of the breathturn, that moment between inhaling and exhaling, Celan so often invokes? As Gadamer remarks (speaking of snow in another poem), "It cannot be answered." It cannot be answered, because here the poem, presenting itself, re-presents nothing. Then what has all this to do with the cat now in my lap, or the earth split open outside my window? What, as the enraged junior professor asked, does it have to do with a picketline? Indeed. Or with smoke? Or with Goethe's beech tree among the fields and hills of Buchenwald?

Before exploring a few of these issues a bit further and allowing, as I said above, this piece to begin to dismantle itself, let me offer a second emblem as interlude, following from the Stevens poem and once again cited by Creeley in *Day Book of a Virtual Poet*. William Carlos Williams:

These

are the desolate, dark weeks
when nature in its barrenness
equals the stupidity of man.

The year plunges into night
and the heart plunges
lower than night

to an empty, windswept place
without sun, stars or moon
but a peculiar light as of thought

that spins a dark fire—
whirling upon itself until,
in the cold, it kindles

to make a man aware of nothing
that he knows, not loneliness
itself—Not a ghost but

would be embraced—emptiness,
despair—(They
whistle and whine) among

the flashes and booms of war;
houses of whose rooms
the cold is greater than can be thought,

the people gone that we loved,
the beds lying empty, the couches
damp, the chairs unused—

Hide it away somewhere
out of the mind, let it get roots
and grow, unrelated to jealous

ears and eyes—for itself.
In this mine they come to dig—all.
Is this the counterfoil to sweetest

music? The source of poetry that
seeing the clock has stopped, says,
The clock has stopped

that ticked yesterday so well?
and hears the sound of lakewater
splashing—that is now stone.

A curious, twisted century, to say the least, among the poems,
"among / the flashes and booms of war." A century bracketed by
so many repressions and returns, often horrific. Yet in the face of
the storm, frequently in the teeth of it, there occurs an outpour-
ing of defiant, exploratory and amplifying work, as the recent,
two-volume *Poems for the Millennium*, edited by Jerome Rothen-
berg and Pierre Joris, forcefully reminds us, whatever its inevitable
omissions and occasionally contestable inclusions. How perverse
might it seem to think of it as a century, that is a poetic century,
also bracketed, if approximately and imperfectly, by works on, of
all schools, that of the troubadours? This thought came to me

recently, as I read through Ezra Pound's *A Walking Tour in Southern France*, assembled by Richard Sieburth from Pound's notebooks dating to the summer of 1912. That in turn brought occasion to reread Jacques Roubaud's indispensable study of the troubadours from our end of the century, *La Fleur Inverse*. Two major poets who choose to look not only at the poetry of twelfth-century France, but also to use it as a lens for examining our own works and days. Not so strange perhaps, when we consider that the troubadours and the *trobairitz* represent a distant European origin (with, undoubtedly, Judeo-Arabic and other influences) of a certain research into the paradoxes of voice, subjectivity and address, silence and violence, cognition and desire, stillness and history we know as the contemporary lyric and its mirror, the antilyric. For our purposes here, I would simply draw attention to Roubaud's first chapter, "La tenson du néant et le dilemme du trobar," and the closely related "The Seventh Day," of Giorgio Agamben's *Language and Death: The Place of Negativity*. What happens when song arrives at the intimacy of the other, that "more or less distant, unknown addressee," as Mandelstam phrases it (as cited by Bruns in *Gadamer*)? Beyond the "self-same"? With a question? In our time, facing the discourses of control (which asks no question) and of exploitation, dual coercions, it is a question to be asked for our time, if time is to be recovered as (h)ours, unconstrained. So Khlebnikov, in full, and fully ironized possession:

> To No-man's-land!
> To that green field in *Niemandland*,
> beyond the leaden Nieman river,
> To Nieman-land, to No-man's land, follow, believer.

The translation, I should note, is by Paul Schmidt, from his almost unimaginably vital and authoritative five-volume edition of Khlebnikov's works for the Harvard University Press. I received word of Paul's death from AIDS two days ago, as I was preparing to deliver this talk.

✴

As we walk
beneath, as we
pass through, as
we wander among
these arcades of
iron and glass
and stone, what
is first for
sale? Time here,
then light, a
shoe, then another
shoe, hundreds of
shoes, soap, thousands
of soaps, candy
in barrels, jewelry,
scents, shirts and
pants, pads and
pens, machines for
processing numbers and
words. Access is
for sale, as
well, to virtual
arcades. There is
Politix, the store.
There are mountains
of books: best
sellers, manuals, how-to
and how-not-to, romances,
mysteries, guides for
foreign lands, *One
Hundred Favorite Love
Poems of the
English Language*, poems

> about marriage, dying,
> divorce, childhood, childbirth,
> sex, the seasons,
> dreams, exotic pets,
> our cells adrift.

★

Language and Death

27 December. My mother now, so close to the end, so fervently gasping for breath.

28 December. Visit to the doctor today. Her valvular heart disease now far advanced, so that she has anywhere from days to weeks to five or six months to live. Her 92nd birthday next month.

The doctor's words, "It will take its course."

Note for Temple talk: this is part of the moment of making such a talk, not apart from it. As is the renewed bombing of Iraq, as is . . . ?

13 January. It isn't the death so much, its prospect, that causes pain (though it does), but the disappearance, bit by bit, word by word, of the one known. Or is it that another side of the self, previously unknown, is coming to be at the end? (And that we are—*I am*—reluctant to acknowledge it?)

Sarah visiting her grandmother for two and a half hours today. My mother's regret that she won't see what will become of Sarah, that they won't have adult conversations together.

Even as, for a moment, she apparently confuses me with her brother Michael.

This sudden onset of intermittent dementia in recent days, confusion of the names.

Confusion of the names.

Now and then, I, you, he, she and it, suddenly loose from their moorings.

And yet the address, the call, has an openness and directness and a fierce intimacy she has never before allowed herself. ["utterly direct, shadowy uncertain and constantly changing . . ."]

Note for Temple talk: a poet, whoever that may be, should never offer an essay—still another essay—but instead something closer to the truth, its confusions and hallucinations, if we might recover such words from discredit.

She has begun to confuse one name with another, a presence with an absence, and so those absent return and those present disappear. Son Michael becomes the brother Michael, dead these forty-more years.

Note for Temple talk: We would always like to offer a form that has not existed before, as a gift to the conversation. It is our only one, even as it echoes other forms, even as they recur within it.

15 January. The sadly beautiful flow of my mother's "liberated" language as she lies, near death, in dementia in the hospital. She who was always so constrained, now freely mixing times, names and events in a final temporal/narrative journey.

16 January. Today, my mother gradually regaining some lucidity in the morning, then a substantial bit more in the afternoon. Almost unbelievable, given where she was when brought to the hospital. So, she is back to the familar, endlessly retold stories, the ones that locate her in the world, that fix her as just this, here and nowhere else, herself and nothing else.

18 January. This afternoon and late into the night, my mother slipping back into extreme confusion, now darkly colored with paranoia. "Why are you doing this to me?" "Are you trying to kill me?" "You don't sound like my son." "Don't you believe me? Look, that one has a gun!" A look of terror in her eyes, when I first arrived, beyond any I had ever seen before. So we are joined in those eyes, with such others as brought her here and are keeping her from her home.

The attending nurse explains to me that the phrase used for such behavior is "twilighting." As the light of day fades from the room, estrangement, disorientation and fear increase.

I think of David Levi Strauss, at Robert Duncan's hospital bedside, when Robert was hallucinating and appeared near death, though in fact he would return and survive another few months. Levi Strauss was listening to Robert's words, the flow of images of color, of lightness and darkness, when he suddenly began to hear that it was the imagery of the Bardo realm, almost exactly as described in *The Tibetan Book of the Dead*.

The realization that this slippage, this disconnectedness, this revisioning of time and person, is always there, within us, but under surveillance and control, except when through fever, mental disturbance, physical extremity, it surfaces to present its alternatives to the story as we would otherwise fashion it. So too, as in dream, the dead are always with us, waiting to put in an appearance, given the opportunity. The subject is no longer fixed by time and place and habit of self-presentation, nor is the Other so fixed as X or Y or even other. Much of this is what the poem knows, all along, even if most verse does not, or does not want to know.

At various points during the afternoon, I am my mother's husband, father of myself, father of Michael, discussing how "I" —the father—loved and raised my child. She speaks to him, to me as him, as a man she had had to learn to love, and tells of an excursion one afternoon, when he had played at length with me, and she had understood then that he was a good father and had begun to love him. The intimacy of this is difficult to describe, impossible to transcribe. I look on and listen in (overhear) with a deeply sad and deeply uncomfortable fascination, see myself as a four- or five-year-old, that day we visited the Cloisters in New York, an outing I remember very clearly, as I remember my father's death late one night in the summer of 1964.

At another point, I am again her brother Michael, from whom comes my middle name, which I've adopted as my first. I am Michael the brother before Michael was born. Michael "who is having trouble breathing." Michael who died still young.

22 January. Note for Temple talk: Maybe it would be enough

simply to list titles of books lying on the floor of living room, bedroom, hallway and study. But enough for what? To graph the expenditure of a cretinous life?

Incomprehensibility of the day as such, and of the everyday.

24 January. 11:10 p.m. The call early this morning (c. 4 a.m.) from attending nurse, saying that my mother had died in her sleep some minutes before.

The end of it, two days before her 92nd birthday. The infinite sadness and infinite distance in her face when I went to the hospital, two days ago, to accompany her home in the ambulance. A sadness that had gone far beyond me, that would not brook address, one that I have glimpsed in certain Rembrandts. [Days later, the word "departure" comes to mind, and the word "elsewhere."] There are poets who might make poems of this, good or more likely bad, but I cannot.

In deep exhaustion, yet unable to sleep, I find myself reading about the trial of the Nazi collaborator Maurice Papon, this Papon who after his World War II depravities would resurface as the head of the Paris Police and oversee the slaughter of Algerian protestors in 1961. Their bodies witnessed there by Irving Petlin, who took part in the protest. Now Papon's face hangs like a towel inside one of Irving's pastels, and the bodies of the dead have reappeared in his *Seine Series*.

✳

By another, much earlier notebook entry, I am reminded that one of the scatter of ideas for this talk came while reading *Confronting Silence*, the great Japanese composer Toru Takemitsu's selected writings. In particular, a little piece called, simply, "John Cage." Here are a couple of excerpts:

> John Cage speaks of the "insides of sounds." This may seem
> like mysterious talk, but he is only suggesting that we include
> all kinds of vibrations in what we accept as musical sound. . . .

> Music is something to be listened to, not explained. . . . *Listening* to his sounds is what John Cage's music really is. . . .

> Genuine art always defies classification. Shallow and flimsy works are always measured by conventional criteria; they do not survive. The deep impression created by some art is not the result of the individual nature of the artist. Naturally, that cannot be eliminated entirely, but it is by our taking in the quiet revelation beyond the artist's individual nature that we are inspired anew each time we confront the art. Because that quiet revelation defies classification it is alive. It has various characteristics and it changes according to who takes it in.

And then a bit further along:

> In Japanese we have the word *ikeru*, a colloquial form of *iku*. It has two meanings. One is "to place flowers in a vase to revive them." The other is "to bury a corpse." Isn't there something basic in this word? Isn't this combination of life and death a measure of the world?

In turn, reading this led me back to Cage's early gathering of writings called *Silence*, and in particular to the now famous "Lecture on Nothing." In fact, it was the first text I taught in the first class I ever taught, an expository writing workshop at Harvard many years ago. I suppose I was bent, even then, on sending students off on the wrong track. It is a text to be sounded, a text that is now, I suppose, a classic work in poetics, though it was then greeted with much ridicule, like Cage's music, by the codifiers and classifiers, may they too rest in peace:

I am here   ,   *and there is nothing to say*   .

To my ear, this gently anarchic piece bears directly upon the *sagesse* of the *tenso de non-re*, the tenson of nothing, where the poet discovers not the subject, but the "taking place of language as originary argument" (Agamben) and thus discovers self as nothing in itself, as only coming-to-be at the moment of greeting, along the way. The poetic here, the obligation here, involves both greeting, or acknowledgment, and disclosure of that which is left, in dailiness, largely unheard and unspoken. Here then, as Cage and Takemitsu tell us, the speaker speaks as "listener to the sounds." Or as Stevens puts it, "the listener, who listens in the snow." There is an exchange of names and a sharing of places, not apart from the world of events but in full contingency among them, "a peculiar light as of thought . . . among / the flashes and booms of war" and among the stopped clocks.

There is another figure, a figure of negativity, whom I must at least mention in relation to the questions of concern here, and that is the great Portuguese poet Fernando Pessoa, who was born in 1888 and died of drink in 1935. Under the assumption that he is still little known here, certainly much less than he is throughout Europe and the Portuguese-speaking world, I'll summarize a few details just to gesture toward his work. My main guides are a little text on Pessoa by the novelist Antonio Tabucchi (in *Fernando Pessoa*, Maria José de Lancastre and Antonio Tabucchi) and Richard Zenith's very informative introduction to his volume of excellent translations entitled *Fernando Pessoa & Co.* Pessoa spent his life constructing a labyrinth of selves and non-selves and placing them in conversation and argument with one another and one another's work. These he called heteronyms, and they must be distinguished from the familiar personae of modernism, such as Pound's Mauberley, Rilke's Malte, H.D.'s Helen, Valéry's M. Teste, Eliot's Prufrock, by the way Pessoa spent his life constructing their dramas, replacing himself with them, and erasing his traces through them. By the end, we seem to be witnessing an elaborate shadow-puppet play, where the puppeteer has vanished or become a shadow himself. (Think once again of Gadamer's "shadowy-uncertain" as applied to Celan's pronouns.) As Zenith states:

. . . no one took the game as far as Pessoa, who gave up his own life to confer quasi-real substance on the trinity of co-poets he designated as heteronyms, giving each a personal biography, psychology, politics, aesthetics, religion, and physique. Alberto Caeiro, considered the Master by the other two, was an ingenuous, unlettered man who lived in the country and had no profession. Ricardo Reis was a doctor and classicist who wrote odes in the style of Horace. Álvaro de Campos, a naval engineer, started out as an exuberant futurist with a Walt Whitmanesque voice, but over time he came to sound more like a mopey existentialist.

As Zenith notes, the supreme fiction was Pessoa's orthonymic creation, the poet known as Fernando Pessoa, not to be confused with Fernando Pessoa, if indeed there can be said to have been a Fernando Pessoa, since none other than Álvaro de Campos denies that he, Pessoa, ever existed. Not just a labyrinth of discourse, but one with mirrored walls, and a hydra-headed creature hidden deep within. Or perhaps the labyrinth is simply empty. Here is a poem, a nihilistic parody of the symbolist *voyage imaginaire,* by the very same Álvaro de Campos, bisexual dandy and aesthete:

> Pack your bags for Nowhere at All!
> Set sail for the ubiquitous negation of everything
> With a panoply of flags on make-believe ships—
> Those miniature, multi-colored ships from childhood!
> Pack your bags for the Grand Departure!
> And don't forget, along with your brushes and clippers,
> The polychrome distance of what can't be had.
> Pack your bags once and for all!
> Who are you here, where you socially and uselessly exist
> And the more usefully the more uselessly,
> The more truly the more falsely?
> Who are you here, who are you here, who are you here?
> Set sail, even without bags, for your own diverse self!
> What does the inhabited world have to do with you?

The answer to the poem's final question, by the way, is, of course, "everything." One more fragment, from Pessoa:

> The poet is a faker
> Who's so good at his act
> He even fakes the pain
> Of pain he feels in fact.

Pessoa created entire hosts of other heteronyms (72 altogether, by one count), poets, astrologers, essayists, sociologists, philosophers, who would occasionally communicate and comment on one another's work. The best known of these others is Bernardo Soares, a "semiheteronym" who wrote Pessoa's fictional(?) diaries, which exist in dated and undated fragments that have since been assembled in various combinations and editions. Soares the rebarbative, enunciator of the unspeakable, debunker, artisan of morbidity, assassin of motion, of the senses, of the present, of the self, misanthropist, onanist, oneirist of the false life, eremite of Douradores Street. Pessoa might seem an unlikely, even heretical, figure to invoke here, beside the names of Celan, Jabès, Stevens, et al., but it is precisely how he casts his voice outward, out from the self-same or self-identical, and how he subverts conventional notions of voice, identity, lyric impulse and subjectivity that bring him close to such company even as he (or do I confuse him with Soares?) repels all company.

Finally, the dedication to Robert Creeley, "Figure of Outward," as Charles Olson once presciently designated him, should need no explanation. To him, to Barbara Guest, to Lorine Niedecker and to many others over a close couple of generations, we owe the recovery of the exploratory tradition in American letters from institutional revisionism, a revisionism we now witness at its work of forgetting once again, in many sectors, cultural, political, historical, of the public world. We must ask whether the subject, in the face of such reaction, will once again become something less, something given. I think not, if we all remain present, as listeners and speakers.

I can only hope that the section concerning my mother's last days will be interpreted in the spirit in which it was meant, one of homage and farewell, rather than as the exploitation of some last, intimate moment. It all seems to me part of the insistently human: the words, "in the same bare place," as they ask to be there.

The final poem I've sampled from Creeley's *Day Book of a Virtual Poet* is a brief one by Wisława Szymborska:

The End and the Beginning

From time to time someone still must
dig up a rusted argument
from underneath a bush
and haul it off to the dump.
Those who knew
what this was all about
must make way for those
who know little.
And less than that.
And at last nothing less than nothing.

[*Talk given at Temple University, February 1999. First published in* Fulcrum *2, 2003.*]

OCTAVIO PAZ:
CIRCULATIONS OF THE SONG

By way of a brief preface, I am reminded of a moment many years ago at the house of a friend. On her wall was a Diego Rivera from his so-called Cubist period. Rivera had indeed taken on the compositional means, the simultanism of the Cubists. Yet there were already signs of a formal transformation, an overcoming. The palette itself was less restricted than early Cubism, hinting at a nascent new style. More important, in the place of the newspapers, carafes and ashtrays of the Cubist still life was a sky bristling with the guns of the Mexican Revolution. And it occurred to me that these guns were also pointing back toward Cubism itself, that they were saluting a new pictorial language even while paying homage to the old. (It's an ironic recollection, no doubt, given Paz's multiple reservations, over time, regarding the Mexican muralists other than Orozco.) Roughly cognate with this is a trip to São Paulo some years later, where I was to introduce an anthology of contemporary Brazilian poetry I had helped to edit and translate. The other editors and I discussed the arrival of Blaise Cendrars there in the 1920s and how his presence had been a key to Brazil's entry into the field of both modernism and vanguardism. The immediate result was Mario de Andrade's *Hallucinated City*, Brazil's first vanguardist work and one that still speaks to that self-devouring entity, São Paulo. It is no imitation of Cendrars, but a response, and a call to arms. Later in the same visit, Haroldo de Campos presented me, from his astonishing library, with the liberated cosmopolitanism, the wild literary collaging, of sousândrade, a proto-vanguardist of the most exemplary order. We could multiply without effort a thousand-fold instances of the complex back-and-forth, call-and-response, that constitute the cultural flows of our century and that explain the spread of vanguardism beyond the small urban coteries where they are initiated. They are transactions that are at once personal and artistic, as much a matter of chance, a chance encounter, as of any abiding cultural logic or necessity.

It is perhaps the agony and joy of the poem itself, as Paz and others have conceived it: We write not from but toward an emerging subject and a reconfigured subjectivity. We wonder, continually, how the pronouns, how the *I* and the *we*, the *you* and the *they*, the *he* and *she*, are spoken, invoked and meant. Here we ask, What is it? and wait anxiously for some response from the other side of the page. The ostensible is something of a cloak, beneath which is found the body, or a snow-layer, beneath which is to be found . . . whatever is to be found. So, in Paz's writings, beneath the question of vanguardism, its origins and the narratives of its practice, are to be found irony and analogy, passion, negation, the lineaments of desire, alienation, conversation, history and time, the political and the atemporal, revolution and reaction, hermeticism, reason and dream, identity and difference, rupture and recurrence, the aesthetic and the anti-aesthetic, the present, the social, the Great Wheel, the movement ("revolution" once again) of the spheres.

What is beneath, but equally what precedes and what follows. Have we finally witnessed the last "last avant-garde"? Are not all avant-gardes, in their self-imagining, the last, the beyond, beyond which no other beyond is conceivable? And also the first, the origin? And is there a before to these eruptions, a presaging? Or does such thought in linear, historicized time betray the active imagination itself, the movement of words and forms among the communicating vessels, the circulations of the song, to borrow a phrase from Robert Duncan in his homage to Rumi?

A disclaimer is perhaps needed here. I will not pretend to engage directly in this brief talk with various theories of modernism and vanguardism, such as those of Peter Brger, Renato Poggioli and Andreas Huyssen, Habermas and Jameson, or Adorno's theory of modernity, relevant as they may be (or, indeed, may not be) to an examination of Paz's critical and poetic practice, and to his place among the various movements of recent times, and to difficult questions of social and political agency. I am more interested in exploring the poetic conversation he establishes, asystematically, across time and the vision of discordant community it implies. I will also pretend neither to objectivity nor to comprehensiveness, but will rather strive for a continuance of the conversation, as best I'm able, leaving it open and fluid, subject to its own inconsistencies and paradoxes, as Paz himself might have preferred. From Baudelaire, Paz borrowed the term "partial criticism" as his own mode of critical thought, and now I will borrow it from Paz, with its paronomasia intact.

Both modernity, as Baudelaire understands it in *L'art romantique*, and vanguardism as it later developed, belong for Paz to a "tradition against itself," a paradoxical tradition of discontinuity, rupture and change. A tradition, that is, with paradox at its heart, far from the fantasy of "tradition" invoked by Eliot as reactionary cultural critic but rather closer to the actual vision of textual circulation, citation and human circumstance envisioned by Eliot, the modernist poet of "Prufrock" and "The Waste Land." The modernity of modernism and the vanguards, is, then, never self-identical, but always its own other, taking difference as identity. From this central paradox, vanguardist theory (whether Russian or Italian Futurism, Dada, Surrealism, Expressionism, Negritude, Ultraism, et al.) will generate a host of other paradoxes and internal contradictions and inconsistencies. Far from disqualifying them as generative movements, as more than one critic has claimed, Paz will plead that their particular energies arose from the irresolvable tension between reason and dream, the personal and the political, the spontaneous and the formal, the negation and the invocation of the past, the critique and celebration of the present, the yearning for, and sometimes dread of, the future. In a broken age, broken time: exaltation of a utopian future of social emancipation and of the liberated imagination, a future of the never-to-become, or appositely, a revenant, a Golden Age that never was. At the same time, these movements, in their various ways, sought to vitalize the present, to strip it of the habitual, the given, and replace that with the actual, the act. The poem as act, displacing the institutions of art. To anneal by rupture and displacement. To enter the social by assaulting it. To cure time of itself by means of time itself, rhythm, recurrence and difference within language, the fashioner of consciousness. Extension of the Romantic paradigm of the poetic imagination, yet also an echo of the most ancient magical and incantatory practices in language. Breton as magus, Khlebnikov as shaman, Lorca as medium for the duende, Artaud as ritual sacrifice.

A further paradox might include the historical moment of Paz and this aftertime of the (pseudo-millennial) present. Paz himself came into his first maturity as a poet at a time when historical vanguardism was either in its waning stages as a movement, as with Surrealism, or had been annihilated by the forces of history, as was the case with Russian Futurism. Perhaps, Paz notes, only Brazilian Concretism can be seen as a genuine extension of historical vanguardism into that now recent past. In addition, we should at least mention a host of neo-vanguardist movements, such as Xul in Argentina, the Vienna Group, Fluxus, the Situationists, the Novissimi in Italy, Language Poetry in the United States, all of which share certain characteristics regarding the place of theory, and political and aesthetic (or antiaesthetic) practice, with the historical avant-gardes. Yet there is the essential difference, that they arrive with a precedent, a model, they are not self-fashioned. For the present writer and his generation in the United States, it may well have been, again paradoxically, the historical amnesia of the Anglo-American critical tradition in the fifties and early sixties that kept the earlier movements vital. The critical histories and classrooms of the time not only erased or simply ignored the fact of artistic vanguardism, but in their Cold War fervor, they tended to ignore as well the recent history of all radically resistant movements within the culture. Thus a generation was able to rediscover them, in the turmoil of the Vietnam years, with the "shock of the new" still affixed. The particular ways in which the principles of Surrealism, among other movements, remained vital for Paz we will discuss below.

Vanguardism is historical fact, of course, a phenomenon of our century, its wars and political upheavals, its bourgeois hegemony, its tyrannies, its anti-colonial movements. Yet it is also a contended, discursive site, defined and historicized in multiple, conflictual ways according to the agendas and attitudes of the artists, cultural theorists, literary and social historians fashioning the narratives. Paz's own view is inseparable from his poetics. In fact, this alone may make his perspective, his poet's perspective, of special interest, since his sense of the Romantic origins of vanguardism, even of its occasional anti-romanticism, is, as Paz himself admits, widely, if not unanimously shared. However, as a practicing poet of world acclaim, and, it must certainly be emphasized, a Mexican poet, he brings a singular point of view not only to vanguardism, toward which his own relationship is complicated, but to its place in relation to the poetry of past, present and future. Paz's method is at once subjective in outlook and universalist in range. His thoughts tend to overflow, beyond any neatly bounded limit of the subject, in all senses of that word. In that regard, his approach mirrors his sense of the poem itself, and ultimately Paz is always, one way or another, writing poetics, writing it into the social, into the imaginary and into history, whether the history of our multiple futures or multiple pasts. And always, one need hardly add, in search of the present. The governing figure for such work is analogy, which is to say, similarity among things otherwise dissimilar. That in turn means that his work is by nature expansive, almost endlessly so.

The first stirrings of vanguardism in the nineteenth century can be glimpsed here and there, at least retrospectively. They can be found in the theoretical matrices of German and English romantic theory, with its revolution of forms, its conflating of genres, its collapsing of life into art and art into life. They can be found in the circle of literary eccentrics around Nerval (*les bousingos*, "the rowdies"), walking their lobsters on the boulevards, eating ice cream out of human skulls, holding literary seminars in the nude, while attempting to subvert the new, official aesthetic of "realism," as decreed by Louis Bonaparte's *apparatchiki*, soon after the Eighteenth Brumaire, history as farce. Two decades later, at the time of the Commune, Rimbaud and his circle would create the *Album Zutique*, mocking both authorship and high literary values, to say nothing of conventional morality. Perhaps the comic-nihilistic side can even be glimpsed in prototype among the *incohérents*–of Montmartre, the Paris pranksters of c.1875–1905, with their empty canvasses, Eugène Bataille's "Mona Lisa with a Pipe," their cabarets, their shadow theaters and mock exhibitions. Difficult to imagine Pataphysics without such a precedent. Difficult to imagine Oulipo without Pataphysics. Yet the ground of an altered subjectivity and consciousness is to be found less, for Paz, in such epiphenomena than in Rimbaud's *alchimie du verbe*; in Nerval's oneiric defiance; in Baudelaire's double vision and his envisioning of the poem as the universe's double, a new cipher for the first code (the poet in Baudelaire's view becomes the translator of an unknown language into an unknowable one). One must add to the list Fourier's society of desire and Mallarmé's void, his dice-cast, and the silent explosion of the arrival in Paris, from Montevideo, of Isidore Ducasse, le Comte de Lautréamont. (He would die at 24 during the Siege.) These, to cite only a selection, will form the system of communicating vessels that in turn will enter and alter the dreams of certain twentieth-century writers and activists. In turn, their own preceding works will be forever altered. Hölderlin, Kleist, Novalis, Schiller, Shelley, Coleridge and others will never again be the same.

Paul Celan, a poet to whom, within my very restricted

knowledge, Paz nowhere refers, has spoken of the poem as "a conversation ... along the way."* Paz, too, speaks often of the same thing, stressing the poem's dialogic nature, its completion not as an object but as a thing always in process. The poem converses first with its first reader, the poet him- or herself, as Other, then others in the world, the present world, and the world of the future, should the poem survive for a time. The conversation, of course, is also with figures from the past, such as poets who may be said by their works to read and modify and make place for the poem, even as the poem reconfigures the space of reception for their work and our sense of temporality. Returning now to Romantic theory, I hear it differently through the work of Paz.

Novalis, in his *Aphorisms and Fragments*, writes, "Ordinary experience of the present connects past and future through contraction and limitation. This results in contiguity, a kind of crystallization brought about through reflection. But there is a kind of spiritual sense of the present that identifies the two by means of dissolution, and this mixture is the element, the atmosphere, of the poet."

We sometimes forget the central place of wit, humor, irony in the theoretical writings of the Romantics. Paz reminds us that irony, ironic subversion, is the crucial antipode to analogy both for the Romantics and their inheritors. It is these two functions, in play, that lead to the totalizing claims for life as art and art as life, and for the endlessly dialectical *becoming* of the work. Friedrich Schlegel, in his *Dialogue on Poetry*, writes, "Romantic poetry is a progressive universal poetry. Its mission is not merely to reunite all separate genres of poetry and to put poetry in touch with philosophy and rhetorics. It will, and should, now mingle and now amalgamate poetry and prose, genius and criticism, the poetry of

---

* Eliot Weinberger has since discovered what he believes to be the only published reference to Celan by Paz, in a 1973 memoir of the poet José Carlos Becerra. Paz recalls having lunch with Becerra in a Chinese Restaurant on the King's Road. Michael Hamburger unexpectedly arrives and joins them. "The conversation turned toward Paul Celan and German poetry, and from there to Hölderlin, and from Hölderlin to the relationship between poetry and madness." (Octavio Paz, *Obras completas*, vol. 4: *Generaciones y semblanzas: Dominio mexicana*)

art and the poetry of nature, render poetry living and social, and life and society poetic, poetize wit, fill and saturate the forms of art with solid cultural material of every kind, and inspire them with vibrations of humor. It embraces everything poetic, from the greatest system of art, which, in turn, includes many systems, down to the sigh, the kiss, which the musing child breathes forth in artless song. . . . The romantic type of poetry is still becoming; indeed its peculiar essence is that it is always becoming and that it can never be completed. It cannot be exhausted by any theory, and only a divinatory criticism might dare to characterize its ideal. It alone is infinite, as it alone is free; and as its first law it recognizes that the arbitrariness of the poet endures no law above him. The romantic genre of poetry is the only one which is more than a genre, and which is, as it were, poetry itself; for in a certain sense all poetry is or should be romantic."

We see in that final claim a characteristic that would be foregrounded by the Surrealists, that in a sense all true poetry "is or should be" surreal. By implication then, the movement, in essence, claims timelessness. Late in life, when Breton was asked whether Surrealism had waned, the question quite literally had no meaning to him, for Surrealism was the key that unlocked the limitless field of desire. In an essay on Breton in *Alternating Current*, Paz writes, "I have no idea what the future of the Surrealist group will be; I am certain, however, that the current that has flowed from German Romanticism and Blake to Surrealism will not disappear. It will live a life apart; it will be the *other* voice."

As Novalis and Paz may be said to read and thereby modify each other, in the same way the poem moves at once forward and backward, both as a form in time where a last word may propel us back to a first, and as form in the *other* time of poetry, that future-past where it oscillates. We are brought back to the notion of conversation, the open exchange, which is also the mutual acknowledgment, invention and imagining of the other. If Baudelaire offers to Walter Benjamin the definitive figure of the flâneur, and eventually thereby a new understanding of the Surrealists in the crowd, Benjamin at the same time creates Baudelaire anew for his own time. The Baudelaire we have has passed through Benjamin's hands. Nerval is the presiding figure of Breton's *Les vases communicants,* the exemplar of the intertwining of day and night, reason and dream, thought and sensation, reason and madness, life and death. Yet he is also a vessel into which the time traveler Breton will pour the stuff of his own oneiric projections. It is not a matter of influence in a given direction, or one and the other, but the alchemy itself, the mutual transfiguration that, for Paz, lifts the core of the vanguardist intervention out of time and literary fashion and into an *other* company. It is not, of course, uniquely a company of poets and visionaries. Rather it is the company of all who would willingly be so translated out of the self-same, the fixed, and into the open. It implies also the courage of losing one's self, of coming to nothing. So Keats, "The Sun, the Moon, the Sea and Men and Women who are creatures of impulse are poetical and have about them an unchangeable attribute—the poet has none; no identity . . ." (Letter to Richard Woodhouse, October 27, 1818). It is interesting to speculate that even a poet of such famously abiding ego as Breton, and one so fixed on realization of the resonant core of *self,* might agree.

Breton is, for Paz, the paradigmatic figure of vanguardism, as Surrealism can be said to offer the model against which other vanguards will, inevitably, justifiably or not, be compared. The cause of the latter must be found in the unprecedented international reach of the movement whether through the nations of Western Europe, or east into what is now the Czech Republic and Romania, further east to China, and west of course to the West Indies and the states of the Spanish- and Portuguese-speaking Americas. In the case of Breton himself, Paz will state that it is above all Breton's commitment to "the language of passion—the passion of language," that attracted him. "To him," Paz writes, "the powers of the word were no different from the powers of passion, and passion, in its highest and most intense form, was nothing less than language in its wildest, purest form: poetry."

Paz first kept company with Breton at what must have been

a curious and troubling moment in the history of Surrealism. In adolescence, he recounts that at a moment of "isolation and great elation," he had come across what he would later learn was Chapter 5 of Breton's *L'Amour fou*, and that this, along with Blake's *The Marriage of Heaven and Hell*, had "opened the doors of modern poetry to me." During the war, some years later, he had "met Benjamin Péret, Leonora Carrington, Wolfgang Paalen, Remedios Varo and other Surrealists who had sought refuge in Mexico." In Paris in 1946, he met Péret again, who took him to the Café de la Place Blanche where Breton often held court.

Arriving in Paris at that moment, Paz encountered a Surrealist group much altered from its earlier years. Aragon and Eluard had long since defected to the Stalinist camp. Soupault, Picabia, Desnos and many others had wearied of Breton's iron-fisted control of the movement and departed, or else had been excommunicated for various heresies. Breton himself was under attack from Tzara and others for having the temerity to judge the Occupation from exile, "from high atop the Statue of Liberty," as Tzara phrased it, with striking mean-spiritedness. Replacing earlier generations in the Surrealist camp, as Mark Polizzotti relates in his biography of Breton, *Revolution of the Mind*, were now such younger figures as "Alain Jouffroy; philosopher and sociologist Nora Mitrani; Stanislav Rodanski, a scholar of Hegel and Tibetan yoga; poets Yves Bonnefoy and Claude Tarnau; and Henri and No Seigle, painters who worked in collaboration." It has usually been assumed that this was an unfortunate moment to associate with Surrealism, for evident reasons. Yet I would suggest that for Paz it was a most useful time. The principles of Surrealism were in flux and undergoing adjustment to post-war political, social and artistic conditions. Breton's control was certainly weakening, to the advantage, I think, of the group's younger members. Most of all, however, he was under increasing, often virulent attack. Had Paz associated himself with Breton at a moment of acceptance and adulation, the gesture would have been less meaningful. Instead, he was able to witness Surrealism under assault, as it had been in its earlier years. I would also imagine he was never to forget the rhetoric of the Stalinists and the Sartreans as it filled the air with accusations and admonitions during that time.

Breton is celebrated by Paz less in terms of historical vanguardism itself or the technical elements of the Surrealist program. For Paz, Breton is a quest figure, free of the morality of Christendom, in search of the "originary word," when language and thought were one. Automatic writing is downgraded by Paz as a "method" for writing poems (the trap into which so many aspiring Surrealists fell) while being praised as representing "the belief that speaking and thinking are the same thing. Man does not speak because he thinks; he thinks because he speaks." Once again, we confront both the Romantic paradigm and *l'alchimie du verbe*. The poem overcomes time, even as we die into time. In the face of instrumental reason, the poet steeps him- or herself (invariably "him" among the Surrealist poets) in a magical practice that will dream of restoring a lost unity. We must not forget Breton's sincere, if somewhat exoticist, reverence for Mexico as itself a magic site, a hieroglyph of the lost Book. Breton, then, represents analogy in its transhistorical power. That Paz chooses to disregard or deny Breton's arrogance and occasional self-caricature, his replication of some of the worst aspects of the discourse of power, and his hand in the often farcical political machinations within the movement, is understandable, and perhaps necessary. Breton is meant to exemplify the tragicomic artistic figure caught in the double bind of magic and revolution, two faces of death. With *Les vases communicants,* Breton offers Paz one of his central metaphors, one Paz will expand well beyond Breton's initial meanings. Breton also offers a text where an oddly resistant critical prose is set beside the narratives of dreams and objective chance. It is a text where dream and action, night and day, are not opposed, but interpenetrate to create an *active* world of poetry. As always, Breton is interrogating the poet's domain of liberty. At the end, truth appears at the dark window, "its hair streaming with light." It is a vision of the vessels united. Breton, for Paz, is Mount Analogue.

If Breton is the Master of Analogy, then Duchamp is the Me-

taironic Master of Irony. He responds to Breton's fire with cool-
ness and distance, to Breton's interventionism with inactivity. He
is Rimbaud's refusal of labor, as well as Bartleby. To Breton's judg-
ments, Duchamp responds by suspending judgment, sometimes
by a wire from the ceiling, sometimes between panes of glass. By
means of the eye, and the word, he annihilates the ocular, and
the verb. By means of the gaze, he opens the gaze to itself. Pass-
ing through the great Arensberg collection at the Philadelphia
Museum of Art, we confront a sequence of stoppages, at once
termini, endings, and measurements or ratios with no basis other
than chance, and no necessary end in sight. Stoppages without
end. If he is a Surrealist at all, he is one without portfolio, without
papers, the singular in the face of Breton's many, the exception.
If Breton spent a lifetime denying he was making art, then Du-
champ spent a lifetime cultivating an art of denial itself, denial of
the hand and eye and object, while often secretly constructing, by
hand, his objects of denial. The aesthetic is displaced from mat-
ter onto thought, onto speculation itself, if I may be permitted
an obvious pun (and Duchamp was a great fan of the obvious
pun). Each of his works enfolds and embraces contradiction. To
Paz, Duchamp mirrors Mallarmé, in the use of silence, of course,
but also in the way both "turned criticism into myth and nega-
tion into [a provisional] affirmation." And elsewhere, "Duchamp,
critic of the subject who looks and of the object looked at . . ." For
Paz, he is the necessary Other to Breton, on "the axis of erotic af-
firmation and ironic negation." He is the final point of Romantic
irony, the moment of closure that we now can see also as (perhaps
an ultimate Duchampian irony) the opening of a path in artistic
exploration for the final years of the century.

Two other essential, vanguardist precursors must be men-
tioned here, one a poet of sky, the other, as Paz says, a poet of
earth. Vicente Huidobro was born into a wealthy family in San-
tiago, Chile, in January of 1893. His early work was profoundly
influenced by the Modernismo of Darío, but by his second book
he was (apparently) already experimenting with the calligram.

(There is significant scholarly controversy over the provenance of that first edition.) After four more youthful books, tired of "the senseless mockeries, the unbreathable air," he left Santiago for Buenos Aires. As he writes, "It was there that they baptized me a Creationist for having said in my lecture that the first condition of the poet is to create, the second to create and the third to create." There he published his first book of Creationist poems, *El Espejo de Agua* (*The Mirror of Water*). From there he sailed for Paris, where he arrived toward the end of 1916, and where he immediately fell in with Apollinaire and various of the Cubists. In 1916 and 1917, with Apollinaire and Reverdy, he published the influential review *Nord-Sud*, before moving on once again, to Madrid, where he established a salon. In Madrid, he published two books, *Ecuatorial* and *Poemas Articos*. As Paz notes, "With them the Spanish avant-garde commenced." Huidobro's presence in Madrid, along with Borges' (stopping over, on his way home to Argentina from Switzerland), was at least in part responsible for the birth of Ultraism. The books and statements of this time, including the various Paris periods, are strongly marked by the influence of Reverdy and Apollinaire. The work of this stage is remarkable for its precocity and its skilled assimilation of an advanced idiom, its casting off of provincialism. At the same time, it is a body of work clearly inflected by Europe, whereas *Altazor* (1919-1931) is unmistakeably a flight and a parachute descent into the New World. From the beginning of Canto V translated by Eliot Weinberger:

> Here begins the unexplored territory
> Round on account of the eyes that behold it
> Profound on account of my heart
> Filled with probable sapphires
> Sleepwalkers' hands
> And aerial burials
> Eerie as the dreams of dwarfs
> Or the branch snapped off in the infinite
> The seagull carries to its young

Writes Paz in *Children of the Mire*, "Not a language of earth but of aerial space . . . Words lose their meaningful weight and become not signs but traces of an astral catastrophe." The debt with Europe has been settled.

Huidobro's dark twin, his Other, is surely César Vallejo, born in 1892 in Santiago de Chuco, an Andean town in north-central Peru. In his introduction to *The Complete Posthumous Poetry*, Clayton Eshleman informs us that Vallejo's grandmothers were both Chimu Indians, his grandfathers Spanish Catholic priests. Vallejo's first book, *Los heraldos negros* (1919), is very much within the tradition of Modernismo, yet his second, *Trilce*, published in Lima in 1922, is like nothing that had come before. Its stammerings, wrenched syntax, neologisms and sheer viscerality remain emblematic of the singularity and estrangement that would mark Vallejo's entire poetic life. Each poem in *Trilce* feels like a fevered, incomplete reassemblage of scattered limbs. His work as a whole is a desperate act of internalization. It seems to sum up the agony of a fractured postcolonial consciousness (with its ancient echoes), where the body itself has always already been sacrificed, yet where desire continues to survive as a consuming force.

In 1923, under threat of imprisonment for reasons that remain somewhat obscure, Vallejo would depart from Lima for Paris. There he would meet Juan Gris and Juan Larrea, and Huidobro. Yet, often desperately poor, his experience there could not have been more unlike that of Huidobro's. Vallejo maintained an acute mistrust of vanguardist circles and the "pseudo-new," though his own work seems to almost magically internalize and, as Paz says, "transmute the international forms of the avant-garde." Late in the decade, he took up the study of Marxism and began to teach in workers' cells. Yet his poetry, unlike some of Neruda's, never becomes a conduit for doctrine or ideology. It is too resistant, too ungovernable, and too internal. Its passionate negation is the necessary counterpoint to Huidobro's "miraculous fountain," his "ecstatic bird," and his "dawn with the hope of aeroplanes." Though Vallejo would never return to Peru, dying in Spain in 1938, it could also be said that he never left. Like Huidobro, (whom he is so *unlike*), he assimilated European forms in order to escape both provincialism and assimilation. The two might be said to have imagined the sky and the ground of the coming poetry. The parallels as well as the differences with the experience of Paz and European vanguardism are too striking to ignore and almost too obvious to need much elaboration.

The founding significance and influence of such figures on the poetics of Paz, and what we might call the project of Paz, is unquestionable. From Breton, he learned the primacy of desire, the dynamic of reason and non-reason, and a particular relationship to rhetorical figures and the image without which the following from "Storm," for example, would not be possible:

> The downpour comes into your dreams
> green hands and black feet
> wheeling around the stone
> throat of the night
> tying your body
> a sleeping mountain
> The downpour raves
> between your thighs
> soliloquy of stones and water

Through Duchamp, Paz reasserted the contemporary, critically subversive force of irony. Breton's *nearness*; Duchamp's *distance*. Breton's *heat*; Duchamp's *cool*. The example of Huidobro and Vallejo is less one of strict poetic influence (though that could use discussion), and more one of example: of how the forms and discoveries of international vanguardism can be profitably ingested without loss of cultural particularity. (Parallels in the United States might include the influence of Apollinaire on William Carlos Williams and the young Louis Zukofsky, and of the Surrealists on Frank O'Hara and John Ashbery—many more could be cited.)

Yet Paz's relationship to vanguardism, both as poet and critic, is anything but a simple one. It makes no sense, first of all, to think of Paz as a pure vanguardist himself, if the term is to retain any meaning at all. He is not a poet of coteries (this is not to me necessarily a derogatory term), despite his lifetime's multiple cultural and political interventions and controversies. He became, in his lifetime, a nation's representative poetic voice. For a vanguardist, such a position seems to me unthinkable and self-canceling. And finally, of course, his own poetic and cultural perspective stretched well beyond any given program, indeed, beyond any one historical moment. He freely critiqued both vanguardist leftist utopianism and the fascist sympathies of certain Anglo-American modernists. He says the following in *Children of the Mire* of the postwar period in Spanish-American poetry, the time when he published *Libertad bajo palabra* (1949) and *Aguila o Sol* (1951), the time that would soon be followed by publications from Nicanor Parra, Jaime Sabines, Roberto Juarroz and many others:

> The beginning: a clandestine, almost invisible action. At first almost nobody paid attention to it. In a certain sense it marked the return of the avant-garde, but a silent, secretive, disillusioned avant-garde. An *other* avant-garde, self-critical and engaged in solitary rebellion against the academy which the first avant-garde had become. It was not a question of inventing, as in 1920, but of exploring. The territory that attracted these poets was neither outside nor inside. It was the zone where external and internal merge: the zone of language. Theirs was not an aesthetic preoccupation; for these young men language was, simultaneously and contradictorily, their destiny and their choice. Something given and something we make—and which makes us.

It is a territory, then, of a very real ambiguity and uncertainty, a moment *after*, after both the war and the time of the historical avant-gardes, and also a beginning. "A silent, secretive avant-garde," is in one real sense, of course, an absolute contradiction in terms, as Paz is well aware. Yet it is perhaps only contradiction and paradox which make sense (as evidence of the Holocaust and of Stalinist depravities become public knowledge, as the atomic bomb prefigures apocalypse).

As a critic, a "partial critic," Paz performs what seems to me a two-fold operation on the historical vanguards. He places them within an eternal tradition of innovation and renewal. The affirmation of Surrealist desire and magical-alchemical practice is seen as part of a continuum of change and invention stretching back beyond the Romantics, to the Renaissance, to the poets of *trobar*, and beyond to the sources of magical speech in prehistory. Granting the historically particular nature of vanguardist formations, he at the same time denies them the poetic singularity, the never before and the never after, that was their initiatory impetus. They are recovered within the circulations of the song. This two-fold evaluation in turn frees him to inherit without having to join, and to inherit selectively. He jettisons, for example, not the political agency of the poet, but the particular illusions of both utopian and nihilistic world views. The historical dilemma of the double bind, magic or revolution, imagination or action, is displaced by the vision of the "other voice," whose time is the time of the poem yet whose world is that of the present. The time of the poem, its play of difference and recurrence, is in itself a projection of community, and perhaps of utopia. Paz builds that vision of the poem in time and poetic time on a characteristic set of paradoxes. He writes, "The time of the poem is inside history, not outside it." He continues, "Text and readings are inseparable, and in them history and ahistory, change and identity, are united without being dissolved. It is not a transcendence but a convergence. It is time which repeats itself and is unrepeatable, which flows without flowing: a time which turns back upon itself. The time of the reading is here-and-now: a now which happens at any moment, and a here which exists anywhere. The poem is history and it is that something which rejects history in the very instant of affirming it." The poem, Paz seems to say, must have it both ways—or not at all.

[*First published in* Tribute to Octavio Paz, *a joint publication by the Mexican Cultural Institute of New York & the Mexican Cultural Institute of Washington, D.C., and the Octavio Paz Foundation, 2001.*]

THE DANISH NOTEBOOK

"The sun," noted Reb Gabbar, "is a flaming hoop which a little girl trundles around the earth. Nobody has ever discovered the child even though she plays in broad daylight."

—Edmond Jabès, *Return to the Book*

Dear Iselin,

You ask me to connect the dots. You ask whether I remember the "old childhood drawings" where you connected the dots until a figure appeared. I remember connecting the dots; I remember the dragon that appeared, the angel that appeared. A winged horse once, a small wooden house. I remember sitting on the floor in a house, connecting the dots of a wooden house. Sitting on a coco rug on the tile floor of a house, my grandfather's house. Connecting the dots of a wooden house, a dragon with an enormous tail, a horse with wings outspread. But I remember as well refusing once in a while to connect the dots in their numerical order, choosing instead to make a random pattern, with lines crossing other lines.

And you ask about the sun. You remind me that I never wrote about the sun for *Brondum's Encyclopedia,* and I realize that I know nothing about the sun. I remember it less well than the black, angular purse you were carrying that day we visited the press in Nansensgade. The day you asked whether I knew a French poet named Claude Royet-Journoud. Yesterday I received a letter from Claude, saying that a book of mine published in France, *Cites*, a collaboration with the painter Micaëla Henich, had been reviewed on "France-Culture." I don't believe I've ever had a book of mine reviewed on radio here.

Soleil noir, soleil acéphale.

Mean distance from the Earth: about 150 million kilometers. Diameter: approximately 1,390,000 kilometers. Mass: about 330,000 times that of the Earth. We'll have to do better than that, of course.

There is, by the way, no sun today. It's a Wednesday in late February. Wind and rain have been blowing in from the west, off the Pacific, for several days, and we've hardly seen the sun at all. It is the 28th, normally the last day of February, but I see that this is a leap year. I will have an extra day this year to attempt to connect the dots. To consider the sun, the question of the sun:

> We sat on the cliff-head
> before twin suns.

At the same time, the question of "fault." I am working on a new, evening-length dance piece with Margaret Jenkins and her company. Its title is "Fault." This city, in which I live, is built on a network of faults. These have the capacity, under certain conditions, to destroy the city. Seismologists and fault readers attempt to connect up the dots, to determine where and when an "event" (for so it's called) will happen next. In Prague last spring, people spoke of the perilous transition from Soviet occupation to independence and free-market capitalism. Several times I heard or read the expression, "It's like crossing a series of fault lines."

Today's mail just arrived. In it, another letter from Claude, containing a postcard designed by him, a representation of what I will call, for now, "the sun." It is postmarked 24 dec 1995, that is, a little over two months ago.

I once thought I should find a form for this little book you have asked for, but now it seems to me that unformed would be better, a book at fault. Displaced. I accepted your invitation because it seems an impossible thing for me to do, against my nature as a writer. Of course one should never have such a nature. If you discover that you do, you must erase it, as violently as possible. *Coup de torchon.* Clean slate. One of our cats, the apricot-colored one, is sleeping on the computer as I write this. He doesn't give a shit one way or the other. As long as the machine stays warm.

". . . following an arc that ultimately has no tangent." (Deleuze, *Le Pli*).

In the new dance, by the way, one section is titled "The Fold." It explores the possibility of endless movement, endless surfaces, the folds of clothing and the folds of the body, folds within the earth, folds and creases on the surface of a rock. Deleuze again, "The movement never stops."

One day recently, a professor of physics we have been consulting brought a piece of moonrock to the studio for us to look at. It was very small and very dark, like the sun.

The sun, which is missing from your encyclopedia:

> An indefinite calculus
> watches, writes and rewrites

*

So as a result of my failure to respond, there is a lacuna, a black hole, in your encyclopedia, where the sun was meant to go. I can at least direct your attention to the entry, "Sun," in the *Critical Dictionary,* edited by Georges Bataille. It is the only entry attributed to Zdenko Reich. I have never before come across this name. Is it a pseudonym? An anagram I cannot unravel? A joke—one of those fictions created from time to time by the *Documents* and the *Da Costa* groups? A note in my edition simply reads, "Zdenko Reich—Biographical details remain few; before publishing in *Documents* he was part of the *Grand Jeu* group. . . ." The entry itself is an exemplary rendition of surrealist ethnography, where oneiric and scientific imagery, and the sacred and the profane, become indistinguishable. The sun itself is not the subject. Instead we are offered the festival of a solar cult in the *Hautes-Alpes,* dating from the early nineteenth century, a festival of dancing and omelettes, celebrating the sun's return. The omelette, the sun's likeness, draws the sun down, once again, to expend itself.

★

Leap Year Day: an invention of Julius Caesar's astronomer, Sosigenes, in 46 BCE. No sun today, but I am listening for the first time to some preliminary musical materials for the new dance work. They leave me in a state of uncertainty, as was perhaps intended, since I can't make out their origins in the world of sounds. Listening again, I think I hear electronically modified wind instruments in one section, high-pitched bells in the next, like rain, muffled and variously altered industrial sounds in the third and fourth, building to a state of profound disquiet.

In my notebook for Leap Year Day four years ago, I find no entry. The closest to it is the entry for March 3rd, which consists of a single word, "Tasseography," starred as if I should be certain to return to it. I can find the word in none of my dictionaries.

The entry for Leap Year Day, 1988, contains a note on the word "float" in one of my own earlier poems. Nearby are references to the deaths of Robert Duncan (Feb. 3) and René Char (Feb. 19).

No entry for Leap Year Day, 1982. On the first day of the month, I had woken at 4:45 a.m. and recorded the following, "Dream this night about going to film 'Ragtime' (I haven't seen) with C. We are shown to separate seats and mine faces away from the screen, or 3/4 away, so that I must turn and look over my shoulder to see. I then change seats to one nearer C, but in this one I can only see the film in a reflection on a large column, mirror-surfaced and decorated with Art Deco-style flowers (so that I can't tell whether the film itself is affecting a 'deco' style). I tell C I have to leave and she is somewhat reluctant, finally agreeing (I tell her, 'This is insane.'). The manager is perfectly agreeable when I go to him for a refund, though instead of giving me my money back (C doesn't want a refund for herself), he hands me six tickets, good only at the 'Sacramento Street Theatres.' He then explains where some of these are ('There's one at 2nd and Market') and I look at the yellow tickets, which are printed in the conventional way but also have some handwritten instructions, the only one which I can make out reading, 'Doors never to open at 4 p.m.' My only hesitation in leaving the film is that many others are leaving as well, apparently out of dissatisfaction, leading me to think that either it is in fact interesting or it is pseudo-literary and pretentious. When I wake, Teresa Stratas singing Weil's 'Youkali' is running through my head."

The despair that invariably overwhelms me when I "look back" in this manner:

> In a certain way all this still exists
> but the scene and the mirror no longer exist

Crows have suddenly appeared in the branches of the trees up and down our street. Abrupt, sharp auditory memory of the rustling wings and the cries of the crows, nesting in the trees above the Jewish cemetery in Prague.

European crow. Jackdaw. In Czech, *kafka*.

＊

I've been thinking about dots. Two years ago, in the intense heat of August, I was wandering with a friend through the streets of Paris. We crossed the Pont Neuf to the Ile de la Cité and entered the Place Dauphine.

＊

I broke off the above some weeks ago, unable to continue, fearing that I would fall into novelistic language in telling what, after all, is a fairly simple story, but one that I had repressed from my memory for many years. Now, the heat today once again brings me back to it. I'll start again.

I've been thinking about the dots. Two years ago, in the intense heat of August, I was wandering with a friend, the poet Norma Cole, through the streets of Paris. We crossed the Pont Neuf to the Ile de la Cité and entered the Place Dauphine. As we traversed the Place in the direction of the Rue de Harlay I was overcome with the kind of obscure emotion which, for me at least, often precedes the recollection of a vanished thought or experience. I turned to look over my right shoulder and recognized the weathered exterior of the Hôtel Henri IV. We continued walking to a nearby café as the pieces of this memory rapidly reassembled themselves. I felt, quite literally, as if I were being drawn downward into a dream state where fiction and fact, imagination and recollection, could no longer be separated.

At the café, I offered to tell Norma of the incident, of which I had never previously spoken to anyone. Over thirty years before (had I in fact recently turned seventeen?), I was spending part of a summer in Paris and had met and become friendly with a young dancer from Hungary who was studying, perhaps as an apprentice dancer, at the Paris Opera Ballet. We were introduced by a mutual acquaintance, an American, who had met Alexandra while browsing through bookstalls on the Boulevard Saint Michel. We had dinner that evening, and over the next few days she introduced me to her small circle of friends, most of whom, like herself, were a year or two older than I. During the following weeks we spent as much time together as possible. I would pick her up after her classes, and we would wander around the city, visit museums, go to films and at night often listen to music in clubs (Bud Powell with his trio once, maybe at the Blue Note). On a narrow street in the Sixth, she indicated an atelier where her grandfather, a composer, had lived for a number of years. French had become the second language in her home in Budapest. Thus it was to France part of her family had fled after the failed uprising of 1956.

On one of our walks, I pointed out to her the window of my room on the third floor of the Henri IV. Some days after that we were at a party where I was taken aside by two men with thick Hungarian accents. I was told that Alexandra was in immediate danger and would have to leave France. They could not say to what country she would be taken, and she herself did not yet know. She had asked to spend her last two nights with me at my hotel, and this had been agreed, provided I assured them that she would not leave the room until they came for her.

I think it was while lying awake the first night, after we had been taken to the hotel, that she asked, teasing, Why poetry? I had replied, with a pretentiousness that immediately embarrassed me, Because we're made of language. At my then obligatory question,

Why dance?—*Alors, pourquoi la danse?*—she had laughed and answered, Because we're made of legs and arms!

I would go out for sandwiches, mineral water, beer, cigarettes in blue packets. She requested tangerines, a copy of *Aurélia*. Each evening we would smoke a little more from the small stash of pot given to me by a friend. We wondered what her new name and new country would be, what language would be spoken, whether she would be able to dance. The stained and peeling wallpaper depicted scenes along a broad river, figures in Levantine clothing, loading and unloading small sailing barks.

How sweat models the body.

The idea of a narrative, that, let's say, X and Y might have been; that to say something is possible, or possibly true, is to say that it is not necessarily false.

Very early on the morning of the third day, the same two men who had first approached me came for her. I watched from my window as they took her from the still darkened square to a waiting car.

In the same heat and the same month, I told the story to Norma as she ate ice cream and I drank a beer, a few hundred meters from where it had occurred. I felt it turning into fiction as I did so and wondered at this betrayal.

Returning to the United States, I wrote a tortuous version of it as a piece called "Autobiography 11." On December 2 of that same year, 1994, after completing the latest draft of "Autobiography 11," I came upon this passage in Mark Polizzotti's biography of André Breton:

> "A kiss is soon forgotten," Breton had said elsewhere in "Soluble Fish," speaking of an amorous encounter in Place Dauphine—

a square that always caused him an indefinable malaise. On the evening of October 6, it was the same Place Dauphine that Nadja led Breton to in a taxi. On the way she had offered her lips for the first time. . . .

A footnote reads in part, "Breton later attributed this malaise to the realization that, for him, Place Dauphine was 'unmistakably the sex of Paris.' "

In the *Critical Dictionary*, "formless" (*l'informe*, better translated as "unformed"):

> A dictionary would begin as of the moment when it no longer provided the meanings of words but their tasks. In this way *formless* (sic) is not only an adjective having such and such a meaning, but a term serving to declassify, requiring in general that every thing should have a form. . . .

I am leaving in a few weeks for Paris, and I have promised to tell this story to Claude, if he will agree to meet me at the Place Dauphine on May 23rd, Nadja's birthday. Then this little notebook will be done.

(I hear from my French publisher that Emmanuel Hocquard's translation of my book *Sun* will appear in Paris during that same week.)

In Persian mystic poetry and folklore, the sun is a round-cheeked girl *(korshid)*.

*

Parmenides' journey in the sun's chariot, accompanied by the daughters of Helios: crossing the divine threshold of night and day, he came to grasp "the unshakeable heart of well-rounded truth."

*

The Manichean sun god, known as the Third Messenger *(Nery-osang),* who lives in the sun and sets the sun and moon in motion, creating the changes of the seasons.

*

Going back through my notebooks, I come upon the day of our first meeting, Iselin, when I agreed to write the entry for "Sun," and when you told me of the first encounter between Jens Birke-mose and Claude:

23 sept 1993 / Copenhagen

At Brondum Forlag today, Iselin Hermann ("forlagsredaktor") and I discover that Claude Royet Journoud is an old mutual friend. She tells me the story of Claude's first meeting with Jens Birkemose (the painter who has provided illustrations for my Danish book, *An Alphabet Underground*), when both were living on the Rue du Dragon. Claude admired Jens's work but was shy about approaching him. Finally, after some weeks or months, encouraged by Jens's wife, he bought a large bouquet of flowers and rang the bell of the apartment of Jens and his wife. Jens opened the door and, upon seeing Claude, immediately grew deathly pale. Claude, of course was terrified that he had somehow given offense and offered to leave immediately, but Jens said no. It turned out that the week before, in the street nearby, Jens had found a roll of film which he had immediately developed. It contained twenty-four pictures of Claude.

✳

Iselin telling me today that Editions de Minuit sells (X) copies per year of a Beckett title in France. Brondum sells (X divided by 10) of the bilingual edition in Denmark. The smallness of both figures astonishes me.

✳

Later in the day, Bob Creeley tells me the story of his meeting Beckett, via their mutual publisher, John Calder, and his wife at that time, Bettina. An entire night spent in a café, with Beckett telling how he had looked for one word that might stand, upright, alone. As Bob put it, not, obviously, "The Word," nor even "a word," but "word," pure and simple.

Bob and I then talk about Michael Ondaatje, whose *The English Patient* I am reading here in Copenhagen for the first time. "All day they have shared the ampoules of morphine. To unthread the story out of him, Caravaggio travels within the code of signals."

I think about the collection of writings on poetics I edited many years ago, and its title, *Code of Signals*, part of a citation from Osip Mandelstam's "Conversation about Dante," "Poetic speech is a carpet fabric with a multitude of textile warps which differ one from the other only in the coloring of the performance, only in the musical score of the constantly changing directives of the instrumental code of signals." This seems to sit perfectly beside Ondaatje's usage.

✳

As I am copying the above, I receive a call from the Brazilian Consul in San Francisco, himself a novelist. In the course of our conversation, he mentions to me that Bob Creeley is in Brazil and just spent an evening with Haroldo de Campos, one of the poets in Copenhagen with us that September. And Bob telling Haroldo that Bob and I have not seen each other since Copenhagen.

*

A letter arrives from Rosmarie Waldrop, wondering whether I have completed my "notes" for Denmark and telling of her anxiety about finishing on time. I reply that I have completed the notes for the notes but have not filled in all the words. Then I wonder when exactly is/was the deadline. But the work now wants May 23rd as its deadline.

*

There is a sixth-century golden medallion from Mersina (ancient Turkey) in the Hermitage in St. Petersburg. It shows the emperor Constantine flanked by figures embodying the sun and the moon. Above the headdress of the sun, who is handing a crown to the emperor, there is a solar sign, an eight-pointed star. The emperor is larger than the sun, who is paying him homage.

*

The "sun game" of polo, played during the time of Akbar (1542–1605) with an ignited "sun ball."

*

From about the middle of the fourth century, it becomes permissible to depict Christ with a crown of sunrays, like the Roman emperors before him. Around the sixth century, such haloes begin to appear on portraits of Mary and other Christian saints. By Carolingian times, the pagan sun symbols have been entirely absorbed into the Christian tradition.

∗

Robert Smithson's idea of "a surd map," that is, a map without a central logic.

∗

Yesterday, for the new dance work with Margaret Jenkins ("Fault"), I wrote:

> What do you see?
>
> I see signs of movement in the leaves, the wind beginning to pick up.
>
> What do you see?
>
> I see a blind woman in a dark scarf and overcoat tapping a path with her cane along a sidewalk bordered with snow.
>
> From the window, what do you see?
>
> I see the burned-out shell of a streetcar, frozen in midturn. I see children playing amid the debris, people gathered here and there in groups, some looking up and pointing, a few dogs wandering aimlessly.

And it occurs to me that this new work is about connecting the dots, above and below, about dance as a way of seeing rather than as, so often, something simply "to be seen."

✳

A letter from Iselin, saying that she has been to Paris and has met with Claude, and that she too believes in deadlines.

✳

Today, for the dance, I wrote:

What can you see?

I can see the winter sun, low and pale above the garden fence, a hawthorn without leaves, some bare fruit trees and vines of bittersweet, a sun-dial that's . . .

What do you see?

I can see what looks like a face. Maybe you can see it as well. A face half turned away, of a girl or a young woman, her hair drawn back tight, the way a dancer might wear it. I don't know what it means—maybe she's in the process of leaving, yet still undecided, hesitating for some reason. There is apprehension and, I think, sadness, but it's hard to say.

What did you see?

At noon, precisely, I saw the lights go out and the doors clang shut in the cafés and bookstores and souvenir shops around Old Town Square. I heard a single bell tolling in the turrets of Tyn Church. In the middle of the square, hundreds of young women with babies in carriages gathered at the statue of Jan Hus. The whole city, maybe the whole country, seemed to be in the streets. I saw a line of high school students in the old ghetto, chanting freedom slogans as they passed the synagogues.

✳

Sun n. 1. A woman's bag for carrying keys, a wallet, and other personal items. 2. A small bag or pouch for carrying money. 3. A pocket-sized, usually paperbound, book.

✳

If, otherwise, he were to write the episode of the Place Dauphine, it might appear thus:

> And eyes: he is eyeless
> A mirror sees for him

✳

The death of Heiner Müller; death of Levinas.

✳

Sun-disc between the thighs of an Aztec terracotta figure.

✳

I've found an old notebook fragment, "And here in the Zero Quarter, below ground the sun is shining, the stars are out, the . . ."

✳

Iselin, I should explain my delay in returning the contract for this book. I held it for a month before signing it, frightened and disabled by the nature of such a document, the mystery of its linguistic transparency. Or do I mean opacity? The curious thought that you will agree to deliver a text, that there will be words when you need them. Who can guarantee this? And yet the thought of the project, of the dots with lines extending between them forming an angel's wing or a solar halo, gradually lifted me from a period of drift and anomie. In a room with a group of people soon after sending off the contract, I found myself standing with my hands outstretched, held about eighteen inches apart. Someone asked, "What are you doing?" Embarrassed—I had momentarily forgotten there were others in the room—I said, "That's the Denmark book."

✱

Waimea, Hawaii. Arrived today at Kona airport with the dance company and drove up through the lava fields to our hotel in the hills near the base of the Mauna Kea volcano and within sight of Mauna Loa. Intense sun, but a landscape that absorbs the light into its blackness.

We attend the ceremonial benediction for a new grove of trees at the theater. A native Hawaiian woman performs the ceremony with simplicity and evident emotion. We speak afterwards. In response to my question she tells me that her first prayer called back her ancestors and greeted them. The second spoke to the nature of the place, the above and below, the four poles, dawn and dusk. I do not ask why she was frequently in tears throughout the ceremony.

At dinner I am introduced to the people who support the local theater. All are white, elaborately dressed and earnest about culture. I wonder how they will react to our performance on Friday. I wonder what I can possibly read to them next Monday. Halfway through dinner, the community chorus enters and sings selections from Gilbert and Sullivan, from *Brigadoon and Kismet*, a Billy Joel tune arranged for chorus, a series of saccharine contemporary madrigals. I can feel my brain beginning to wobble, a familiar prelude to a wave of depression.

Out for a walk after dark, I hear scattered dogs barking, a car with a bad muffler sputtering to a start, just before the rain begins. Scent of plumaria.

*

Waimea. The construction of entire new towns here in the hills, for the workers who will service the tourist hotels on the coast. This afternoon, we traveled in a four-wheel-drive truck through the lava fields of Mauna Loa and up to the top of Mauna Kea, 14,300 feet, where several astronomical observatories are located. Mauna Kea has not erupted since before the last ice age, but Mauna Loa's most recent flows date from 1986. We see them on the west side of the road, free of almost all vegetation, stretching toward the sea.

Two-thirds of the way up Mauna Kea, we stop to put on layers of sweaters and down clothing. The wind will reach fifty or more miles an hour, the temperature drop to thirty or forty degrees below zero. Ancient Hawaiians lived in caves high up on the sides of the volcano, where they would fashion arrows and tools from volcanic rock for use and for barter.

At the summit, well beyond the cloud layer, is the world's clearest atmosphere. As the sun declines, a brilliant crescent moon in Venus appears, with Orion to the west over the ocean. The Comet Hyakutake is clearly visible below the handle of the Big Dipper, its tail not that sharply defined, perhaps due to the brightness of the moon. As the sky darkens further, myriad other constellations become visible, but as always I have trouble identifying all but the most obvious. I can see the dots of light, the countless suns, but I cannot connect them: Pegasus, Andromeda, Cassiopeia, Ursa Major and Ursa Minor, Draco, Pisces, Aquarius, Libra, Eridanus, Perseus, Leo, Hercules, Aquila, Coma Berenices, Cygnus, Vulpecula, Camelopardus, Auriga, Cetus, Delphinus, Lacerta . . .

★

From his room within sight of the Mauna Kea volcano, he sends a postcard of a tropical waterfall to two friends in Bordeaux. On it are nothing but the words, "Tristes Topiques?" On other cards, however, he writes vivid descriptions of his trip through the lava fields, the ascent of Mauna Kea, the surrounding craters, the sun setting over the Pacific, the view of Orion in the western sky (the shining belt, the sword, the two stars marking the shoulders), the patches of snow, the ferocity of the wind at the summit, the view of the comet beneath the Dipper's handle, the cluster of metallic observatories, the sight of Mauna Loa not far off, the difference between the two principal types of lava, the various flora that soon begin to spring up in the fissures of the lava (one, tiny, with bright orange flowers), the military base in the lava fields, established during World War II, the occasional helicopters, the physical hazards of ascending to 14,300 feet—how, for example, you must monitor your breathing—it is no longer purely autonomic, the wild sheep, goats and pigs, the various exotic trees and brilliantly plumed birds, the periodicity of the comet (it appears every 10,000 years), native artifacts to be found there (axheads and arrowheads, the ancient sleds discovered in the caves), the meaning of the mountains' names (Mauna Kea, "White Mountain," Mauna Loa, "Long Mountain"), the fact that the discoverer of the comet was an amateur Japanese astronomer, the many abstruse technical problems in constructing an observatory, the not unpleasant light-headedness at the summit, the changed pressure on the eyeballs which alters vision, the thickening of the blood as the body draws needed water from it at that altitude, thus the danger of dehydration, the enormous berms of iron oxide occasionally visible during the climb, the subtly shifting color spectrum as you ascend, the absolute clarity of the atmosphere, the sacred myths associated with the two volcanoes (the wars of the goddesses), the passion of our guide in offering us information, the special photographic plates that must be "baked" on site for the observatories, the fact

that one successful photographic plate can provide an astrono-
mer with as much as five years of information to investigate, the
three deaths during the construction of the Japanese observatory
(prayers and offerings had been made to Shinto gods at the start
of construction, but none to the gods of the Hawaiian people), the
environmental controversies that explode each time a new observa-
tory is proposed, the bizarre, chalet-style building that houses the
scientists well below the summit, the dangers of the road itself, on
which people continue to die with regularity, and the fact that, at
the summit, one's intelligence quotient is reduced by about 10%.

*

Yet to two friends in Bordeaux, he has written only the two words,
followed by a question mark and the greeting, "Love, Michael,"
with the date at the upper right. Over the following days, he grad-
ually comes to understand why.

*

In his notebook, on that same day, he writes, "I am, here, how many
miles from Copenhagen? from San Francisco? from Paris?"

He writes, "My face a bright red from the wind on top of the vol-
cano last night, and the intense glare of the lowering sun in the
thin atmosphere."

The following day he writes, "In the window of Waimea's Authentic
Western Wear Shop, I see a T-shirt with a picture of palm trees and
the lowering sun just above the horizon. For the Danish notebook,
this would comprise part of the subsection: *Sun, as ornament to casual
clothing.* I am suddenly reminded of how, north of San Diego, kids
gather each day along the beaches at sunset, to watch the sun dis-
appear, and to hoot and applaud appreciatively, almost as if it had
never happened before or, at least, not in quite that way before."

"Sitting in Lanahila Park, I turn and see a woman riding by on a unicycle, her dog trotting beside her on a leash. Four cedars, four pines, five bushes of brunfelsia."

"Pen found on the table of a Waimea café, with name taped to it: Michelle Hotchkiss."

" 'Banality of marigolds,' the man thinks, looking out the window of the café. Later, approaching the flowers in their border, he realizes that they are not marigolds, but some form of succulent he has never seen before. The shape of the flowers, however, and the gold and yellow hues, are virtually identical to those of marigolds."

He remembers the words of the guide, "And at this altitude, your lungs may suddenly begin to fill with water, and if they don't get you off the mountain immediately, you will drown."

*

He is four, maybe five years old. In the swirls of marble over the fireplace, the child sees the face of a woman with long, flowing dark hair. Years later, he would scan Pre-Raphaelite paintings for that same face and hair.

*

He reads that the dead are still dead in Srebrenica, the black churches still burning in the South.

*

Perhaps, Iselin, what I am doing is entirely redundant. As I sit here in Waimea, reading Keith Waldrop's *The Locality Principle*, it occurs to me that he has written what I would like to write for this project—has in certain instances written beyond what I can offer. An example is the section entitled "Two Musicians," which I heard him read in San Francisco some weeks ago. The question of tuning. Its cover photo by Ben Watkins, who also did the cover of my book *At Passages*. On that same program Keith read from his recently published translation of Claude's *A Descriptive Method*.

✱

This feeling of things beyond my abilities (as in reading *The English Patient*), a mixture of rapture and, inevitably, regret.

✱

Life on the road—what I keep in my room: Japanese rice crackers wrapped in seaweed, grapes, bananas, dried fruit, single malt scotch, mineral water.

How this varies according to location. For example, in Paris the time before last, in my room at the Hôtel des Grandes Ecoles: *clémentines*, bread and cheese, calvados, mineral water. A friend had brought me the *clémentines*.

And in Leningrad, 1990, whatever we could fit into our luggage, from a Helsinki supermarket, before our trip to the Finland Station: crackers, grains, dried soups, bottled water, fruit juices.

✱

Did I mention solitude, which in traveling across multiple time zones seems to deepen and darken? I could only describe its taste by the dreams it provokes, their sharp, hallucinatory character. In Stockholm the first night, on the way to Russia, a dream of islands in the bay, their castles guarded by gates resembling mouths with enormous teeth. The castles' mouths constantly opening and closing, under twin, nocturnal suns.

And that total solitude that stimulates memories and dreams of all the women you have ever been with, and those you've wanted to be with. The pure experience of loss, limitless regret.

✱

Tremor, 4 p.m., rolling through my hotel room, northeast to southwest, as I'm trying to take a brief nap.

✱

Before the mirror, shaving, as he approaches the age of his father the summer night he died.

✱

Horse pulling a Bronze Age sun chariot, in Trundholm, Denmark, bearing a sun disc gilded on one side to represent the day-sun, while the obverse, ungilded, represents the night-sun.

Rg Veda: "the horse of yonder sun, rising from the water like the spark of life . . ."

✱

A woman approaches me after last night's dance performance, holding a copy of *At Passages*. "Your poems are all so sad! Couldn't you write some happy poems? I'm too old for sad poems. When I was young, I read Edna St. Vincent Millay (she recites a few well-known lines). And Ogden Nash—I always liked Ogden Nash."

✱

I had first thought to finish the Danish notebook on April 1st, All Fools Day, but it wasn't to be.

*

Reading in San Francisco last night, with Milosz, Snyder, Ginsberg, Thom Gunn, Adrienne Rich and several others before an intense, anticipatory crowd of 700–800 people, so different from the poetry reading as we otherwise experience it. How is the intimate voice heard in such a space? How is silence heard? My instinct was to read my quietest work.

*

The place where Levinas's ethics invariably founders: where "the Other" cannot be equated with "someone else"; where "the Face" is faceless.

*

When people ask me what I'm doing "these days," I reply that I'm working on a new dance piece and on my Danish notebook. I do not tell them that I don't know what these things are.

*

Or what "these days" are.

*

"Flesh-eating Virus Takes Another Life"

*

Cunningham's "Ocean" today, performed in Berkeley, a few days after Merce's 78th birthday . . . watching Merce arrive at the theater, walking now so arthritically. His question to me of some years ago, asking whether it was a mistake to go on performing with the greatly reduced skills of old age. My reply (meant with complete sincerity), that he should continue to perform until he couldn't move at all, then perform some more.

The shift in the reception of his work in recent years. Now it has an almost classical feel, closer perhaps to Balanchine than to what we see in contemporary "modern dance." Its pure, unapologetic sense of movement as its own excuse for being.

✶

I've felt death with me all day today, as sometimes happens, not as adversarial "Grim Reaper" but as silent companion, even friend. Present as I translated from the Russian all morning, and then in the seat next to me in an auditorium at Stanford University as I listened to the sweet, Scots-inflected voice of Alec Finlay lecturing on his father's poetry garden not far from Edinburgh.

✶

The lovers coupling on the walls of the sun temples at Khajuraho and Konarak.

✶

At Sonoma State University today, I began my reading with my translation of Alexei Parshchikov's "Flight II," with its references to the Chernobyl disaster. Not realizing that it was the tenth anniversary of Chernobyl. At the time of the explosion, my wife and daughter and I were at the Fondation Royaumont outside Paris. Everyone gathered before the television and listened to the reports denying that any radioactivity was detectable in France:

> At the start of the war of the worlds harsh
> wormwood's scent intensifies.

Preparing to set out, I was scraping bugs
from the radiator when a new fire scorched
half our lands, targeting, but missing us.

Gas station's ashes. Sea-foam and dust. Nothing
around but this control panel with its eternal lies.
Was a horseman there, or was it sand scattered
from the sky along the tide . . .

✷

A brief visit to Boston, for the wedding of Bill Corbett's daughter.
At lunch with Paul Auster and Siri Hustvedt before the wedding,
I discuss the Danish notebook. I tell the story of Claude's first
meeting with Jens. I mention that when Iselin first told it to me,
I felt as though I might have read it previously, somewhere in
Paul's work. I wonder whether Claude has already told him this
story, but Paul says he's never heard it before.

✷

On the television news in Boston, we hear of a relatively mild earth-
quake in the San Francisco region. Slippage along the Hayward Fault.

✷

A brief letter from Claude today, mentioning a plant that he has
had for more than ten years. How, a few nights ago, while he was
reading at about one in the morning, he noticed that it had be-
gun to flower for the first time.

✷

In Aquitaine in the fourth century, a flaming sun-wheel rolls
down a hillside.

*

My realization today that I have lost my awareness of words, single words as themselves, material elements, soundings. I have become too used to *using* them. Does this mean I've learned nothing at all from listening to Scelsi all these years?

*

For "Fault":

From there, what do you see?

In the window opposite I can see a table covered with artist's materials. A man enters. He goes briefly to the table, only to turn away suddenly, even violently, and hurry from the room.

What can you see now?

I'm looking at the diagram of a hand covered with writing in a language I don't know.

What do you see?

I see a stone, a large boulder suspended in the afternoon sky. Creases and folds crisscross its surface. At its top, the ramparts and towers of a castle.

What do you see?

I see Cassiopeia, Cepheus, Draco, Ursa Major and Ursa Minor in the northern sky, Andromeda and Pisces in the east, Capricorn and Sagittarius at the ecliptic to the south.

*

Rehearsal of "Fault" tonight, for the preview performance just prior to my departure for France. The first half is almost ready, the second half not close.

To the Text I add:

> What do you see?

> I see a young woman gazing at the comet below the handle of the Big Dipper. She is playing distractedly with the dark hair at the nape of her neck, curling it between her fingers.

✷

Prehistoric sun images on the rock walls of the Dudumahan caves on the Kei Islands of eastern Indonesia: rayed circles, circled crosses, concentric circles, spoked circles with a smaller circle at the center, and various combinations of these forms.

✷

Kazakhstan: the bronze feline coiled within solar rays.

✷

Spider web: symbol of the sun god Sûrya's night garment in Hindu mythology. Woven by Ushas, the goddess of dawn.

✷

Etruria: the winged boy with body and skin of a reptile, emerging from the sea.

✷

Rereading the early entries for these notes, I find a comment on "Leap Year 1982." Of course, that was not a Leap Year. I should have been looking in my notes for 1984, where there is also no Leap Year Day entry.

Under February 11th: " 'Forgive the world, however terrible it is.' William Bronk, *Costume as Metaphor.*"

February 12th: "Now I know I would rather embrace the flaws."

February 14th: "Robert Duncan, 'The form is a revelation of the story.' "

February 15th: "LEC(RI)TURE, à Claude Royet-Journoud." (This, apparently, a work never realized.)

✶

I arrive in Paris at 10:10 a.m. On my *Carte d'Entrée,* under profession, I write *poète/professeur,* then cross out *professeur* and replace it with *traducteur.*

That evening I have dinner with the American painter Irving Petlin and his wife, Sarah, on the Rue du Cardinal-Lemoine. We talk about Claude, Ron Kitaj, Antonio López, Leon Golub and many others. He mentions his recent portrait drawings of Susan Howe, Jacques Roubaud, Keith and Rosmarie. I leave about 10 p.m., taking the Rue Clovis up past the Panthéon and the Bibliothèque Sainte Geneviève. To my left, I see the Hôtel des Grands Hommes, where Breton stayed when he first came to Paris. Since my last visit they have put up a plaque, officially commemorating it as the site of the discovery of automatic writing by Breton and Soupault. Descending the Rue Soufflot toward the Boulevard Saint Michel, I hear snatches of conversations among young people standing around in small groups:

> "I have absolutely no accent in German, but English is something else."

> "The Socialists have all the money and the peasants—le Droit— have none."

Near the Rue Auguste Comte, at the edge of the Luxembourg Gardens, I see a kiosk advertising "Un Vampire de Brooklyn." It pleases me to walk along this street named for a man who believed that knowledge of the world arose from observation, one who held that the causes of phenomena and the nature of things-in-themselves are not knowable. It pleases me even more never to have read his six-volume *Cours de philosophie positive*. I imagine M. Comte as a vampire from Brooklyn. It begins to rain as I enter my apartment, very close to the Dome and the Rotonde. My bed lies under a Man Ray lithograph of a woman's heavily rouged lips hovering in a cloud-filled, crepuscular sky above a landscape. In the apartment, as I turn on the lights and wander around, I find other paintings and graphics by Matta, Bacon, Petlin, Seymour Rosofsky.

I attempt to phone Claude but only reach his *répondeur.* I leave a message, asking whether we are still to meet on the 23rd.

✴

You cannot forget that you are *embodied.*

You cannot remember whether, at this corner, years before, you turned left or right.

✴

I go to Irving's studio to begin to take notes on, and to "write toward," his *Seine Series*: the river at flood, two winters past; the bodies of the dead, afloat, October 17th, 1961; those "figures-which-are-not"; the sky escaping its frame.

"Paris is white." Edmund Jabès.

> What is submerged
> behind the liquid—flooded—
> eye

"To bring together the expired space with its origin and full self."

The dialogue between the near and the far. How the center empties as details accumulate. How the absent reappears, and the present . . .

Paris dream: Claude and I are at the summit of Mauna Kea in the early darkness, where I am explaining to him the intricacies of the optical devices, the technical problems posed by extreme fluctuations of temperature, violent winds, snow, and the unfiltered rays of the sun. We turn to leave, but our car and driver have departed. We can make out the lights of the car as it follows the winding road down.

*

An inventory of Irving's studio: erasers, boxes of pastels, brushes, paint daubs arrayed in a half-oval, pencils, pens, charcoal, chalk, pushpins, tubes of oils, sawhorses, notebooks, cans of fixative, jars, draughtman's triangle, masking tape, measuring tape, photographs, sketch pads, books, cassette tapes, radio/tape player, painting smock, scissors and tools, picnic knife (Opinel), film canisters, dusting brush, stapler, wine glass and water glass, pile of exhibition catalogues, two gooseneck lamps, resin bags, palette knives, rolls of sketching paper, dustbroom and canister, reading glasses, rubber bands, mirror, c.7" x 9", draughtman's T-square, large clips, chamois.

✱

We go to see Robert Altman's *Kansas City* at the Grande Action on the Rue des Écoles. I recognize a few musicians I know in the cast. Very good musicians, maybe better than the film which, itself, is better than people will think.

✱

Dear Iselin,

I spoke with Claude by phone yesterday. Tomorrow, the 23rd, we will meet for the first time since last May, when I passed briefly through Paris after a stay in Prague.

✱

Graffiti on the wall of the Eglise Sainte Geneviève, across the street from the Lycée Henri IV:

> Excelle dans l' art
> de ne rien faire

And to the right of it, hastily scribbled:

> Luke
> la main froide

✱

Dear Iselin,

I picked up Claude at his apartment around noon today, where he showed me a suite of astonishing erotic drawings by Jens Birkemose, published last year by Brondums in three volumes. We walked over to the Place Dauphine, and Claude offered a glass of champagne in honor of Nadja's birthday. I then told him, as I remembered it, the story you had told me of Claude's first meeting with Jens. He approved of this version but then proceeded to tell me the story as he remembered it.

After much hesitation, at the urging of Jens' wife, he finally made an appointment to meet Jens. He doesn't recall whether he brought flowers, though he is certain that he brought along a copy of Keith Waldrop's *The Garden of Effort* as a gift. Their first meeting was very pleasant, with nothing out of the ordinary. A few weeks later, Jens discovered a canister of film that he had picked up from the sidewalks of the Boulevard Saint Germain some months before. He had brought it home, placed it on his desk, and forgotten about it. Opening the can, he found a roll of already developed film. On it, twenty-four images of Claude. He noticed that in one frame Claude was holding a book, whose title was too small to read. Getting out his magnifying glass, he saw that the book was *The Garden of Effort.*

My story or stories about the Place Dauphine followed. Claude responded with the obvious questions: what had become of her? had we ever met again? He mentioned that the manager or proprietor of the Hôtel Henri IV often ate in the restaurant where we were sitting, and that the hotel was still known for very inexpensive rooms. He then went across the square and returned with a card:

>   Hôtel Henri IV
>   25, Place Dauphine—75001 Paris
>   Tout Confort—Prix Modérés

We crossed over to the Ile Saint Louis for a long, late lunch.

*

The shouts and screams of children playing in the courtyard of a nearby school, pouring in through the windows each day as I work in Irving's studio.

An event witnessed—a nonevent, invisible; the inversions and anachronisms; what was there is not, what was not, is; traces; "compressed into conflagration"; Titanium White; Zinc White.

The Arab Rider: Cobalt Blue and Delft Blue.

*

This evening at dinner, as I discuss the Denmark book with Dominique and Sandra, Dominique mentions a show that has just opened at the Beaubourg: *l'informe: mode d'emploi*.

*

Today, Irving and I review the last three canvases from the *Seine Series*.

Dominique and I meet later at the Beaubourg to see the show. It is introduced by the quotation from Bataille that I cite above ("A dictionary would begin . . .").

*

First day of clear, hot weather since my arrival. I walk to the offices of POL to sign copies of the French edition of *Sun* and to pick up my copies.

*

On the 29th, the Dürer show with Dominique at the Petit Palais, then back to San Francisco to edit these notes.

*

Newspaper article after my return. Measurements taken at the sun's corona indicate that oxygen particles streaming from the sun in the solar wind are heated to more than 200 million degrees Fahrenheit, hotter than any temperature previously measured. The readings focused on a point 310,000 miles above the edge of the solar disc. (A constant current of electrically charged gas issues from the sun, creating the solar wind. At 775,000 miles from the sun, the oxygen has accelerated to more than 500,000 miles per hour.)

*

Solstice fires, dancers leaping through the flames.

*

Tasseography: reading from the dregs left in a cup.

*

> These words on
> parole.

> K.W., *The Garden of Effort*

[*First published in* An Avec Sampler Two *and by* Avec Books *(Penngrove, CA, 1999); and as* Den Danske Notebog *by Brondum Vorlag (Copenhagen, 1998).*]

A LANGUAGE OF THE UNSAYABLE: SOME NOTES ON IRVING PETLIN

I.

In a culture so much of the moment, of nowness, one all too susceptible to the luxury of forgetting, Irving Petlin's art offers a temporal window. It is a window that looks out at the immediate world, certainly, but more significantly, it looks beneath surfaces, beyond appearances, toward the undisclosed, the enfolded and the disapppeared. His is a body of work that, for this and other reasons, lies largely outside the accelerated play of the art world, that often frenzied quest for currency. Its present is a complex vision of temporal folds, times inhering within other times, tenses we might name the future-past, the first-and-last, the lost-and-found; that present of what he has called an "I impregnated presence," and "something in a sense plucked from the mind and not from nature itself." The art is insistently exploratory, searching for the meeting point of the interior and the exterior, and for a language of the unsayable. It returns again and again to certain resonant objects and figures, recalled or imagined, in order to see them again from a slightly altered perspective and thus discover their undisclosed or alternate meanings. (Hence the crucial importance of the "series" throughout his work.) It is understandable that such a quest might prove baffling to many critics, however skilled in decoding the contemporary swirl of proliferating styles and ideologies, since it asks for another kind of silence and reflection, another way of seeing, with the mind's eye. Though it is by no means literary painting in the accepted (these days usually deprecatory) sense of that term, it nonetheless elicits a kind of reading, a sounding and resounding of its characteristic figures, objects and landscapes. As in Bacon and Kitaj, whose work his own work at various times has been compared, Petlin's narrative—or anti-narrative—emerges obliquely, through its multilayered, metamorphic representations. Again as in Bacon and Kitaj, though in his own distinctive manner, his work foregrounds a deliberately articulated tension between astonishing draughtsmanship and expressionistic rawness, the latter a legacy of his Chicago School background.

I have followed the evolution of Petlin's art for well over twenty years and have watched its figural imagination grow more and more assured, its signifying capacity deepen, its palette and subject matter expand; so I eagerly accepted the invitation to visit his Paris studio in May of this year, to view the *Seine Series* and to respond in whatever way I chose. Before arriving, I thought a great deal about the multiple risks of the project that he had undertaken. How once again to depict a site so laden with representations that it has been virtually abandoned to weekend painters of the scenic for more than seven decades? How possibly to engage anew with some of the central signifiers of European cultural life and history?

I spent parts of ten days in Petlin's studio off the Rue du Cardinal-Lemoine (located in the same complex of apartments where James Joyce completed *Ulysses*). Each day we would discuss the individual canvases for a while, and then Irving would leave me alone with them to look and take notes. What I gradually came to realize was that, across this set of oils and pastels, Petlin had attempted to depict a series of silent conversations, conversations between the visible and the disappeared, the living and the dead, multiple pasts and multiple presents, conversations at once synchronous and diachronous. Historical and spatial anomalies are deliberately and systematically invoked to create a fracture in the apparent scene or site, and within this fracture the drama of historical and personal memory is enacted. We witness too a convergence and conversation between the language of oils and the language of pastels, the two media in which Petlin has most often worked. Here they are dramatically juxtaposed, in a sequence of mutual, sympathetic interrogations.

The *Seine Series* was first suggested to Petlin by the sight of the river in January of 1995, swollen from torrential rains, inundating the quais. To Petlin's eye, it was as if the river, in the force of its flooding, were reasserting its primitive self, its aqueous memory, while simultaneously stimulating a flood of personal recollections and associations. Thus the first canvas, *The Seine (in flood)*, sets what is the essential, methodically compressed frame for the entire series (for, though these are indeed panoramas, there is an almost claustral feel to the majority of them). To the viewer's left is the Pont de Tournelle; at the approximate center of the canvas, on the Ile Saint Louis, the Cathedral of Notre Dame, in Petlin's words, "the disappearing apex, the emptying center," of the series; and to the far right, Jean Nouvel's Institut du Monde Arabe. Near the base of Notre Dame, tacit and invisible to the viewer, lies the Holocaust Memorial. Wisps and streaks of atomized, grainily dispersed reds and yellows dot the sky. Spidery aerials and chimney pots establish their listening and watching, remnantal presence. The river is seen from a high vantage point, as if at once from multiple, subtly shifting points of view. The "now-and-then" and the "near-and-far" have been set in play. Beginning there, the work resonates through its various echo chambers. From my Paris notes, I would like simply to offer a few points of orientation.

To the viewer's right in the second canvas, *The Seine (The Arab Rider)*, floats a figure in blue, taken from *Le Cavalier Arabe*, a drawing in the Louvre by Fromentin. It hovers like an ephemeral witness to this canvas, which appears almost to have been flooded and stained by the river. Rather than painting things on the surface of the picture, the brush seems to be in the process of bringing up submerged forms. The foreboding evident in the first canvas has become more manifest. A dematerialized, woundlike Notre Dame is represented in red.

The Seine ... October 17th, 1961 refers to a nightmarish incident witnessed by Petlin in his youth during a protest against the Algerian war. Walking along the Seine, he saw countless bodies floating by, the corpses of executed Algerian activists. The void of the river fills with white stains, white absences or erasures, figures-which-are-not. The Institut, not yet built in 1961, nonetheless stands as a brightly colored, enigmatic signifier of a world as yet unacknowledged, invisible. Light has been wrenched from the sky, which in turn is now flooded with terrestrial hues and textures.

The fourth canvas, *The Disapppeared, I*, is the first of two dedicated to the great post-Holocaust poet, Paul Celan, who lived in Paris after the war and committed suicide in 1971 by leaping into the river from the Pont Mirabeau. The painting evokes the Paris of World War II, a shrouded, blacked-out city, its bridges spectral, its sky filled with puffs recalling anti-aircraft fire. One window is illuminated, for Celan, who is not there. A remnant of the recently destroyed city of Grozny appears as an echo within this echo.

Paris is White is dedicated to the poet and author of *The Book of Questions*, Edmond Jabès. Forced into exile from Cairo as a result of the Suez episode, Jabès lived in Paris for the rest of his life. The title derives from a key moment in Jabès's *Return to the Book*, when the doomed lovers, Sarah and Yukel, first meet. The whiteness of the page, the city, the canvas, the desert. The white of the third picture in the series has been transmuted into a ground of light. The spiritualized verticality of the painting contrasts with the horizontality of the others in the series. The city's architecture has dematerialized, and everything is in flux. Lines and masses waver, refusing fixity, completion.

As the title indicates, *The Seine in Sleep* is an oneiric canvas, a portrait of the river as dreamed, eyes closed. What is to be seen, after the visible has been withdrawn, detail has been submerged? What comes forward when "it" disappears? The pastel functions here as a kind of mute after-image to *Paris is White*. Yet the dream is, paradoxically, full of light. The red of the sky in the homage to Jabès has now been pushed to the far right-hand edge of the viewer's gaze. The Institut, virtually transparent, seems almost to be made of light.

There is an armored and riveted character to the colors and masses in *La Guerre des Deux Eglises*, a tautness of representation, yet at the same time an apposite, manifestly oriental, delicacy in the way the city itself has been depicted. Two languages of representation, at once at odds and in dialogue. Language to language, *Book* to *Book*. A form can be seen in the water below Notre Dame, emerging from the point behind the cathedral where the Holocaust Memorial is situated. Except for this form, the river is now empty, blank. The skin of the canvas itself appears raw, but the "war" referred to in the title is silent, submerged, to be known only by inference. It exists wordlessly, as a kind of weather, an atmosphere. In fact, the identity of the "two churches" is left ambiguous. Christian and Jewish; Jewish and Arab; Arab and Christian, etc.?

The Disappeared, II, a pastel on raw linen, is the second of two for Paul Celan. It asks, "What is it when someone disappears or takes his life?" The atmosphere or weather mantles everything here. Color and event have been suppressed (the usual bright character of pastel itself has been suppressed, as an empathic gesture toward what is depicted). Things are seen through a scrim. Forms that in many of the other canvases are solid have become hollowed out. The disappeared, and the suicide, are also the unrealized, the incomplete, the mute. Browns and greys dominate, along with the linen itself.

The vantage point in the final two canvases shifts to the top of the Institut du Monde Arabe, where the view extends beyond Notre Dame and the atmosphere expands. These are eventless canvases, celebrating what enfolds and underlies the act of depiction. After exploring his most paradoxical of subjects, the river

that at once recalls and conceals, Petlin now pays homage to
air and light as defining that subject. In a sense, the last two
pictures explore the canvas, actual and metaphorical, on which
the others appear. In so doing, they bow toward the Monet side
of the Impressionist spectrum. This is a surprising acknowl-
edgement for Petlin, whose sympathies among French painters
have always lain more with Seurat and Cézanne and the Post-
Impressionists. The making of the *Seine Series* might then also
be viewed in part as a process of personal, pictorial dialogue
and reconciliation with artistic currents he struggled against
in his youth.

II.

The White Notebook

But we have painted over the chalky folds,
the snow- and smoke-folds, so carefully,
so deftly that many (Did you bet

on the margins, the clouds?) that many
will have gone, unnoticed,
under. Water under water,

"earth that moves beneath earth."
We have added
silver to the river, dots of silver,

red, figures-which-are-not. Tell
me what their names might have been,
what were last and first, what spells

the unfamiliar, awkwardly whispered, syllable?
And what of the blue rider, the Arab
horseman, the *cavalier* composed

of two shades of blue, one
from Vermeer's Delft, the other
from that metallic element called

cobalt, *Kobolt*, goblin? What scene
is he watching? Is it expired space
the fixed eye observes? Is it

the river which has no center, the
whiteness of the city when you say
Paris is white? Is it the arches

of the bridges now narrowed to slits?
Is it the liquid
voices themselves

he watches grow silent?
The voice of closed eyes?
Or the two

impossibly young
in the lighted room
who speak only of rain?

Scene which has no center
or whose center is empty,
elsewhere. The way white is said

rejoining an earlier whiteness
between the done and the not-yet
rolling off the tongue

almond, almond-eyed,
eyeless, denialwhite
as the zero code, wordless,

a language of rhythm and breath.
(In erasure the chestnut
flowering toward origin

among the names for white:
blanc de titane, blanc de zinc.)
I met her there at the crossroads.

I don't remember who spoke.
Two breaths, two patterns of echo.
We have painted a bridge's eyes

narrowed, its mouth spurting sand,
dots, more dots, bright,
not visible to the eye.

River of dots rising,
stream of sand with no center.
This was both before and after.

Palette knife beside a photograph.
At recess the children's cries
through the studio windows,

station clocktower to the right,
ochre of expanding sound,
tongue to mute tongue, tendrils—

tendons—over rooftops.
Didn't it turn me—
he asks of his eye—

didn't it polish me
like one of its stones,
remingle and remake me

and draw me quickly down
to where each night in sand
the hour sounds?

We met there at the crossroads
near the small arcades.

I can't recall who first spoke,
who said, "the darkness of white."

We shared one shadow.
In the heat she tasted of salt.

III.

For many years now, Irving Petlin has been working in the se-
ries form. Each of these series extends, echoes or elaborates, in
particular ways, the thematic core of the others, while form-
ing within itself an elaborate cluster of metaphorical and
metamorphic pictorial "sites." By working in series, Petlin em-
phasizes the open and endlessly exfoliating character of signi-
fication, and the play of identity and difference at work in the
act of representation. In a time, historically, of fragmentation
and loss, no single signifier can pretend to be stable, no one
point de repère to be definitive. Hence, the multiple, or displaced,
perspectives he often incorporates into the work. The gaze is
not singular, not fixed; instead it probes the recurring figures,
objects and images before it for the facets of meaning they may
release. A kind of visual hermeneutics is at play, where what
signifies is not just the wall but the number and texture of the
stones, not just the stair but the number of its steps, not just
the expression on a face, but what lies, not quite visible, behind
that expression (a given face will also resonate with ancestral
likenesses or traces, a plural singularity). So a river in Petlin's
Seine Series tells as much by what it hides as by what it discloses,

and a Paris street resonates with what is absent, what has disappeared.

Petlin's 22 pastels in response to Edmond Jabès's *The Book of Questions* complete a circle. They are the last in a trilogy of series begun with Primo Levi's *The Periodic Table* and continued with a group exploring the work and world of Bruno Schulz. Intimately related to these are the *Seine Series*, consisting of five pastels and five oils, with the river as the governing "text," and the sequence of *natures mortes, The Four Seasons*.

Schulz, Levi and Jabès encompass the before, during and after of Petlin's exploration into the period, the cauldron, of World War II, and the horrors and residues and survivals of Shoah. Each series represents an attempt to grasp the nature of this moment and its aftermath, its aftermath of wounds and absences and revenants. Each as well speaks by indirection to Petlin's own experience, his life, and to the "possible lives" of this painter of Polish-Jewish descent: Schulz, whose city, Drohobycz, and fate "could have been" Petlin's; Levi, whose experience in the camps "could have been" Petlin's; Jabès, whose city of exile, Paris, Petlin has shared during two significant periods of his life as a painter. In the renditions of Schulz's world, Petlin immediately recognized physical and cultural cognates to the tenement landscape of Chicago immigrants in which he was raised. For Petlin, Primo Levi's questioning of the chemical elements for the meanings of a life would suggest parallels to what occurs in the painter's "laboratory," where the elemental means of representation are interrogated, the cobalt blue, the zinc white and titanium white, the cadmium white of absence.

The appeal to Petlin of these writers, the call that results in dialogue, can be understood in several ways. Petlin has said that with each he experienced a "jolt of recognition." All are profoundly innovative writers for whom conventional forms of narrative realism are unacceptable. In each there is an embeddedness of figures, an ancient character to persons and things paradoxically combined with an expressive immediacy. For Petlin, this resonance of the new with the old is the mark of profound innovation, the search for what is old to understand the new in things.

Looking at it another way, the question becomes, how do you arrive at an art that is not simply one of surfaces, an art that participates in the palimpsestic nature of what is before the eye, discovering the withheld beneath the disclosed. I must emphasize that we are not speaking of hermetic meanings here, but of buried history by which the present itself is buried in turn. It is in this regard that Paul Celan, to whom Petlin dedicates two of the *Seine Series* canvases, objected so strenuously and justifiably to being characterized as a hermetic poet. Yet, the unsayable cannot be narratized without betrayal of the meanings at its core. Confrontation must come, paradoxically, by indirection. The truth must be told but, as Emily Dickinson (a favorite poet of Celan) notes, we must "tell it slant." For each of these writers, and for Petlin, the narrative is within, is inside the way of working: materials, shape, form, touch and trace. As a result, the work of these writers has acquired a universal character, for it is finally questions of identity, of being and non-being, good and evil, and the limits of language that are at issue, questions, that is, of the nature and limits of the telling. How, possibly, can the aesthetic illuminate the social and historical dimensions of experience when the aesthetic itself has been so problematized and deformed by the events of history?

It is the questions behind *The Book of Questions* that first drew Petlin to Jabès's work. How do you respond to Theodor Adorno's earnest cry that it would be "barbaric" to make poetry after Auschwitz? By this often misunderstood statement, he means in part that questions of pleasure, consolation, *divertissement*, must be entirely rethought; the activity and signification of art must be rethought. It was, after all, the Nazis who appropriated the aesthetic dimension into the political, and the Nazis who listened to Schubert quartets within sight of the ovens. How do you think the unthinkable? What happens to human feeling and to the aesthetic intelligence "after"? For Petlin, such questions involve a "conversation with the soul," and Jabès offered a syntax for such a conversation. The circling and errancy of *The Book of Questions*, the multiplication of voices, provoked a new thinking about exploratory means. Petlin was drawn as well to what he calls Jabès's "alphabet of attachments" in language, which seemed parallel to Petlin's nonlinguistic or silent alphabet. This alphabet forms the trail of Jabès's words and things, a path of constant invention, of iteration and reiteration, and the testing of meaning. Midrash, perhaps. But it is finally this: how do we ask a question and allow it to resonate in all directions, without the illusion of a possible answer?

These were the issues that began to swirl through Petlin's head when he sat with Jabès in the writer's apartment on the Rue de l'Epée-de-Bois for a first portrait session. It was a month before Jabès's death. The attendant conversation lasted four hours, at the end of which time Petlin's drawing paper was blank. He would never see Jabès again but would complete the portrait the day after his death.

Petlin chose to work with the first three volumes of *The Book of Questions* (*The Book of Questions, The Book of Yukel, Return to the Book*), using the exemplary Rosmarie Waldrop translation that had been supervised by Jabès and his wife, Arlette. Rather than foregrounding one narrative voice, *The Book of Questions* presents a kind of *theatrum mundi*, a multiplicity of voices within a variety of forms. Imaginary rabbis ("rabbi-poets") converse. The doomed lover Yukel speaks from his diary. Absences converse. Events are narrated, witnessed, recalled, prefigured in a first-person voice impossible to identify or stabilize. "I" as we, or you, or they. "I" as everyone or no one. The exilic "I" may stand in utter isolation or in turn become the voice of all exiled "persons of the Book," persons exiled into the book. In fact, it is all of these things at once.

The site? Paris and the desert. Paris as the desert. The desert as the book. The book as the body. The Seine and the Nile. The buildings and the wells. The alleyways, the streets and the skies.

The skies and stars, skies and smoke. The cemetery of Bagneaux, the cemetery of sand in Cairo, of marble in Milan, the cemetery in Rome.

And within this labyrinth, the fragments of the tale: the first encounter of the young lovers, Sarah and Yukel, at the Carrefour de l'Odéon, her death in the camps, his suicide. Fragments of a tale enfolded, buried, with countless others.

After the Suez crisis, the Jewish community of Cairo was forced to emigrate. Paris became the home of Edmond Jabès, his new landscape. The whiteness of the city echoed, not without multiple ironies, the whiteness of the sands of Egypt. Out for a walk on his first day of residence, he came upon a graffito in French and English: MORT AUX JUIFS/JEWS GO HOME, a literally graphic reminder of France's enduring anti-Semitism and its all-too-recent, dark chapter. So Paris was double, at once welcoming and rejecting. For Petlin too, upon his return, Paris was a multilayered site of rich personal experience, stored history, beauty and complicity. Like Jabès, he would look at the city with an eye that was at once familiar, accustomed and foreign. The apartment he and his wife, Sarah, eventually found, coincidentally, was a few minutes walk from that of Edmond and Arlette Jabès. They would share the same streets and markets, would walk the same trajectories.

From *The Book of Questions*, Petlin would extract a series of recurring images, figures and viewpoints that spoke both to his plastic imagination and to his lived experience. As in *The Book of Questions*, he would continually return to these sites from different angles, in the attempt to fathom the full range of their meanings. Thus the wells, the alleyways, the trees, the door, the brothers, the streets or roads, the boats, the Book, the scream, the sail, all of which have their own history in Petlin's earlier work. He would look as well at the way these images continually metamorphose into one another ("the door—a book," "the tongue of dry wells," "the word—a fir tree"). The site, then, is always multiple, consisting of the scene before the eyes and the site within the text. The site, therefore, is at once a present and a presence and an absence and an elsewhere. The latter, a shadow, informs the present with memory, with unforgetting. It is an act of anamnesis. Before the eye/I is also what is gone, silenced. The site is always a place of confluences, its temporality multidimensional. Hence the "ancient character" of these depicted places, events, gatherings, figures, cloaked in time but of no identifiable moment.

There is not space here to examine the entire series, but I would like to take a brief look at a number of the pastels in relation to the generative textual passages, to give some idea of the process involved. Many of the pastels, of course, are linked to multiple passages, where the same image recurs in the text. Only a reading of the book would offer a full sense of the unfolding of a given image.

In Vézelay on January 6, 1994, as Petlin is contemplating figures from the Old Testament, his conceptual work on the series begins to come into focus. Here he takes the photographs from which a composite will be constructed. He will work from this composite to create the somberly elegiac, *The tallest tree, feet buried in the snow, hears our screams*, and its companion piece. It is from the cry of Reb Kamoun in *The Book of Yukel*, and it can be seen as the iconic, mournful initiation of the series. The tree itself strongly suggests a torso, arms upraised, with a bright slash or wound of red against the winter sky. It is a picture of silence, a silent scream that will sound through the entire series.

"A neighborhood lives through its streets, as a tree through the strength of its branches." So begins a passage in *The Book of Questions* that will be the source (along with many parallel passages) of several images in Petlin's series. The street as a site of passage, of encounter and reencounter, chance events, violence and play, apparition. "A street is never the same," states Jabès:

(The street stirs with the passer-by.
My street stirs in her sleep and speaks, now
softly, now loudly. My alley-way is an adolescent

> in the middle of a noisy neighborhood, where her
> sisters have lost the habit of rest.

Petlin wandered the streets spreading out from the Place de
la Contrescarpe, the Rue Mouffetard and the Rue Monge, in
Jabès's neighborhood. He was struck by the ancient scale and
singular curve of the narrow Rue Saint-Etienne-du-Mont, how
its atmosphere seemed to contain another time within its pres-
ent. He decided to posit this as the street/alley-way of encoun-
ters suggested by the text. (Jabès himself never remembered the
specific street, if any, he was referring to.) It will appear and re-
appear, "never the same," throughout the series in works such
as *The Street* (I & II), *My alley-way* (I & II) and, finally (though it
is in fact the earliest pastel rendition of it), *Paris is White*. In the
first of these, *The Street* (I), the street is empty, but stained with
slashes of red, the same red which scars and crosshatches the
sky and highlights details of the buildings. *The Street* (II), on the
other hand, is inhabited by five spectral figures. At the extreme
left edge, a screaming figure; behind him a man "who might
be Yukel." Behind Yukel, a figure "from an Egyptian past," car-
rying an infant. To that figure's left, parallel with Yukel, the
ghost-double of Yukel, the lover and suicide. Farther back on
the street there is a fifth figure, half-naked, drawn from Petlin's
The Street of Jews. Now, windows are lit and stars are visible ("a
bonfire in the starry night"). In *Paris is White*, we have the first,
tentative attempt to represent the drama of absence that is the
story of Sarah and Yukel. It is what, like *The tallest tree . . .* , Pet-
lin refers to as a "white pastel." The "false," nonoptical perspec-
tive gives the feeling of being expelled from a tunnel-like space,
rather than entering it. The title is drawn from the section in
Return to the Book immediately before Sarah speaks of first meet-
ing Yukel ("We were two breaths, two echoes."). "Paris is white.
Paris rejoins the old Paris in its whiteness." Petlin, of course,
will return to this section for one of the panoramic pastels of
the *Seine Series* dedicated to Jabès, and once again for *Winter* of

The Four Seasons. My alley-way (I & II) follow *Paris is White* with more developed and articulated views of the street. The identities of the figures are fugitive and shifting, unstable. They seem to metamorphose into one another. No one can be identified as Sarah or Yukel. The clouds in the blue sky of #I have become vertical smoke plumes, as if from factories or other chimneys. The power and menace of the images evoke the horror of conflagration, engulfment, flight. Nowhere is the expressive potential of pastel more evident.

Several in the series depict the Egyptian landscape. These derive from numerous references throughout *The Book of Questions* to Jabès's homeland and to the formation of his poetics under the influence of its culture and its landscape, in particular the desert and its silences, the river and its commerce, the wells and their gatherings. The pastels, however, also refer to a range of Petlin's own personal experiences, stemming in part from a trip to Egypt and the Sinai with his wife, Sarah, some years ago. The new works echo those produced directly after the trip, a trip in which for the first time Petlin witnessed a landscape of sand and rock strikingly close to that which much of his earlier work had, half-unknowingly, evoked. *Watching the Nile flow with its cargoes,* from a passage in *Return to the Book,* is a virtuoso, panoramic evocation of the river that derives in part from a semi-hallucinated dream Petlin experienced in Egypt in a state of extreme dehydration. It is a work in which nothing happens. A state of slowness and spatial extension creates, in the painter's words, a "historic haze." The boats seem almost unmoving, and the river-as-canvas/ river-as-text, as well as the elevated perspective, remind us immediately of the renderings in the *Seine Series.* On the right bank are overturned boats, hints of activity but no figures. On the left bank, we find a combination of new and ancient architecture. There is a sense of distance, of endless vistas dotted with minor events in their soundlessness and voicelessness. Here we see the influence of Renaissance martyr landscapes which has touched a number of Petlin's earlier works. Things occur at the edge of the frame, at the edge of history, obscured by the inexorable flow of ordinary life.

The wells of my brothers and *Wells of the desert, buds of fire* refer to the not always comfortable memories of difficult discussions at the wells in *The Book of Questions*, the experience of leaving the city to walk and talk along the Nile. For Petlin, they are reminders of walking and talking in the streets of Chicago with his brothers. Meetingplace as a site of disputation. In striking contrast to *Watching the Nile . . .* , the scale here is dramatically reduced. In each, a night sky is represented, rich and turbulent. In *The wells of my brothers*, there is an almost Bacon-like distortion and merging of the figures, a sense of lamentation. The sky is a site of unsettled activity, with the suggestion of patterns and figures emerging and merging. A yellow tear rends the sky's fabric, hinting at another dimension behind. In *Wells of the desert . . .* , the sense of contention seems partly diminished, as a male figure somewhat stiffly and tentatively reaches to enfold the naked, orange-tinted female, while an ancient child-witness watches. The events of the sky appear less troubled, if still unsettled.

The desert, Paris is a large pastel on linen, accompanied by a small study with the same title. The desert, like the city in such a view, represents an accumulation of infinite detail, and therefore a kind of emptiness. It is a space at once full and empty, sounding and silent. There is a brooding, darker character to the large work, a sea of flickering, rooftop details creating at once a multiplicity of signs and a void. Rising over the horizon is the spectral outline of one of the university buildings from the Jussieu campus as a kind of sentinel or witness. The sky is leaden, composed of grey and white pastel shades and the texture of the linen itself—a source of weight rather than of light. It is a work that, like many of Petlin's, brings into question the boundary between the abstract and the representational through its sense of field and pattern. The primary reference in Jabès is to the "Letter to Gabriel" in *The Book of Yukel*, which begins with an evocation of Cairo in contrast to the pyramids and sphinx of the desert and ends with an eruption of the desert in the city:

> This morning, between rue Monge and la Mouffe (after the rue des Patriarches and the rue de l'Epée-de-Bois where I live) I let the desert invade my neighborhood. The Nile was not far. . . .

This autobiographical moment must have immediately struck Petlin, whose son is named Gabriel, by its dual proximity.

Closer still to abstraction are the two pastels on paper, *The soil shifted (for a long time)* (I & II). The title is drawn from *The Book of Yukel*:

> And Yukel said:
> "In a village in Central Europe, the Nazis one day buried some of our brothers alive. The soil shifted with them for a long time. That night, one and the same rhythm bound Israelites to the world."

Petlin has stated that both works "almost made themselves," and that "certain things can't be drawn, instead they are materialized." It is the paper itself, the defining shapes in it, that Petlin allows to model his patterns. In each, what is described is a surface; the unspeakable, beneath, is both implied and screened. Additional commentary seems unnecessary. The eloquence is evident—and tacit.

The door, the rabbis go in refers to an early sequence in *The Book of Questions* which for Petlin carries an almost mystical weight:

> "What is going on behind this door?"
> "A book is shedding its leaves."
> "What is the story of the book?"
> "Becoming aware of a scream."
> "I saw rabbis go in."

The two rabbis here hearken back to the "white negroes" who populated some of Petlin's work in the sixties. Figures of multiple and inscrutable identity, their bodies are wound with philacteries. They climb a stair toward a door, a door of the book. Inside the door is a third figure, angelic, youthful, wrapped in a ruffled cloth, the air around her animated. The rabbis are entering a mystery, a space of youth and living spirit. A line, perhaps a thought line or a sight line, or both, passes through the central figure.

Day breaks. The night has conceived (I) follows immediately from *The door* . . . In a passage directly preceding the one quoted in the title, Jabès writes:

> We know the word which makes us see, hear, dream, and judge does not exist except in terms of the reality it creates and yet eludes.

> Thus opens the book. What is traced there is the shadow of the gold which gleams by inner necessity.

Through the opening of the door, of the book, once again the angelic figure, but here enveloped in a red night filled with stars, reminding us of Jabès's description of the Egyptian night and its "buds of fire."

In the second *Day breaks* . . . , all that is left of the young woman is the ruffle, a trace of innocence. An orange-yellow *tâche* effaces the figure and seems to bear it toward the upper air, following the vertical lines in the paper itself. Behind her, before what has become a deep blue night sky, the "tallest tree" reappears, now more than ever suggesting a male torso, its pectorals clearly visible. The door has become a window. Outside its frame stands a figure naked except for a cap, a mason or some other kind of workman. He is one of those displaced figures from no identifiable time who populate Petlin's work. He is at once depicted (within the frame of the pastel) and off-scene (outside the frame of the window and its events). Thus the laborer, the silent witness, semi-invisible, offstage, without whom the event, or the events of history, cannot take place, and without whom the monuments, the temples and pyramids, cannot be built.

The final image in the series is drawn from one of the last and most poignant images in *Return to the Book*:

> I am haunted by the memory I mentioned of a buffalo tied to her wheel to spread the bountiful water.
>
> Have I given drink, I who know only thirst,
>
> I, absent from myself,
>
> I, Yukel Serafi, whose life and story are summed up in a few sentences?
>
> I share the fate of the worn-out beast in its self-willed night.

As artists, in Petlin's words, "We trade on freedom but live in slavery." The tension between these poles is central to the dynamic of artistic production. The versions of *The water buffalo, tied to her wheel* (I & II) form a coda to the series and explore this image of resignation of the artist at his or her task. In the first we view the animal, passive, beaten and scrawny, from behind. A yellow curtain, perhaps a shroud, hangs over the beast. In the second, the white, ghostly face comes toward us, again attached to the pipe-turnstile, in Petlin's words "the plumbing of our lives." The shroud has been replaced by a light, the animal is healthier, less mortified. Two views of the (Sisyphean?) artistic vocation or task. To paraphrase Jabès, "a task to be completed without question," since *we* have tied *ourselves* to the wheel. Petlin expressly intends an echo of Van Gogh's portrayal of inmates at the asylum of Saint-Rémy, and he may also have in mind Van Gogh's *Prisoners' Round (after Doré)*.

The Four Seasons follows from the vast panoramas of the *Seine Series* as a kind of mirror turned inward. Now it is the seasons of the studio, and of the artist's life and psyche, which are to be portrayed. Details of autobiographical memory are scattered throughout, as the painter contemplates the experience of passage, of transiency, and of the still life, the *nature morte* itself. Personal history and the interior life displace the focus on historical event and public space that dominate the *Seine Series*.

Spring represents an astonishing confluence of the quotidian with the oneiric. It is as if the imagery of the dream were voyaging into the everyday or, conversely, the things of dailiness had been transported into, and been illuminated by, the slant light of dream. Out the window of the artist's Paris studio one sees the grey roofs of a gently subdued Paris under a grey sky lit by a patch of orange. Within the studio, to the right, a boat is arriving. The boat is a recurrent image in Petlin's work and can take on various shades of meaning. Here the image is clearly a hopeful, liberating one, as the boat sails toward the "harbor" of the artist's palette mounded with paints directly beneath the window. In his notebooks, Petlin makes clear that this is "Gabriel's boat," the boat his son Gabriel used to sail during the summer. The boat is sailing across a pacific "mare bianco," its passengers garbed in cheerful colors. Above the heads of the passengers are brightly detailed brushes, and to the right of the brushes hover two indistinct hands holding sticks. To the lower left, the pastel is anchored by a folded, glowing pink cloth. Beyond we see the paraphernalia of the studio, including a jug of brushes glowing with light. The interplay of the material and the imagined, the studio and the harbor, proposes that in any fully realized work, the two will blend seamlessly into one plastic vision.

The mood of *Summer* is strikingly different. There is a sense of intense nocturnal heat, fierce reflected light, airlessness. To Petlin, this work summons memories of the suffocating heat of Chicago during his childhood. The half loaf of bread at the center suggests the oven of summer but also the young artist's head baking with ideas in that same heat, trying to imagine art in the airless environment and sensual deprivation of the Chicago tenements. To the viewer's right, there is a blue head on a stick, and beside it a white skull. Next to the skull, the pair of blurred hands reappears, holding now intensely red sticks (a recollection of Petlin's early, quasi-allegorical Rowers). Beneath the sticks, two glittering, yellow forms send off showers of sparks. To the left, once again the painter's materials, his brushes and mounds of paint, modeled with an iconic character. Through the window, we see Paris at night, sweltering.

Fall, like *Winter,* is close to a *grisaille.* It is the time of last light, before the descent of winter. Only a scrim of muted green to the right of the window and one last brush still aglow provide relief. The tubes and mounds of paint are partially desiccated. The tubes and brushes to the right have been set in rough alignment, while the tubes, the tubular bodies, to the left lie in a contorted embrace. Everything is grounded, fallen.

Winter offers a divided canvas with an exaggerated recessional perspective. The "lake" of the painter's table has frozen, and whiteness mantles the air. Here is a third reading of Jabès's "Paris is white," one to be juxtaposed with the versions in the *Seine Series* and *The Book of Questions.* Certainly the whiteness of winter implies another white page, another silence and another kind of desert, where life has come to a stop. To the lower left are tubes, glasses, the things of the studio strewn about and abandoned. At the center the now thoroughly aged and shriveled tubes and paint mounds meet. Through the window, the city and sky in winter. To the right, from bottom to top, whiteness has invaded the studio.

[*This essay was originally written as two separate pieces: "Irving Petlin: The Language of the Unsayable, Some Notes on Irving Petlin and the Seine Series" published in* Irving Petlin: Paris is White (*Exhibition brochure, New York: Kent*

Gallery, 1996) and "A Bonfire in the Starry Night" published in Irving Petlin:
Le Monde d'Edmond Jabès *(Exhibition catalogue, Geneva: Galerie Jan Kru-*
gier, Ditesheim et Cie, 1997) and in Irving Petlin: Pastelli / Pastels *(Exhibi-*
tion catalogue, Venice: Galleria Contini, 1998). See also "The Rightness To Be
Depicted," a conversation between Michael Palmer and Irving Petlin, Sulfur *18,*
Winter 1987.]

ON JESS'S *NARKISSOS*

A first impression of Jess's *Narkissos* drawing is one of daunting iconic complexity. Literary and pictorial references abound. Multiple homages to writers, painters and illustrators are secreted within the work. A swirl of images drawn from radically disparate sources confronts the viewer. An image from popular culture is juxtaposed with the sacral; a fragment of auratic, "high" art finds itself counterbalanced with the familiar, or at least, the familiar-made-strange. Jokes and puns proliferate, all pointing toward the linguistic unconscious. Spatial perspectives establish themselves, only to dissolve, like a Baroque facade, before our eyes. Yet there is an equally paradoxical stability to the whole, a sense of an operative and consistent counter-logic, which lends an undeniable coherence and unity to the visual field.

A poetics of representation is at work which must be understood if the underlying relationships among the images are to be comprehended. It is a poetics of enigma, play and resistance to meaning, one that celebrates an eternal strain within the arts, which Jess himself would define as "romantic." It is a celebratory strain, in that it acknowledges the "play" of meaning, the endless desire of meaning to expand, and the endless play of desire within meaning. Yet it is, equally, subversive in its determined outsidedness, its refusal of canonical culture and linearity. Its goal is to represent difference, the hidden or undisclosed, and the metamorphic fluidity of the signifying process. Using the myth of Narcissus as the generative seed, Jess has created what might be taken as an echo chamber, a labyrinth or a hall of mirrors. The *Narkissos* also serves as a quite comprehensive guide to the world of gnostic, hermetic and spiritual lore constructed over a period of more than thirty years by Jess and his companion, the poet Robert Duncan.

The work was first conceived in 1959 and completed in 1991. A preliminary, quite simple (4"x 4") *Narkissos* drawing exists from the time of Jess's first "imagining" of the work, in 1959. There is another, slightly larger and more complex, dated 1963. The final work, measuring 60"x 70", consists of graphite pencil on differing papers, with paste-ups. Material was collected from 1959 to 1979. The piece was sketched and pinned up from 1976 to 1979, and transferred to canvas and pasted up in 1978 and 1979. The drawing was originally conceived as the mirror (enantiomorphic) image of a painting of the same size. Painting and drawing would form an emblematic reflection of Narcissus and his reflection. The idea of the mirror image was eventually abandoned as impractical, and in 1991, nearing completion of the drawing, Jess also abandoned the idea of the painting for artistic reasons. Thus the *Narkissos* drawing stands alone, as ghost or reflection or double of a nonexistent other.

The history of the *Narkissos* includes the history of the evolution of Jess's style from the early, thick, gestural line developed under the influence of instructors such as Elmore Bischoff, Hassel Smith and particularly Clyfford Still at the California School of Fine Arts (which soon became the San Francisco Art Institute). Jess realized immediately that to execute the *Narkissos* a new, lighter line and a thinner process of paint application would have to be learned. He would have to slow himself down from the rapid "flux painting" of his earlier style and find a process that would allow for precise detail. (Jess would later describe himself then as having been "struck by the inadequacy of expressionism to achieve sensuosity without pornographic emphasis.") In 1959, Jess began the *Translation Series* with this goal in mind, of teaching himself a new method. From the first (*Laying a Standard*, 1959), the turn away from abstraction is obvious. The lessons of abstraction, however, and of "all-over" composition, remain evident, as they will even in the articulated field of the *Narkissos* itself. The *Translation Series* was originally intended as a set of twelve, a "sun clock." This number was eventually doubled to allow the process of learning to continue. Yet by the end of the series (which would finally, in fact, number twenty-six, and would be exhibited at the Odyssia Gallery in 1971), a feel for the *Narkissos* had still not been established, and another set, or series of "lessons," the *Salvages*, interposed itself. In these, Jess reworked early abstract and semi-abstract canvases of his own that he had set aside. He would see where these non-objective works pulled him, and what images he could happen upon within them. The *Salvages* were to help him locate (recognize) and then to paint often minute details. Before such canvases (paraphrasing Plotinus), Jess placed himself in the position of Narcissus "falling into nature . . . his consciousness recognizing a fact." Jess emphasizes that the *Salvages* are also a form of translation. This metaphor, of *translatio* or "bearing across," will remain central to the *Narkissos* drawing as well, both in its metaphysical implications and as a description of the actual process of image appropriation, the transfer from one domain to another. Process itself, of course, will be foregrounded throughout the work, reflecting Jess's complex and ambivalent relationship to High Modernism, as well as his grounding in Romantic aesthetics. At all points the process of the continuous production of meaning (and nonsense as another form of meaning) will take precedence over a stable narrative or a fixed *point de repère*. It is not Modernism *per se* which Jess rejects, but Modernism's ideological exclusions, its war on sentiment and decoration, its separation of the arts into "high" and "low." Even as he assimilates modernist and avant-gardist practices (the *Narkissos* would be inconceivable without them), he rejects the militant and authoritarian aspects of avant-gardism, and Modernism's estrangement from spirit.

It is in 1977, having completed five of the *Salvages*, as well as *Translations for a Villa* and *Arkadia's Last Resort*, that Jess began pencil development of the work. The complex process of drawing and image transfer continued until the work's completion, with many interruptions for other commissions, as well as for the profound personal crisis of Duncan's kidney failure in 1984 and death in February 1988.

In his "*Narkissos* Notebook," (the painter's personal compendium of source materials and procedural notes), Jess writes of "seeking finally to maintain intense homoeros unprofaned, sensuous, joyful-fearful." He had attempted to portray homoerotic romance in many works painted in his earlier, Expressionist style, such as *Imaginary portrait #9*, *Cafe Sodom*, *Feignting Spell*, *A Meeting Ground*, *Imaginary portrait #17*, and *A Duino Icarus*, to cite only a selection. In 1959, however, he had interrupted work on the first state of his *Apollon-Hyakinthos* upon realization of the inadequacy of his means. In his discouragement, he felt that he must do nothing less than "learn how to paint." This decision results from the larger ambition of the *Narkissos*, a work of far greater inclusiveness and complexity than any he had previously attempted. It was a work quite literally impossible to execute, an unrealizable act of *gnosis*. As such it would in itself represent a kind of alchemical search, one that might well be envisioned to last a lifetime. The commitment to pursue such a project is consistent with Jess's lifelong antimaterialism and anticareerism, that is, with his singular romance of representation. Its approximate parallel in Jess's personal life might be found in Robert Duncan's decision, upon the publication of *Bending the Bow* in 1968, not to publish another collection of poetry for fifteen years, lest career strategies distract him from the design of his final volumes. The *Narkissos* would embody not only a transformation, or metamorphosis, of Jess's artistic means, it would also come to stand for a hermeneutics of desire, an exploration of both the darkness and the light of Eros, the play of desire and loss, and of the visible and the invisible.

The myth of Narcissus, actually the various tellings of the myth and commentaries on it, would serve as the vehicle for this exploration. (Jess would adopt the Greek spelling when he was led from Ovid back into Greek origins and parallels.) As he explored the relevant texts, and was drawn both backward and forward in time by them, he began also to accumulate the images that would be interwoven in his own "telling." These, in Jess's words, were "images which found me along the way." Some would directly portray characters and elements from the myth itself, but far more would offer oblique rhymes, visual puns, displacements and substitutions. Many function also, as I have noted, as homages to writers, painters and illustrators of special significance to Jess. Other than Robert Duncan, the primary literary influence on the work is undoubtedly Joyce's *Finnegans Wake*. Yet traces of Edward Lear, Lewis Carroll, Blake, L. Frank Baum, George Herriman, Andrew Lang, George MacDonald and Christian Morgenstern are evident as well. (I will refer to gnostic, hermetic and neoplatonic authors later; they represent a different kind of influence on the atmosphere and philosophical inclination of the work.) As we explore the visual imagery, homages to various visual artists will also become evident. For the moment, we should note the formative influence of Max Ernst, represented in the drawing by eyes borrowed from what Jess refers to as *The Avenue of Sphinx Eyes* (*Troisième Poème Visible*) in Ernst's *Une Semaine de Bonté*. (They peer out and across from both sides of the chasm into which the figures of Echo descend.) In 1952, Duncan had purchased the original, multivolume 1934 edition of the work and brought it back to their Baker Street house. Jess stresses the work as a key to the evolution of his later use of paste-up and collaged images. Equally significant in the *Narkissos* is the dark eroticism of Ernst, with his frequent representation of rape and atmospheric intimations of other forms of sexual violence and intrigue.

The version of the Narcissus myth in Book III of Ovid's *Metamorphoses* is the standard one. It tells of the rape of the Oceanid

Liriope by Cephisus, river-god of Boeotia. Liriope gives birth to an infant so beautiful that even as a child he inspires girls with thoughts of love. Liriope visits the prophet Tiresias to discover whether her child will live a long life. He replies enigmatically, "Only if he never comes to know himself." As a youth, Narcissus is courted by both boys and girls, whom he spurns. One day the Oread Echo sees him hunting and falls under the spell of his beauty. Yet in a previous act of revenge, Juno had deprived Echo of the full power of speech. She can do no more than repeat the last few words of what another has said. Narcissus, of course, rejects her advances. In despair Echo retreats into the forest where her body gradually wastes away, first to a shade, then to a sheet of air, then to bones, leaving only her voice with life in it. A love-sick boy (perhaps Ameinias?) raises the curse, "May he love himself alone." Nemesis hears the curse and arranges fitting punishment for his cruelty. Leaning over a spring in order to drink, Narcissus becomes enraptured with his unattainable image. Eventually he perishes of longing and exhaustion. He perishes, as Ovid expresses it, *per suos oculos*, "by his own eyes." His sisters the Naiads, and the Dryads, weep and tear out their hair in mourning. He is then changed into the flower which bears his name.

Already present within this single version of the myth are many of the themes Jess will expand upon for the drawing, those that will form its constellation of possible meanings and possible readings. Eyes, mirrors, mirror-images, twins, rivers and springs, water-as-mirror. Echo and reflection. Prophecy, violence, infatuation, transformation. The theme of the other, or double, as both self and non-self (Narcissus does not recognize *himself* in the reflection). The eternal force of desire and the destructive side of the erotic. Polysexuality, or hermaphroditism, as represented by Tiresias, and androgyny in the figure of Narcissus. The homoerotic theme is present both in the unrequited longing of the boys for Narcissus, and in his infatuation with the image of the boy—himself—in the spring. (Another version of the myth tells of the death of Narcissus' beloved twin sister. He consoles himself by gazing at her features in his reflection in the spring.) Present as well are Orphic echoes and echoes of Dionysian ritual below the surface of the text.

In 1959, as Jess tells it, Duncan had been reading gnostic and hermetic texts, and it was to these that Jess was drawn for further elaboration of the meaning of the myth. From these, as well as from a vast number of more recent commentaries and retellings (including, for example, Marcuse and Freud), he would derive the open set of variations around which he would weave the found imagery of the work. They form, in effect, the semantic underpinning or grid, the submerged cluster of narratives that ties the disparate images together. There is, of course, a parallel visual logic, derived principally from collage technique, which is at least equally responsible for the ultimate coherence of the drawing.

Figures will be added as new sources and mythic interconnections are discovered. For example, the Greek writer Longus tells that Echo rejected the advances of the god Pan, who then drove the shepherds mad, and they tore her to pieces. Gaia (Earth) buried her limbs, but allowed her to retain the power of song. Pan appears in the cliffs high above the Monadnock Building at the center of the picture, behind the figure of Eros with his bow and arrow. Pan is a composite derived from the photograph of a Panamanian flute player and festival dancer, found in *Pacific Discovery* magazine, with horns on his head from another source. The Monadnock Building ("monadnock" meaning a mountain rising over a plain) by Burnham and Root, 1891, was America's first skyscraper, and serves as the "clearly echoing cliff," part of the composite of mountains from various sources. Above the head of Pan, slightly to the right, is the figure of Nemesis, a Fate, in the form of a woman riding—or "spinning"—a hilarious early tricycle across a bridge by Maillart, toward the prognosticating Sphinx (a double for the oracle Tiresias?). Her feet work treadles, just as the Fates spin their thread. Perhaps to complete the pun, Nemesis the Cyclist was discovered in an old issue of *Life* magazine. Gaia appears as a bag lady, with arms folded and a sad, distracted

expression on her face. She sits above the dark pool at the bot-
tom of the canvas, directly below the fallen Echo, reclining on
the "puy" of Mont Ségur at the base of the Monadnock Build-
ing and to the right of the hand of Narkissos, which languidly
grasps a backscratcher-*cum*-wand or caduceus. (There are many
Echoes in the canvas, beginning with the diver Pat McCormick
plunging from the source of the painting's light at the far upper
right.) This Echo is borrowed from Claude Lorrain, the hand of
Narkissos from Dürer, the backscratcher from a woodcut in the
Reineke Fuchs. The replaced ball at the handle of the backscratcher
comes from a fairy tale vignette. A woman's face appears in it, as
if in a crystal. Beside the right elbow of Narkissos is a seated nude
boy, from a Pontormo drawing. Here he is meant to represent the
spurned lover, Ameinias. He clutches the sword said to have been
thrown to him by Narkissos, as a sign of contempt, with which
Ameinias committed suicide. Behind him is a threatening and
jeering mob (taunting Narkissos?), taken from Fritz Lang's *Me-
tropolis*. Images of desire, of pastoral calm, and of violence appear
in close proximity, impinging on one another and subverting the
possibility of any single, overriding emotional atmosphere, as if to
affirm that the heaven and hell of desire are not separate realms.
Mont Ségur is the site of the final siege against the Cathar culture
of the Troubadours by the orthodox Catholic crusaders from
northern France. As such, it held a central place in Duncan's per-
sonal mythology of artistic resistance. Its presence here, as part of
the landscape, is also a reminder of the endurance of the imagery
that permeates the Narcissus myth, since eyes are mirror to the
soul throughout the poetry of the Troubadours, which is domi-
nated by the figure of Love. In his notes, Jess quotes a stanza from
"Can vei la lauzeta mover" ("When I see the lark moving") by the
Troubadour poet Bernart de Ventadorn (c.1150–1180), translated
by Frederick Goldin:

> I have never had the power of myself,
> I have not been my own man since that moment

> when she let me look into her eyes,
> into a mirror that gives great pleasure, even now.
> Mirror, since I beheld myself in you,
> the sighs from my depths have slain me,
> and I have lost myself, as fair Narcissus
> lost himself in the fountain.

In the eyes of the lover the speaker sees himself reflected, and the self is entranced and extinguished by this self that is another. In such imagery we hear the distant echo of the creation myths and neoplatonic commentaries that lend further metaphysical resonance to *Narkissos*. Similar themes are sounded in Duncan's "Star, Child, Tree" (1981):

> So that the History of what Man has been
> falls away, crumbles, is blown about and
> mixt in the wind—Christ, His Mass,
> with Kybele and Thanatos-Eros pass away
> members of the play of what we divine,
> constant initiations of there being a Way—
> this the Mirror of Narkissos
> myth and mystery of what we mean to be
> speaks in the downstream of what Is

In Pausanias, Plotinus, Boehme, Henry Corbin, the Homeric Hymns, Thomas Taylor, the texts of the *Thrice Greatest Hermes*, Mead's *Orpheus*, Cook's *Zeus*, Wasson's *The Road to Eleusis*, Kathleen Raine's *Blake and Tradition*, and Hans Jonas' *The Gnostic Religion*, Jess would trace the precursors to the metaphors and figures of the Narcissus myth, searching for the undisclosed, or tacit, connections among them.

In *The Eleusinian and Bacchic Mysteries*, the neoplatonist Thomas Taylor interprets the "secret meaning" of the tale of Narcissus as directly connected to the story of the rape of Persephone. He cites Homer, meaning the Homeric *Hymn to Demeter*, which tells of Proserpine gathering crocus, iris, jonquil and narcissus. During her state of distracted play and enchantment the earth opens, and she is carried off by the Lord of Hades into the underworld. This enchantment mirrors that of Narcissus. Both have become enthralled by the material, or vegetable, world. Both represent souls whose attention has been drawn away from the contemplation of eternal, or noetic types. In his negative reading, Taylor closely follows his philosophical master Plotinus, for whom the myth of Narcissus is a cautionary tale against absorption in sensory images, copies, as opposed to archetypes. The soul must instead follow the upward path back to true likeness, identity with the *nous*. Referring to the mirror of Dionysus, as G. S. Mead recounts, Plotinus says that "the souls of men, when they have seen the image of their true selves, hasten above." The soul must retrace its path to its first state, and must contemplate its type in the suprasensible world. Notes Kathleen Raine, in *Blake and Tradition*, ". . . the image of the glass goes far back into antiquity to the glass of Isis, the mirroring pool that drowned Narcissus and the dangerous toy of Dionysus—dangerous because in the mirror shadows take on the power of substance." "For all the form of a spirit is seen in the reflection or in the mirror, and yet there is nothing which the eye or mirror sees," says Boehme in *Six Theosophic Points*, a work of devotional Christian neoplatonism, replete with mystical paradox. This world of paradox and devotion is not unlike the situation of the painter contemplating the impossibility of representation while losing himself in the mirror of nature. The enchantment of the artist while contemplating likeness and unlikeness, while regarding the self in its own estrangement, and while in some quite real sense losing himself to *sight* (*per suos oculos*), would seem to be another critical subtext of the *Narkissos*.

It is certainly from the "spirit of romance" that Boehme writes, ". . . all is together an eternal *Magia*, and dwells with the center of the heart in itself, and by the spirit goes forth from the center out of itself, and manifests itself in the eye of virgin wisdom endlessly." As in Boehme, so in the *Narkissos*, a contention is drawn between a "light-world" of desire and a "dark-world" of loss. It is appropriate then that the work only exist, finally, in black and white, shading from the absolute blackness of Narcissus' spring, in which the *Narcisse* of Brancusi appears, to the various gradations of light around and above.

In *The Road to Eleusis*, R. Gordon Wasson further explores the link of the Narcissus myth with the rape of Persephone and extends the thread back into the Eleusinian mysteries themselves. He identifies Hades, the abductor of Persephone, with Dionysus, the Zeus or Dios of Nysa, the "Divine Bridegroom." As others have noted, the narkissos flower is so named for its narcotic powers, and may well have played a role, along with ergot of barley or rye, in the rituals of death and regeneration acted out in secret at Eleusis. To the *Narkissos* drawing, this means that the Thespian fields, home of Narcissus and dedicated to Eros, also resonate with elements and symbols from the fields of Eleusis. The mythic meaning of the flower itself, and of the flowering fields, expands to include chthonic echoes of ecstatic rites. Simultaneously, Jess moves forward in time to incorporate additional figures from medieval echoes of the Narcissus tale, such as are to be found, for example, in Chaucer's *Romaunt of the Rose*. There the dream traveler discovers the crystal mirror of Narcissus in the well, is caught by the mirror, sees the Rose and is entrapped by the rose garden. Jess is establishing the diachronic landscape, or ground, of the work as one where multiple times intersect and are collaged together, just as diverse styles of representation are juxtaposed and symbols from diverse cultures are placed side by side. Assumptions of decorum, notions of incongruity, both in a visual and an intellectual sense, are being offered a radical challenge. To the formalist ideology that dominated the official narrative of contemporary American art when the *Narkissos* was first imagined, such syncretism would undoubtedly appear illegible and incoherent.

The theme of the double, in all of its manifestations, lies at the heart of the *Narkissos*. It is through the *Corpus Hermeticum*

that Jess traces perhaps the most astonishing prefigurations of
this theme, which are reflected in the "above" and "below," what
might be termed the "metaphysical dimensions," of the draw-
ing's space. In the *Poemandres* (from the collection of writings we
know as the *Thrice-Greatest Hermes*) we find, "And God-the-Mind,
being male and female both, as Light and Life subsisting, brought
forth another mind to give things form, who, God as he was of
fire and spirit, formed Seven Rulers who enclose the cosmos that
the sense perceives." And a bit further on, "But All-Futher Mind,
being Life and Light, did bring forth Man co-equal to Himself,
with whom He fell in love, as being his own child: for he was
beautiful beyond compare, the Image of his Sire. In very truth,
God fell in love with His own Form." In the same volume, "For
either sex is full of procreation, and of each one there is a union,
or—what's more true—a unity incomprehensible; which you may
rightly call Eros or Aphrodite, or both." ("The *Prayer of God* is His
aspiration to manifest Himself, to see Himself in a mirror, but
in a mirror which itself sees Him. . . ." writes Corbin.) Here, in a
Hermetic creation myth, we find once more those themes that
Jess derives initially from the Narcissus: the twins or Dioskuroi,
the hermaphrodite, enchantment with one's double, the union of
sexes in a transcendent vision of Eros. It is the positive, or procre-
ative side of the narcissistic vision, a union with Logos or Reason
through *reflection*. Duncan's "The Face":

> Be still, whatever deep onward current flowing, steady
> your face entirely receptive, my soul, to mirror this
>   presence
> needs, as if in the eternal holding of a breath, to sound
>   your depth
> needs hear   this dark glassy surface clear surface wait-
>   ing upon
>
> reflections.   It is time to reflect,   to let the feeling
>   come forward

> from the foundation of the pouring waters of a face so
>   steady
> as if sleep tranquil and gleaming had ever a ready place,
> a letting go of striving, protesting, knowing, grasping.

As Marcuse comments in *Eros and Civilization,* "He [Narcissus] lives by an Eros of his own, and he does not love only himself. (He does not know that the image he admires is his own.) If his erotic attitude is akin to death and brings death, then rest and sleep and death are not painfully separated and distinguished: the Nirvana principle rules throughout all these stages. And when he dies he continues to live as the flower that bears his name." The Orphic and Narcissistic Eros "transforms being." Marcuse continues, "Narcissus' life is that of *beauty,* and his existence is *contemplation.* These images refer to the *aesthetic dimension* as the one in which their reality principle must be sought and validated."

The viewer's gaze falls first upon the composite figure of the kneeling Narcissus. From the angle of his face, one wonders whether he has as yet seen his reflection. Is he in fact at the very point of noticing it, the point of his own transformation? In his left hand rests the backscratcher or sceptre noted above. In his right he holds a composite of panels from various *Krazy Kat* cartoons, each suggesting the Narcissus myth or one of its associations: Ignatz Mouse in a jail with a moat; Krazy floating in his bath; Krazy testing the myth itself. An eruption of the mythic in the culture of everyday life, but also the eruption of cartoon figures into what we had taken—what otherwise has been framed—as the space of high art. Yet to what degree has it been? Narcissus' reflection is a marble bust by Brancusi, *Le Narcisse,* 1914. The model for the upper part of the body of Narcissus is Michel Chevalier (*The Young Physique,* 1964), but various of his limbs have been borrowed from diverse other sources. The lower body is taken from the Narcissus fountain of Minne. He is part stone and part flesh, entirely graphite and paper. A frog by Sendak peers up at him, or else at the cartoon. To the frog's right, just beneath the cartoon panels, are two enantiomorphic crystals from an organic chemistry text, a reference to Pasteur's discovery of enantiomorphic or mirror imaging in crystals, and perhaps also the lightest of allusions to Jess's background in science. Approaching Narcissus' right shoulder is a bat with a glove in its mouth (from Klinger's *The Rape of the Glove*), echoing the theme of abduction, but also offering a precursor to the Surrealism of Ernst. The bat passes in front of the figure of Arethusa, echoing once again the theme of rape. (The "pursuing river" lies behind her, and above her is represented *The Rape of Persephone*, from the Bernini marble group of 1622.) Just beyond the bat we find a snake from Gaudí's *Sagrada Familia* coiling downward along a rain pipe below a sphinx close to the top of the canvas. Near the snake's mouth stands Tiresias, represented (with deliberate incongruity?) by a young man in outdoor walking garb, carrying a coat and accompanied by hounds. (The proximity to the snake refers us back to the myth of Tiresias.) The sphinx is not the "actual" sphinx, but an imitation verging on kitsch from the Scottish Rite Temple in Washington, D.C. Beside it, at the very top of the canvas near the left corner, is a sketch of Gemini by Gaudi, which here represents the Dioskuroi, the archetypal twins Castor and Pollux. Opposite the sphinx is its own mirror image, a sphinxlike monadnock, Mount Ennedi in Chad, discovered by the Surrealists, then found by Jess in *Le Surréalisme même, no.3*. Over the shoulder of the monadnock-sphinx, at the very upper left of the canvas, is a photograph by Berenice Abbott, the multiple reflections of a girl's eye in a segmented parabolic mirror, echoing Boehme's conflation of eye and mirror. It seems to gaze out, like an *oculus dei*, over the canvas, and to balance the light source that streams from the Constable clouds (a sketch by Constable after an engraving by Cozzens) and the William Morris birds in the sky behind the tumbling Echo at the upper right, where we also see, as Jess's "Diana," a woman in a bubble—Albert Aublet's painting *The New Moon*. (A study could be made of the occulted symmetry of the drawing.) Next to Abbott's mirror, a beehive can be seen, standing as Jess has remarked for "the sweetness and the sting of human community."

Allowing the eye to travel down from the Abbott photograph we find, among many other figures, Blake's *The Soul hovering over the Body reluctantly parting with Life*, from his illustrations to Grey. The soul hovers above a cave, which is the source of what was once the River Adonis. Here it becomes the Cave of the Nymphs.

Below Klinger's bat is the infantilized Ameinias, at whose right foot lie two satyrs by John Hamilton Mortimer (*Two Sleeping Monsters*, 1780), here representing the violent coupling of Cephisus and Liriope, the parents of Echo. Just below and to their left is a model perspective house, taken from an instructional booklet. It is Jess's pun about learning to draw in order to execute this work. Ergot of rye can be found in its vicinity.

Standing astride the "puy" of Mont Ségur, beyond the left shoulder of Narcissus and at the center of the canvas, is Eros, the arrow not yet released from his bow. He too is a composite. His male model figure comes from *The Young Physique*. His head derives from an Hellenistic bronze, and the "aura" behind it is from the *Chromatic Notations* of the Symbolist painter Filiger. There is not space here to begin to speculate on the meaning of such radical juxtapositions, except to note their subversive defiance of art historical *doxa*, and their tacit suggestion of a counter-narrative, one that defies the accepted logic of aesthetic categories.

The dark spring of Narcissus is a kind of well of symbols. In it float (or do they "appear," reflected from an invisible source?): a six-petalled lotus with the seed-syllable HRIH at its center; a six-pointed star, two interlocked equilateral triangles, with the Arabic word for "blessing" at the center; an alchemical emblem of ourabouros surrounding another six-pointed star. A trigram from the *I Ching* is also visible, which translates as "the abysmal water over the abysmal water." A mole with a shovel has popped out, again from the *Reineke Fuchs*, and seems to be observing the strange goings on. Across the dark waters from him, slightly to the right of Gaia, can be seen John Muir, gazing Narcissus-like into the water. Among lotus flowers and narcissi, the spring arrives at a spillway (a Montana dam with sheep crossing over), which leads to the painting's "abyss" in the lower right-hand corner. At the near end of the dam is the *The Dry Bones Coming Alive*, from Doré's *The Vision of Ezekiel*, while at the far end can be seen *Genie Guarding the Secret of the Tomb*, by René de Saint Marceau. At the lower right a snail is crawling on a pot of Narcissi. A "JS" has been incorporated into the leaf design. The snail (by Flinzer, 1876) stands for Jess himself, working at a snail's pace.

My hope is to give an initial glimpse of the complexity and variety of imagery of Jess's *Narkissos*—its open semantic and visual landscape, and its serious playfulness. Perhaps as a final emblem of the purposefully enigmatic nature of the work, we should note the river flowing through the canyon into which Echo descends. The foreground, flowing toward us, is the Colorado, while at the rear, the river becomes Hell's Canyon. It is flowing away. It is as if to say, that in such a metamorphic field nothing is to be assumed. At no point can we posit a boundary between the physical world and the world of the mythic imagination, nor can empirical truth be set above poetic truths. As such, the *Narkissos* represents the reassertion of an enduring Romantic credo, by new means.

[*First published in* Jess: A Grand Collage 1951–1993, *Albright-Knox Art Gallery, Buffalo, New York, 1993.*]

SOME NOTES ON SHELLEY,
POETICS AND THE PRESENT

"But I beg you to take into consideration the conditions under which I am writing, the time and place."
—Heine, *The Romantic School*

As I was first beginning to reread Shelley, a quotation I had copied out from Susan Buck-Morss' *The Dialectics of Seeing* (on Walter Benjamin's *Passagen-Werk* or *Arcades Project*) came repeatedly to mind. Buck-Morss draws the quotation from Benjamin's *Theses on History* (IX). It reads:

> There is a picture by Klee called *Angelus Novus*. An angel is presented in it who looks as if he were about to move away from something at which he is staring. His eyes are wide open, mouth agape, wings spread. The angel of history must look like that. His face is turned toward the past. Where a chain of events appears to us, he sees one single catastrophe which relentlessly piles wreckage upon wreckage, and hurls them before his feet. [. . .] The storm [from Paradise] drives him irresistibly into the future to which his back is turned, while the pile of debris before him grows toward the sky. That which we call progress is this storm.

Certainly a key passage for the understanding of Benjamin's own romantic progressivism and the various contradictory threads which are responsible for the complex and compelling fabric of his social and aesthetic thought. Yet the visual meaning of this image of the Angelus Novus is anything but stable, as I am sure Benjamin would have acknowledged. We may just as easily interpret this figure as gazing "into the future," or at some event in the world of the present, or into some entirely nonspecific space. The expression could be one of astonishment, or incomprehension, or horror, or perhaps all three. The arms might be raised in surprise or benediction. "He" (we lack the angelic pronoun) seems suspended in a kind of cosmic dust, caught between this and some other world in weather he has never experienced. The gaze, then, is multiple and the figure, like so many crucial verbal figures in Shelley, is polysemous following Dante's sense of that word. We might even refigure him as the Angel of Poetry, whose many faces are like the multiple Shelleys which, since his death, have been imagined or posited and projected toward our time. In any case, in its uncertainty or ambiguity, its backward-forwardness, it seems an appropriate figure to preside over this talk, which must look forward and back, as well as at what "now" is now, and finally into the temporal modes poetry itself envisages, such as the future-present and the future-past, to name but two.

There is no question that the future has recently undergone some major alterations. In fact, it is possible to say that The Future as once conceived by utopians and revolutionaries of various stripes has (at least for now) entered into the historical past without ever having been realized, dissipated by its own repressive and totalizing social economy (which imposed the dictatorship of an endlessly deferred future on the texture of everyday life) as well as, no doubt, by the relentlessly ambitious and adaptive force of international capital, which has been busy with the business of creating its own narratives and its own set of possible futures for immediate consumption.

It is in the light of the collapse of various melioristic futures, their implosion into an unstable present, a "now" of uncertain boundaries both cultural and political, that we are asked to reread and in some sense rediscover Shelley for contemporary poetics. Certainly such a reading will be further qualified by the fact that Shelley (as Jerome McGann has noted) is a poet of futurist vision and address. Initially, of course, he is a poet of his present moment who invokes alternative social orders through an evocation of the specific injustices of the present and a highly abstract vision of future redress. He speaks to contemporary injustice at times with an almost agitprop directness, at other times with the layered symbolic language of allegory and myth. Regarding the latter, even his most "displaced" and idealized poetry has a proto-dialectical character to it (to borrow a term from Richard Terdiman); it is part of an argument that moves beyond the self and beyond aesthesis to engage with contradiction and paradox. Everywhere shadowing that future is the specter of another future from the recent past, Shelley's almost immediate past, that of the French Revolution. The self-devouring of the revolution and the age of reaction that follow serve both to problematize and to deepen Shelley's own progressivism. A Spinozistic sense of community and desire will become more and more integral with the vision of radical renewal as Shelley seeks alternatives to anarchic violence and revolutionary chaos. Desire itself will be seen as signifier of resistance and subversion, as well as (quoting *Epipsychidion*) "An image of some bright Eternity." *Epipsychidion* is an act of defiant poetic excess, an act of resistance to the hypocritical puritanism of the time, but also to the idea of a poetry of limits. Like so much of Shelley's work, it is impossible; its suppression is preordained. The poem, in its graphic sensuality, defies the decorum of what was acceptable verse. There is another and more threatening insistence that conjoins in poetically coded language the personal with the social vision. An escape *from* is always an escape *toward*:

> This isle and house are mine, and I have vowed
> Thee to be lady of the solitude.—

And I have fitted up some chambers there
Looking toward the golden Eastern air,
And level with the living winds, which flow
Like waves above the living waves below.—
I have sent books and music there, and all
Those instruments with which high spirits call
The future from its cradle, and the past
Out of its grave, and make the present last
In thoughts and joys which sleep, but cannot die,
Folded within their own eternity.

A passage that, like so much of the poem, operates at many sym-
bolic levels (along with Dante, are there echoes of Shakespeare's
Prospero here as well?). The poet-alchemist asserts the power of
the poetic voice to command historical time, to resurrect the past
for the present, invoke the birth of the future, and in so doing
eternalize an ideal present (a present of living ideas). After the
dystopic and utopian hours (I meant to type "horrors") of our
age, the status of such a claim must of course be at the very least
thoroughly interrogated. What, if anything, do we believe of the
poetic function now? What claims can be made for the poem in
the world? In what margins and at what borders, barely visible it
often seems, does it continue to be heard?

Before attempting a few remarks on the above, there is one
more of Shelley's "futures" to note. In rereading Richard Holmes'
and Kenneth Neil Cameron's essential biographical studies, I was
reminded how much of Shelley's work was left unpublished dur-
ing his life, or else subject to censorship and suppression. Most
of the work would only come into print in one of several futures,
often a distant future, as the forces of censorship and revision
(and perhaps indifference) continued to operate long after his
death. The effect is obviously to remove the work from any possi-
ble influence on its time (which I need hardly suggest in any case
would have been marginal). The effect is also to reduce it to purely
literary-textual status, to reframe and limit both its purpose and

address. It is in great measure to de-realize and acculturate it, to remove it from history to literary history. Such suppression, ironically, as the future—this century—would discover, is also the source of much of the mythic aura and mystification that come to envelope such a poet and his work.

To look at Shelley, or to look for Shelley, in the present is also to confront certain questions of the present itself for poetry, certain paradoxes and contradictions that poetry as a practice both reflects and addresses. What "now" is it, and where do we find ourselves—and lose ourselves—in it? What responses can poetry make, and to whom? Questions at least to be raised for a poetics, even if not answerable by one. Questions too that risk both banality and rhetorical inflation.

Ten years of Reaganbush, coupled with the vicious attacks by the likes of Jesse Helms and Donald Wildmon on free speech, and racial, sexual and cultural difference, have been only the most visible signs of a rightward drift toward a shamelessly exploitive materialism and a know-nothingism worn with a kind of violent pride. At the same time, logically enough, the marketplace has come to seem the all-justifying means of cultural support and distribution. It is not stretching things too much to find at least a few obvious parallels with the public culture of reaction and privilege in Regency England, though clearly the means of cultural dissemination are markedly different, as are the means of control and constraint.

In poetry, as a poet committed to an exploratory prosody, an assertion of resistance to "meaning" and "expression" as givens, and a radical questioning of our means of representation, I have been struck by the quite determined recent movements to reassert order under the familiar flags of "craft," "value," "taste," "excellence," etc. The New Formalists, in systematically trivializing and demeaning the functions of poetry, in reducing form to the formulaic and prosody to a narrow compilation of Anglo-American meters, have in effect turned the poem into a tired but manageable short story in verse, content to sing, rather quietly, of middle-class life. Charles Simic has noted that their ideas of prosody sound as if they came from "Victorian schoolbooks—or perhaps cookbooks." I would say that they are in fact more like Victorian manuals of etiquette, though much less entertaining. They nest, appropriately, in the Eliotic parapets of *The New Criterion* and other neo-conservative venues. There is a nostalgia here, i.e., a pseudo-historicism, which wishes to obliterate history and return to a world where things were perfectly consistent, perfectly clear. Such a program calls for pacification of the means of representation. After years of formless workshop verse, we can sympathize with the perceived need for clearer formal values, but such a *rappel à l'ordre* represents the refusal of significant form. Such "principles" stand as well, quite baldly, for a regressive and authoritarian cultural agenda.

Professor Helen Vendler is of course a highly respected scholar who has produced notable studies of the English Romantics and the Romantic tradition. However, with the rather nebulous *Harvard Book of Contemporary Poetry* (1985), her agenda seems to be to articulate a vaguely liberal, slightly eclectic, and mildly multicultural center. Ominously, the word "charm" appears three times in the first six lines of her introduction (juxtaposed, equally ominously, or is it frivolously, with the word "command"). Launching with the complacencies of the peignoir, the anthology offers initially a very conventional choice of deceased poets, a choice (with the barely possible exception of Robert Hayden) that would have been acceptable in any academic and normative anthology of twenty years ago. As one might expect from Professor Vendler, it is a poetry weighted heavily, if not exclusively, toward that particular naturalized self supported and at least partly generated by American neo-Freudian ego psychology and articulated in the work of the Confessional Poets. (It is a poetry that tends to oscillate between bourgeois anomie and the bourgeois sublime.) One might say that the selection from the living follows conventional cultural doctrine, a doctrine she has played no small role in sustaining. There are good poets beside mediocre poets. In fact it is not so much the inclusions that define such an anthology, but the exclusions and the willful amnesia. There is hardly a trace of those contemporaries who identify with an exploratory counter-tradition in American letters, and the barest hint indeed of those who preceded them: the Objectivists, the Black Mountain Poets, the poets of the San Francisco Renaissance, such as Spicer, Duncan and Blaser, to say nothing of the younger poets of the New York School, the Language Poets, the lineage of Stein, the actual lineage of Dickinson (such as Lorine Niedecker and Susan Howe), and of Williams, and of the Harlem Renaissance. There is no hint that there exists a widespread, vital experimental feminist practice. There is very little sense of interplay or exchange with the international avant-gardist movements of the century, an exchange that has been formative for so many of our more profound and innovative poets from the twenties through the eighties. Such suppression (for whatever reasons of ideology and/or marketplace) results in a domesticated map of American verse. (One cannot help but be reminded of similar efforts on the part of John Ciardi, Oscar Williams, indeed a host of other benighted authorities.) It is American poetry bowdlerized and made safe for readers of the *New Yorker*, and for the classroom, but it is not American poetry. If I seem to have strayed from the question of Shelley and the present, Shelley and contemporary poetics, I would like to suggest exactly the contrary.

For the poets of my generation, Shelley was a poet under several erasures. There was the initial prohibition of the modernists who went, or at least claimed to go, "in fear of abstraction." Shelley's difficult and audacious juxtaposing of (at his best) precise physical detail with philosophical rumination ran counter to the entire economy of modernism. His often baroque syntax seemed to lead a reader toward the "dim grey lands of peace" deplored by Pound. Then too there was the inherited Palgravian Shelley, the Shelley of a lyricism that quickly became the debased currency of entire generations of pseudo-romantic *pompiers*. To recover such a music was roughly equivalent to recovering Debussy after being inundated by five decades of Hollywood film scores. Perhaps equally a problem was the sympathetic but one-dimensional, vatic Shelley beloved by the Beats and embraced by the counterculture. One had the spontaneity and speed, the *enthusiasmos*, of Shelley, but his brain had been removed. This is no less sentimentalized a portrait than Palgrave's, or that of Maurois. Then, too, there is the wild variation in the quality of work from a man who still, near the end of his brief life, was attempting to rhyme "twinkling" and "tinkling" with a straight face ("To Jane"). Shelley, it must be added, was a poet for whom formal perfection, the perfection of static form, was often secondary, however much certain critics of a generation ago strained to discover occulted symmetries throughout his work, as if thereby to justify it.

Let me quote from the well-known and revealing section on Shelley in Eliot's "The Use of Poetry and the Use of Criticism":

> Shelley both had views about poetry and made use of poetry for expressing views. With Shelley we are struck from the beginning by the number of things poetry is expected to do: from a poet who tells us, in a note on vegetarianism, that "the orangoutang perfectly expresses man both in the order and the number of his teeth," we shall not know what to expect. The notes to Queen Mab express, it is true, only the views of an intelligent and enthusiastic schoolboy, but a schoolboy who knows how to write; and throughout his work, which is of no small bulk for a short life, he does not, I think, let us forget that he took his ideas seriously. The ideas of Shelley seem to me always to be the ideas of adolescence—as there is every reason they should be. And an enthusiasm for Shelley seems to me also to be an affair of adolescence: for most of us, Shelley has marked an intense period before maturity, but for how many does Shelley remain the companion of age? . . . I find his ideas repellent; and the difficulty of separating Shelley from his ideas and beliefs is still greater than with Wordsworth. And the biographical interest which Shelley has always excited makes it difficult to read

> the poetry without remembering the man: and the man was
> humourless, pedantic, self-centered, and sometimes almost a
> blackguard.

It is a passage quite astonishing for a number of reasons, not the least its patronizing smugness and condescension. Why, one wonders, does Eliot fear a poet from whom "we shall not know what to expect"? And why must a poet be separable from his ideas? To free him for pure, ahistorical readerly delectation? To isolate him definitively and securely in aesthetic space? Dante and Milton cleansed of ideas? One wonders whether Eliot had equivalent difficulty in separating his friend Pound's poetry from his friend Pound's ideas? And are we obliged to separate Eliot's poetry from its anti-Semitism, High Church elitism and its Podsnappery? Would we then be left with Eliotic *poésie pure*? The passage is replete with unintended ironies. Eliot has generated so much recent, lurid biographical interest, that we too now must be forgiven for finding it difficult to read the work apart from the life. And the final description of Shelley as a self-centered, humorless pedant matches many accounts of Eliot at certain stages of his life. What is most striking, of course, is the rage against Shelley's ideas. Which, one cannot but wonder, seemed to Eliot the worst: Shelley's feminism, his progressive egalitarianism, his ecotopic perspective, his idealism joined with an active interventionism, his atheism, his defiance of conventional amatory codes? Perhaps all of the above. Yet a good deal might be forgiven if the work would allow itself to be separated from its ideas, that is to say, acculturated and pacified. Eliot's (unconscious?) echo of pseudo-Mallarméan ideology speaks to a still insufficiently examined inheritance from late Symbolism, an inheritance that saturates the atmosphere of much of Eliot's work.

In the flux of our present, with poetry everywhere acknowledged as marginalized, what we least need is a poetry of accommodation, whether that be the self-absorbed and anti-intellectual neo-romanticism of the workshop, or the exhausted so-called "middle voice" of so much infinitely replaceable and infinitely consoling magazine verse. Nor, in full retreat, will it do to revive a bogus traditionalism. Shelley, perhaps more clearly than any of the other English Romantics, represents a radical alterity, an alternative to the habitual discourses of power and mystification by which we are daily surrounded and with which we are bombarded. He represents a poetry of critique and renewal, rather than of passive re-presentation, a poetry that risks speaking to the central human and social occasions of its time, yet speaks from a decentered and largely invisible place. It exploits the margins to speak as it will, out of difference, rather than as it is always importuned and rewarded, out of sameness. This "other voice of poetry," as Octavio Paz has noted, speaks to the present from a unique (or at least singularly focused) relation to past and future derived from the exigencies of the art. It speaks to the present, whether a present-now or a present-to-come (or, indeed, one never to be), much as do poets disparate as Dickinson and Akhmatova, Mandelstam and Holan.

Shelley is certainly the most optimistic of the Romantic poets, yet this optimism is drawn on a dark background. It acknowledges despair and loss and thereby deepens its own necessity. *Julian and Maddalo* offers a clear instance of a work in which the emotional and intellectual range is fully realized. It begins with a highly precise physical evocation of landscape, the salt marsh wastes of the Lido, before evolving characteristically into the commentary that will frame what is to follow:

> I love all waste
> And solitary places; where we taste
> The pleasure of believing what we see
> Is boundless, as we wish our souls to be:

The passage indicates that the poem will recount an inner, psychic and intellectual voyage, even as the third line warns us against surface meanings, against appearances. As he deploys the personae of the poem, from the innocence of Byron's young daughter, to the skepticism of Julian/Shelley probed and chided by the aristocratic Maddalo/Byron, to the fragmented desperation of the Maniac, it becomes clear that Shelley is also exploring the levels, stages and voicings of poetic perception, the problematics of desire, loss and belief, and perhaps of representation itself. As in *Prometheus Unbound*, there is a drama of internal and external causes, of the psychological and the political, the oneiric and the empirical. Maddalo ("You talk Utopia") projects Shelley's increasingly clear self-questioning, the thinking-against-himself that occurs in much of the later work. After the model of Dante, Shelley claims poetry as an active mode of cognition, as no less than a means of exploration and interrogation of inner and outer worlds. Even when it expresses the most acute despair, as in the mirror called *Adonais*, the work refuses Wordsworth's apostasy and failure of nerve. Its resistance, as well as its acknowledgments, bring it forward toward our own time when the critical and epistemological authority of poetry stands in desperate need of reassertion.

*

As a brief coda, I would like to make mention of one other event. Months have now passed since the Persian Gulf War, "Operation Desert Storm." Certainly it did not escape poets and concerned intellectuals that, whatever the causes and motives, a nation that designated itself as current defender of Western Civilization had been moved to assert its righteousness by massively bombing the birthplace of written language. It is precisely this kind of paradox or deep contradiction that poetry is structured to address. Yet it could not have been more evident that poetry was entirely silenced, before the fact, by the swarm of images and the cascading rhetoric, leading us once again to ask in what present we do speak, and with whom. And I am reminded one final time of the figure of Angelus Novus, Angel of History or Angel of Poetry, caught up in the rising storm of dust. It is unclear where he is directing his gaze. He wears several expressions at once.

[*Talk given to the Keats-Shelley Society in celebration of the 200th anniversary of Shelley's birth at the meeting of the Modern Language Association, San Francisco, December 28, 1991. Published in the* Journal of Keats and Shelley Studies *and in a slightly different version in* Sulfur *33, 1993.*]

ACTIVE BOUNDARIES:
POETRY AT THE PERIPHERY

For my own sense of poetry, I would like to examine a series, a "discrete series," as George Oppen would say, of sites or *topoi*, places and pages, boundaries, junctures and margins. By "poetry," I mean that poetry often marked by resistance and necessary difficulty, by a certain rupture and refusal, and by the use of exploratory forms. Such poetry has come to be identified, very loosely, with an enduring counter-tradition that encompasses both critique and celebration. There are other poetries, of course, and other poetries of value; that is not the argument.

I think of that "*communauté désoeuvrée*," "idled community" (hard to find an adequate translation) of Jean-Luc Nancy, and of the "imaginary" or "negative community" as defined by Maurice Blanchot, in fact not so much defined as imagined, in all its resistance to definition. "*Communauté impossible*" then, existing at the margins of thought, as the poem so often does, and as the poet all too often exists at the margins of material society. Such an imagined site would be, as much as anything, a place of contention, fractious, even dystopic. As "a community of those who have no community" (Georges Bataille), a community of differences, it is the space of encounter of the poetic imaginary with the social, the space where the poem may be said to disclose its desire for the world, for nothing less than the recovery of identity from loss, and language from the discursive mechanisms of power. It is finally, I think, as one projects it, a site of passages, full of noise and its silence, what Clark Coolidge refers to as "sound as thought."

The title of this talk—meant I suppose in part to disperse or decenter the idea of a subject as such—is "Active Boundaries: Poetry at the Periphery." It derives essentially from the Heideggerean notion of *peras*, of the active boundary in relation to a sense of form, but also to a more social sense of poetic activity as it exists in the margins, along the borders and, so to speak, "underground." It is a term I put to use often in the years when I first worked with dance, and for me at least, it then connected with notions of composition by field so important to the Black Mountain poets, and in particular, Robert Duncan. It suggested to me (how distant this must certainly be from Heidegger's intent is another question) an anti-hierarchical structure of language and perhaps hinted at a politics of poetic form as well. Its origin in this respect, in Heidegger, is not finally determining and may well be deceptive, given his sense both of relentless hierarchies and of poetry as truth or *aletheia*, poetry as disclosure of unconcealment, disclosure of the world. That is, I would strongly disavow his idealization of the poetic function, though I'm not always completely sure, as this talk may disclose, whether my poetic unconscious feels quite the same way. Certainly the issues raised or implicitly alluded to by such a title go back to topics addressed by both the German and the English Romantics, though many have been passed on almost osmotically (and here particularly skepticism is called for). They are concepts that underlie much of the content as well as the rather nomadic form of this talk, as much as they inform, positively or negatively, much of the work of our century's modernists and vanguardists. The title suggests an "elsew(here)" that includes the word "here," as well as a "nowhere" which can be read "now here." Such is the power of juncture, or silence. Here and elsewhere, here as elsewhere, elsewhere too as here: a space or region of paradox, contradiction and polysemy, a space, one is tempted to say, of poetry, where the words we hear are both the same and different, recognizable and foreign, constructed in fact like language itself on the play of identity and difference.

First image: a bird's-eye view of the Serra Pelada gold mine, Brazil, 1986: an almost unimaginably vast and deep open pit, with tens of thousands of mud-covered workers clambering with sacks of dirt along its floor and up the network of almost vertical ladders along its walls. At the time, the mine was said to employ 50,000 workers. Second image: a close-up of the miners surrounding a member of the military police. One holds him by the hair, two others clasp his arms, another displays the pistol which has been taken from him. The policeman's face is swollen from a severe beating, and blood runs from his nose and mouth. Third image: an American slaughterhouse: pigs have been crowded into a room. From nozzles in the ceiling a shower of water descends, in preparation for their electrocution. Fourth image: the refugee camp of Wad Sherifay in the Sudan, starving children lie on rows of cots or palette beds. The desert light burns through the doorway and through openings in the walls. Fifth image: Mali, 1985: a cemetery for refugees on the outskirts of Gao. Since there is no wood for grave markers, scrap iron is used instead. One grave is marked by a half-buried steering wheel, another by what appears to be a rusted brake drum, others by pipes and unidentifiable metal fragments. Sixth image: the interior of Brazil's Northeast: a child is prepared for Christian burial with her eyes open, so that she will be better able to find her way through the underworld.

Such images of elsewhere in the work, the life project, of the Brazilian photo-journalist Sebastião Salgado, evoke a complex series of often contradictory responses. The scene in the Serra Pelada gold mine verges on the incomprehensible, both in its visual scale and its human implications. At the same time it is, one gradually realizes, entirely familiar, a vision of hell prefigured in

Dante and the painters of the Trecento, as well as the earliest of
the Russian icon painters:

from *Inferno* XVIII:

"Luogo è in inferno detto Malebolge . . ."

There is a site in hell called Malebolge
made of stone the color of iron
like the wall encircling it.

At the exact middle of that evil field
opens a pit both wide and deep
whose plan I will speak of in its place.

What we had thought of as an oneiric product of the visionary
imagination was in fact an image of the world, an entirely pos-
sible world. World as it is, somewhere. Other echoes are obvious:
the beaten military policeman, with his swollen and distorted
face, brings to mind Lee Miller's photographs of Auschwitz
guards, similarly beaten. The children in the refugee camp, near
death from illness and starvation, are twin to earlier images from
earlier camps. Nowhere/now here. Yet here, now, means the walls
of a museum of contemporary art in San Francisco. Here, now,
there occurs an almost inevitable aestheticization of Salgado's
(as of Dante's) "moments." One notices the surreal beauty of the
desert cemetery, the exact rhyme (deliberate or not) with Tcheli-
chev's *Cache-Cache*, or Hide-and-Seek, in the picture of children
in Thailand playing in a tree. One takes a certain uneasy plea-
sure . . .

    There is a tension between context of viewing and source,
between here and there, which Salgado exploits to focus atten-
tion and to ironize the act of viewing itself. The subject of Sal-
gado's photojournalism, we must continually remind ourselves,

is *not there*, is in fact not the visible but the invisible: what has been repressed and will not be spoken. It appears always at the edge of the frame or in the uneasy negotiation among the space of origin, the framed space of the work, and the social space to which it has been removed, which is also a cultural space, of the aesthetic.

Here the paradox of Paul Celan's struggle "against representation" comes to mind. It is that in the search for an active mimesis, *Darstellung*, or presentation, the work may be drawn further and further from conventions of affect and accepted norms of narrative, those very devices that function as a kind of agreement or tacit contract (or complicity?) with the mainstream of culture. Let me quote a few passages from Celan's complexly layered and ironic talk he delivered upon receiving the Büchner prize, "The Meridian," translated by Rosmarie Waldrop:

> Ladies and gentlemen, it is very common today to complain of the "obscurity" of poetry. Allow me to quote . . . a phrase of Pascal's . . . : "Ne nous reprochez pas le manque de clarté puisque nous en faisons profession." This obscurity, if it is not congenital, has been conveyed on poetry by strangeness and distance (perhaps of its own making) and for the sake of an encounter.

For the sake of an encounter. The poem speaks "on behalf of the other, who knows, perhaps of an altogether other." A little further on in the same talk:

> It is true, the poem, the poem today, shows—and this has only indirectly to do with difficulties of vocabulary, the faster flow of syntax or a more awakened sense of ellipsis, none of which we should underrate—the poem clearly shows a tendency toward silence. The poem holds its ground, if you will permit me another extreme formulation, the poem holds its ground on its own margin. In order to endure, it

constantly calls and pulls itself back from an 'already-no-more' into a 'still-here.'

In other words: language actualized, set free under the sign of a radical individuation which, however, remains as aware of limits drawn by language as of the possibilities it opens.

In vastly different circumstances and with different means, Salgado and Celan are both drawn to ask, What are the exigencies of witness, where must you go, where is the margin, where the (invisible) meridian? To Celan, the margins may mean margins of language, a necessary distancing from the center for one who in life is already, forever, *distanced*. (Yet such distancing, or estrangement, seems to me radically different from the strategic subversions of a self-conscious and self-designating avant-garde, whose other is often none other than the center itself, to which it incessantly calls like a wayward child. As Lyn Hejinian put it very eloquently to me recently, "It is not only a matter of where you are standing, but also of the direction you are facing.") We can measure degrees of distance by placing a poem by Celan from *Mohn und Gedächtnis*, *Poppy and Memory* (1952, the early collection that contains his "Todesfugue") beside another poem, and a similar form of address, published in the 1976 posthumous collection, *Zeitgehöft*, *Farmstead of Time*, both translated by Michael Hamburger. From 1952:

Aspen tree, your leaves glance white into the dark.
My mother's hair was never white.

Dandelion, so green is the Ukraine.
My yellow-haired mother did not come home.

Rain cloud, above the well do you hover?
My quiet mother weeps for everyone.

Round star, you wind the golden loop.
My mother's heart was ripped by lead.

> Oaken door, who lifted you off your hinges?
> My gentle mother cannot return.

From *Zeitgehöft*:

> Walking plant, you catch
> yourself one of the speeches,
>
> the abjured aster
> here joins in,
>
> if one who
> smashed the canticles
> were now to speak to the staff
> his and everyone's
> blinding
> would be revoked.

In the former, however elliptical, orientation is still possible without too much difficulty. It is work fully realized in an elegiac mode quite characteristic of the poetic literature of the Holocaust, for example that of his friend Nelly Sachs. The latter poem more completely acknowledges, or perhaps inscribes, unrepresentability. It presents the unutterable and leaves the text, in any conventional sense, incomplete or broken. "Tell all the Truth but tell it slant— / Success in Circuit lies," writes Dickinson, a poet whom Celan translated extensively. But what of the untellable, what is the nature of such witness whose center is, necessarily, silence?

It is sometimes forgotten (I'm thinking here of various polemics, notably in Germany and Italy through the seventies and eighties) that there is a profoundly historical and social dimension to such hermetic (a designation Celan himself understandably disavowed) speech, that it is its own form of intervention, and that its resistance to meaning, to paraphrase Stevens, is shared by many types of poetry, including some of the most avowedly public and/or "transparent." Before the contradictions and paradoxes of the real, including the quotidian, those very paradoxes and contradictions may become agents of articulation and the reassertion of meaning. I am thinking of a poetry that "asks to be questioned," a poetry whose means remain in question. I am afraid that this is all too obvious, yet much remains invested in its denial. One is drawn toward ease of assertion and consumption, toward a formal nostalgia and the comfort of the given, the given self and its terms of reception and address, the beloved other always the same, a certain neo-romantic aura, a moving and mysteriously articulate aporia; in short, the standard issue sublime, the Wordsworth of late age still among us, slouching from workshop to workshop, waiting to be reborn. A poem called "Ne'er so well expressed" or "I looked at myself and there I was."

The actual origin of this talk dates to a visit a few years ago, with the photographer Ben Watkins, to the Eliot Square cemetery in the Roxbury section of Boston. (Ben was then in the process of documenting its restoration, along with that of several other local historical sites.) The graveyard was in an extreme state of neglect, with broken gravestones scattered about and others that had been removed from the ground and were awaiting repair. Ben indicated a particular eighteenth-century marker lying among the weeds. On the decorated part of the stone, that which would have been above ground, were the spare "hic iacets" for a husband and wife ("Here lyes ye body of . . ."), followed by dates of death and ages at death.

The cemetery had served an affluent, initially rural community from some time in the late seventeenth until the early nineteenth century. (The eponymous Eliots were in fact forebears of the poet's family.) Now the graveyard, surrounded by a cast-iron fence, was itself enclosed by a struggling and impoverished African-American and Latino ghetto.

On that part of the stone which would have been below

ground, had the marker been in place, Ben pointed to two meticulous lines of letters, among a scatter of other letters. The two lines, he said, were practice alphabets, the product of an apprentice stonecutter learning how to work the granite. They had been buried when the stone was put in place and only rediscovered during the current repairs.

Practice alphabet, alphabet of praxis, alphabet underground, the letters invisible beneath the conventional memorializing sentiments. Layerings and contradictions, both diachronic and synchronic, of the site itself. The stark social reality of the present, things coming to light or not.

The "above" and "below" of Williams' *Kora in Hell*, echoed in "Homage to Creeley," the opening section of Jack Spicer's *Heads of the Town up to the Aether.* Which is the signifier, which the signified? What of the line between? Is it a bar?

Where does one practice the art, and how does such an art respond, in its relative invisibility, to things? And to "things as they are"? Is there a counter-logic in the poem, a possible other voice, which can talk back, cast some light? Or, as certain contemporary theorists have proposed, gathering their accusations under the reductive and deficient rubric of "postmodernism," are the strategies and subversions of contemporary practice merely symptoms of the contradictions themselves, a kind of schizo-mimicry of a desiring machine that has lost its wheels?

I think of Zukofsky's long poem "*A,*" finally published in its entirety only after his death. From "'A'-12," a passage about his father after his arrival from Russia, where syntax, the "orderly arrangement," is drawn into music, so that both survival and mourning can be sung:

> The miracle of his first job
> On the lower East Side:
> Six years night watchman
> In a men's shop
> Where by day he pressed pants

> Each crease a blade
> The irons weighed
> At least twenty pounds
> But moved both of them
> Six days a week

The path is that crossed and recrossed in *"A"*: from the domain of labor and the social, to the world of spirit and family. The one is overseen by a very personal and idiosyncratic Marx (to whom reference will eventually disappear), the other by Zukofsky's omnipresent Spinoza. The syntax is flexible, at times perplexing, and the prosody post-Poundian, a highly disciplined free verse (though, of course, elsewhere Zukofsky will also work with fixed measures, both simple and complex). It is worth considering the economy of such presentation and the effect of its music in the evocation of the marginalized subject. The narrative itself exists in tension with the ellipticality and lyric condensation of the work. A further tension is that between his often stated objective of "rested totality" and the restless multidirectionality and complex layering of language, the "invisible" Zukofsky rendering the invisible subject, "Lower limit speech / Upper limit music." Here I would guess that it is the music of the Psalms he hopes to suggest. In the following part of the passage, there is also the barest, delicately ironic hint of the poet/son's lifelong experience of a minimal audience for his work:

> A shop bench his bed,
> He rose rested at four.
> Half the free night
> Befriended the mice:
> Singing Psalms
> As they listened.
> A day's meal
> A slice of bread

And an apple,
The evenings

And everywhere, the consciousness of alphabet, from the A to which the instruments are tuned, to the terminal Z, the letters B-A-C-H woven by Bach into his fugue and transformed by the poet into a laud for his wife, "*Blest Ardent Celia* . . ." Regarding "Eliot Square," with its high metal fence, I am reminded that it is the first poem of Zukofsky's *All*, his collected shorter poems, which sends up "The Waste Land" and its cultural vision in a cloud of bricolage, a hilarious pastiche of quotes, canon and kitsch, high and low hopelessly intertwined.

The multiple dialects of "*A*" and the pastiching of sources and citations in "Poem beginning 'The' " bring to mind the echoing and multiphonics found in sections of *X/Self*, the final volume of a trilogy by the great Caribbean poet and cultural scholar, Kamau Brathwaite. As Brathwaite sounds out his origins (European, Amerindian, African and Maroon, we are told), we experience the sound of "young Caliban howling for his tongue":

The new man is nubile
and has made his choice
as priest or politician

police or poet
choirboy or cocks
man

da vinci was the last of the genies
and he knew

it

though we didn't seem to believe in it
then

now the word belongs to machiavell and philip
the second of spain

and to that calculating calvin

is them that working all night long in the high
light executive suites

on all the national security commissions
on all the full plenary sessions

is them who is right what is rote in the paper
is them the master gunners in the sweating three piece
        suits

who circumcizing caliban

Caliban cannibalized is, of course, one of the central symbols
of Caribbean anti-colonial thought, representing, among other
things, the dilemma of reclaiming language through the lan-
guage of the colonizer, and the multiple ironies attendant to
such an undertaking. It is a highly specific, other domain of
"poetry at the periphery," with evident differences yet intrigu-
ing and surprising parallels to the work we have been examining
from various "sites." Brathwaite's prosody is personal and ex-
ploratory, echoing at one moment European, at another African
and Caribbean origins. It is generally nonmetrical and cadential,
and has lately drawn increasingly on indigenous, popular music
forms as well as surprising graphical effects. The space of the page
is taken as a site in itself, a syntactical and visual space to be expres-
sively exploited, as was the case with the Black Mountain poets, as
well as writers such as Frank O'Hara, perhaps partly in response
to gestural abstract painting. Such work may appear arbitrary and
illegible to those committed to an imagined orthodoxy. Yet one
could make the case that it is the imagined Anglo-American for-

malist continuum, with its Arnoldean ideological underpinnings, that is largely arbitrary, given the migrations and passages of living culture. Words such as "craft" and "tradition" thus become code words for authority and orthodoxy. As the Ukrainian poet Alexei Parshchikov has stated, " 'New poetry' has never found a place for itself against a conservative, or, as conservatism's overseers themselves continue to call it, a 'traditional' background. 'New poetry' has always compared itself with previous 'new poetry,' and so forth."

"Make it new," of course, is a very tattered banner of the Modernists, rent in part by the tragic lack of self-reflection of the figure who coined the phrase. That Pound's mind sank beneath the weight of his own intuitionism and bigotry represents a betrayal of the very means of representation he set out to renew. It is particularly tragic and ironic in light of his intention to expand the horizons of American culture, to recognize difference as a source of that renewal. "Writing reflects," states Trinh T. Minh-ha in *Woman Native Other*, "It reflects on other writings and, whenever awareness emerges, on itself as writing." It is precisely this awareness Pound came to lack, and it is this growing lack that in his mania eventually became an abyss. It is as if the periphery from which he operated, at times with great generosity and creativity, transformed itself into a lunatic fringe.

Perhaps no one speaks with more creative relevance or urgency to the paradoxical issues raised by "Eliot Square" than Susan Howe. A poet avowedly working at the margins, she addresses questions of disappearance and recovery, identity and absence, by means of a radical reevaluation of the space of the page and the nature of the text in relation to time. At moments her page becomes a virtual palimpsest, interrogating the notion of legibility itself. Though her acknowledged model is Olson, her perspective is explicitly female, as well as feminist, though for the latter term to make sense it must be disengaged, as she has vehemently stated, from certain institutionalized feminist critical practices that have made a place for women's work within the

Anglo-American academic tradition without thoroughly critiquing many of the doxological assumptions of that tradition.

As is the case with the work of another acknowledged model, Emily Dickinson, Howe can be viewed as exploiting, with a kind of dialectical force, the paradoxes at the heart of her project. Though assuredly an outsider to contemporary mainstream New England culture, she is at the same time a pure product of that culture, an admirer of the work of the "Puritan fathers" and a self-proclaimed Calvinist by temperament. Though her work, like that of many of her contemporaries, interrogates the constitution of the self, it is suffused with a passionate subjectivity. As with Dickinson, her "practice of outside" (the words are Robin Blaser's, referring to Jack Spicer), takes place from within, and employs the means of critique and expression provided by that culture. She seeks out lost narratives, the words of the disappeared, while constructing a narrative of loss. Often the result is something like the twin alphabets of the underground stone, one above the other, each carved with great clarity and care, each invisible. In "The Difficulties," Peter Quatermain has written:

> Howe's work, from the very title of her first book (*Hinge Picture*) on, treads borders, boundaries, dividing lines, edges, invisible meeting points. Her language returns to such cusps again and again, for they mark extremities, turning points, limits, shifts, the nameless edge of mystery where transformations occur and where edge becomes centre. Hope Atherton, in *Articulations of Sound Forms in Time*, moves from the centre to the margin, to the wilderness, and (like Mary Rowlandson) thus marginalizes the centre.

Howe's "Pythagorean silence" not only explores the gaps in the record, the silenced witnessings, but also explores the silences of the text, the space between the words into which (as with Celan) meaning erupts, the pause-boundaries between larger units of utterance (the interruptions of sound by silence), perhaps even the phonemic markers of difference. Through these creases, Howe attempts to give voice to the "ghosts" of our wilderness, those who have been silenced. In an interview, Howe has stated:

> Often I think I am an interloper and an imposter. Something Nietzsche wrote I copied out because it both helps and haunts me. "People still hold the view that what is handed down to us by tradition is what in reality lies behind us—while it in fact comes toward us because we are its captives and are destined to it." Because I am a woman I am fated to read his beautiful observation as double-talk of extraordinary wisdom and rejection. *Us* and *we* are disruptions. These two small words refuse to be absorbed into proper rank in the linear sequence of his sentence. Every sentence has its end. Every day is broken by evening. A harrowing reflection is cast on meaning by gaps in grammar, aporias of historic language.

In a revealing moment, Howe both accepts and rejects Nietzsche's words. She accepts his analysis, then reveals that, if in Nietzsche's *we* remains the trace of an exclusionary tradition, then she is doubly excluded both from that tradition and from that *us*. Her poetry will then employ such disruptions, such gaps and aporias, in its interrogation of signs, texts, shifters:

> light flickers in the rigging
> flags   charts   maps
> to be read by guesswork through obliteration

Citation, erasure and over-writing, joined to an emotionally charged lyricism, all function simultaneously to court and question history, and to understand inheritance:

THE KEY

e n i g m a s t i f e m i a t e d c r y p t o a t h

a b c d e f g h i j k l m n o p q r s t u v w x y

z or zed
graphy
reland
I

Susan Howe is of Irish descent. Ireland with the "I" removed becomes a question "re(garding)" land, as geography with "geo" (earth) removed (or else "bio," life, or some other prefix) becomes "writing." A famous code-machine is named "enigma." What "we" can be recovered from Nietzsche's pronoun? In the "Speeches at the Barriers" section of *Defenestration of Prague*, she writes: "For we are language // Lost in language."

Speaking in the margins, at the barriers or boundaries, perhaps the poets I am considering might be thought of as border workers, constantly passing through checkpoints. There are, after all, guards, customs officials, official guardians of custom. Checking the papers. What deterritorialized space or page might poets be said to inhabit, what curious inside-outside, nowhere/now here? What language is (un)spoken here?

Let me attempt to address, not answer but address, such questions briefly at the final site of this talk, Leningrad, from which I recently returned with four other American poets (Lyn Hejinian, Clark Coolidge, Jean Day and Kit Robinson). We were there for the last stop on a tour with five Russian poets, Ivan Zhdanov, Nadezhda Kondakova, Ilya Kutik, Alexei Parshchikov and Arkadii Dragomoshchenko. The ostensible purpose of the tour was to give readings in preparation for publication of a bilingual anthology of the ten poets' work. The deeper purpose was to erode the Cold

War barriers blocking the flow of cultural exchange and communication.

Leningrad, like Soviet society at large, seems virtually constituted of paradox and contradiction, external and internal, visible and invisible. There is the city of endless classical and baroque symmetries, painted in bright pastels, malachite blue and gold—an Italianate czarist fantasy. Ornate bridges, canals, onion-domed cathedrals and palaces can be seen everywhere throughout the old city. Visible everywhere as well are the grey, sullen crowds attempting to negotiate the labyrinthine difficulties of everyday life, people in endless queues for food, tobacco and clothes, scenes now well-known in the West. Rumors of right-wing coups, civil war, famine, are common. The "market," like the ruble, is a kind of free-floating signifier, a sound without a concept or a referent. Conversation is open, anticipatory, anxious and speculative.

"Poet" too is suddenly an open, free-floating term. The poet was previously defined by his or her silence and suppression, and by the refusal of that silence. Available nowhere, the work was read or recited everywhere. Stalin mandated the necessity of poetry. The poet did not exist: *That was when the ones who smiled / Were the dead, glad to be at rest* (Anna Akhmatova, translated by J. Hemschemeyer). Suppression of the subject articulated the subject and its complex encoding, truth told slant.

Strange then to be talking openly and reading in the Red Hall of the Writers' Union, the Neva's embankments beyond the windows, the KGB building with its security cameras a block away. For the American poets, the problem of the static subject of postwar culture, the pervasive "voice" not all that deep within us, and the fragility of community. For the Russians, the almost opposite problem, that of constituting a self (that self beside that X of Brathwaite) in a culture that has relentlessly devalued the individual since long before Soviet collectivism. In "Flight II," Alexei Parshchikov writes:

> Flashing teeth and flying heels in the bar. The dance
> Fans out like a seine net in turtle's claws. In vain
> I search for you—not even an I;
> maybe the earth reabsorbs us.

Yet these supposed opposites are actually part of a common problem, that of articulating a language of resistance to the merely given or apparent, to hegemonic assumptions concerning self and other, voice and text, expression and form, etc. The particular "permissions" (in Robert Duncan's sense) of poetic speech offer the opportunity for an exploratory engagement with questions of voice, identity and place. What Parshchikov amusingly calls "average poetry" (which he distinguishes both from "traditional" and "new" poetry) declines such an offer, settling instead for a rehearsal of the known, the practice of the craft, the profession. Such work represents, in the words of Arkadii Dragomoschenko, "a yearning for nondifferentiation, for indifference, irresponsibility."

"In poetry," writes Mandelstam, "only the executory understanding has any importance, and not the passive, the reproducing, the paraphrasing understanding. . . . Poetic speech is a most durable carpet, woven out of water." Such a figure is in itself an example of language operating in the margins. It articulates by its impossibility that space, that nowhere, which allows poetry to function, to encompass the paradoxes both of sight and the site. Yet at the same time, it offers poetry no place "to be." A further paradox is that, the more it achieves its goal of critique and renewal, of resistance to the rote, the more vulnerable poetry seems to become to cultural arbiters, whether official (as in the Soviet case) or designated by a somewhat unstable, even haphazard combination of established institution and market.

Since I began with photographs, let me conclude with a snapshot. In Helsinki, on the way to Leningrad, the ten poets were to read at the university's Student Hall. During a break in the event, I stepped outside to get some air. A long, double-line of large, identical black limousines was passing slowly down the avenue through the twilight and making the turn toward the airport. The entourages of Gorbachev and Bush were leaving the city after their one-day summit meeting. I had never seen a more precise physical representation of the language of power, that other syntax and alphabet, of linearity, the monotonal, the same.

[*Differing versions of this talk were first given at the State University of New York at Buffalo and at the University of Chicago in November 1990, and later published in* Onward: Contemporary Poetry and Poetics, *edited by Peter Baker (Peter Lang Publishing, 1996).*]

ON OBJECTIVISM

in memory of Claude Richard and Leah Rakosi

I would like to begin with the music, the work as heard, since it is that which in the winter of 1963 provided my introduction to the Objectivists (that and the publication by New Directions in 1962 of *The Materials* and *By the Waters of Manhattan*). Specifically, a tape recording of " 'A'-11" and a section of " 'A'-12," Zukofsky's voice devoid of theatrics, tracking with great care the syntactical and metrical complexity. " 'A'-11": the prosodic grid drawn from Guido Cavalcanti's *ballata*, "Perch'io non spero" (the same *ballata* echoed to different effect twenty years before, at the start of El-iot's "Ash Wednesday"); Zukofsky's, a poem of forty-six lines, one stanza of six, four of ten, with complex end and internal rhymes, each stanza terminating in the word "honor." He threads to-gether the "notes" or words of Guido, of "Spin" or "the blest" (his Spinoza-Baruch or Blessed-lens-grinder and philosopher of the *Ethics)*, the healer and metaphysician Paracelsus, Joseph Rodman Drake (author of the poem *Bronx* (the river in New York named for the forebears of the poet William Bronk)), Henry James and the makers of two books of the Pentateuch, Numbers and Exodus. (Undoubtedly I've missed a few.) It is a song that invokes song as an act of devotion to wife Celia and violinist-son Paul, and as a projected consolation for them after the poet's death. "To live . . . our desires lead us to honor." " 'A'-11" was composed in 1950–51, the first new movement of *"A"* since 1940, and one can read it as well, I think, as an act of mourning for the century. Marx is now if not missing, at least more faintly heard (he will not appear in *Bottom*), but Bach will return with the long movement, " 'A'-- 12," "done in a summer" the poems says, "June–October" reads the manuscript. Its question, "Where stemmed the Jew among strangers" would be asked in various ways by others among the poets we are discussing on this weekend of Rosh Hashanah, the Jewish New Year.

I understood little of either text at first and would not have my own copy to puzzle over until the Jonathan Cape edition of *"A" 1-12* appeared in 1966. To those of us listening, though, two things were apparent: that there had been no equivalent model of syntactical music in American modernism; and that it was manifestly (for all of its "difference") a product of American modernism—the presence of Guido marked instruction from Pound, the density of reference pointed to both Pound and Eliot, while the "open" syntax, the resistance to "meaning" (to "meaning" as a given), pointed to the exploratory and heterogeneous counter-tradition in American writing dating back at least to Whitman and Dickinson. Equally the two texts were drawn from the paratactic structure of a "poem of a life," like (and unlike) *Leaves of Grass* and *The Cantos*, like (and unlike) *Paterson* and the *Maximus Poems*.

"Upper limit music," as Zukofsky had written of his poetics, and " 'A'-11" seemed very close to that limit where the harmonic density at once intensifies and threatens the signifying capacity of words. Certainly the passive reader will make nothing of it; it demands a virtually hermeneutical engagement with its words, playing insistently on shades of meaning within each. As Michael Davidson has noted, it is hermetic in a way even our most difficult poets, such as Pound, never are. Among other things, it is this resistance that sets Zukofsky apart from—and at times in contention with—the other poets known as Objectivists.

In the summer of 1963, at the Vancouver Poetry Conference, Robert Creeley had asked whether I was familiar with Zukofsky's

work. I answered that I'd read very few things in the little maga-
zines, but that they had not made an impression. He sent the
tape that winter. On it were also recordings of H.D. reading from
Helen in Egypt, Levertov, Ed Dorn reading very early, very lucid
work from the book, *Hands Up!*, and Allen Ginsberg reading *Howl*
at Stan Brakhage's cabin in Colorado with the sounds of the "un-
derground" filmmaker's children in the background. Creeley had
discovered Zukofsky through Robert Duncan in 1955. Duncan,
by his testimony, had been reading him, whenever he could find
the work, since 1937. (I do not at all intend by this perhaps ill-
advised anecdotalism to try to construe some specious patriar-
chal lineage or filiation, but rather to give a sense of the tenuous
threads of an "outside" literary community that existed, and
the difficulty of discovering, of finding and finding out about
poets for the most part ignored and in some instances system-
atically excluded by the cultural arbiters of both the Left (for
example, the Trotskyite *Partisan Review* and the Stalinist *New
Masses)* and the Right. The epigones and heirs to the Eliot of
The Sacred Wood and "Tradition and the Individual Talent," and
to Frost and Auden, such as the New Critics, the Fugitives, and
the Agrarians, constructed a new Anglo-American formalist
ideology in reaction to what was perceived as the excesses of
modernist experimentation. The work privileged conventional
(mainly British) forms, a reified subject, consistency of tone,
elaborate tropes, socially coded irony, myth, and Eliot's central
metaphoric device, the objective correlative. The shared ideolo-
gies, both overt and hidden, of such a poetics served in effect to
buttress the cultural institutions whose patronage was essential
to such poets' ambition. Their most conspicuous, if troubled,
heirs in the postwar period were the so-called Confessional Poets
(partly centered in Cambridge, Massachusetts, where the above-
mentioned tape arrived and was played about the time Robert
Lowell was preparing the manuscript of *For the Union Dead* for
publication). Here are two stanzas from the poem "Middle Age"
in that volume:

Now the midwinter grind
is on me, New York
drills through my nerves,
as I walk
the chewed-up streets.

At forty-five
what next, what next?
At every corner
I meet my Father,
my age, still alive.

I would doubt the need for comment on such mawkish posturing
and exhausted rhetoric, except that it quickly became a model for
the drama of the "petit moi" among campus poets and antholo-
gizers across America. In fact, one or another version of a debased
Romantic style has constituted acceptable poetic affect ever since
the official recuperation of the Romantics from the social and cul-
tural challenge they initially hoped to embody. Even when turned
supposedly outward toward the world, such a "voice" tends to
flounder in a veiled, mandarin paternalism. Lowell, Berryman,
Plath, early Adrienne Rich and Roethke, among others, would
foreground personal, psychological narrative, reflecting both the
constitution and the crisis of the subject in a postwar America
preoccupied with individualism ("Yankee individualism") and
self-realization. The popular acceptance among many intellectu-
als of neo-Freudian ego psychology would further reinforce this
myth, or more precisely melodrama, of the self.

The tenets and refusals of the Objectivists articulated in their
lives (as well as their work) stand in contrast both to this form of
public self-dramatization (there were other forms as well, among
the Beats for example), and to that other subjectivism of Ezra
Pound, represented by the virtual compulsion to reduce and sub-
ordinate various fields of information to an emotionally distorted
cultural agenda. (The complex relation of Pound to the Objectivist

poets, particularly Reznikoff, Zukofsky, and Oppen, will I'm sure be raised during this symposium. Let us say for now that, at the very least, it raises another question, that of the many contradictions at the heart of the Modernist project (if we can in fact speak of a "project").) This second question, among other things, includes within it the relation of the aesthetic to the political. Any comprehensive discussion of the Objectivists must address the significance of their progressive social values, as well as the difficulty, in the pre- and postwar years, of integrating those values with the demands of an art and the ideological pressures of a culture. What is obvious is that there is an active social dimension to the work of these poets that deserves our scrutiny.

Within the fractured narrative of modernism, we can probably say that Objectivism begins with the perceived necessity to add active intellect to the verbal and visual economy of imagistic method. In its brief history, Imagism had quickly degenerated into a passive and decorative form, evoking exactly that hothouse atmosphere of the eighteen nineties it was meant to dispel. Yet at its origins it had served the purpose of clearing away much of the rhetoric and poetic furniture inherited from the Victorian period. The refusal of such a rhetoric might be characterized as the first of a series of critical negations by the Objectivists. Throughout his "Day Book," Rakosi repeatedly warns against the dangers of posturing and verbal contrivance and against the "large Romantic tone of greatness." If he is arguing for a "plain style," after Williams, grounded in the rhythms and accents of American speech, this must not be confused with the self-consciously dryly literary "middle style" of so much polite and nondescript American verse. And if, characteristically, he speaks of himself as poet as an "amanuensis of time," it does not mean that his ambitions for the poem are of equivalent modesty. Rather it is a warning against foregrounding personality, whether through avant-garde gesturalism or other styles of self-representation. The work faces the world.

"Rays of an object brought to a focus," states Zukofsky. Proposing "sincerity" and "rested totality" as values, Zukofsky too proposes an ethics of representation "concomitant" (Veblen's word) with desire. Presentation without superfluous commentary. Form resides in the act of (or in an active) objectification. This term, so slippery in its uses and shadings, must not be confused with either scientific or moral objectivism. It is closer instead to a notion of integrity, in the sense of wholeness, retaining faith, as Oppen would say, in the possibility of reference even when faced with the unspeakable and apparently unrepresentable events of our century. I am reminded, somewhat paradoxically, of the novelist Christa Wolf's term, "subjective authenticity." In conversation with Joachim Walther she explains that "This mode of writing is not 'subjectivist,' but 'interventionist.' It does require subjectivity, and a subject who is prepared to undergo unrelenting exposure . . . to the material at hand . . . The new reality you see is different from the one you saw before . . . It becomes more and more difficult to say 'I,' and yet at the same time often imperative to do so." Later in the same conversation she adds, "When I say 'authenticity,' I don't mean 'truthfulness'; I'm not moralizing. Truthfulness must be taken for granted; it is absolutely undeniable that literature cannot exist without it." Now a remarkably parallel passage from George Oppen's essay, "The Mind's Own Place":

> It is possible to find a metaphor for anything, an analogue: but the image is encountered, not found; it is an account of the poet's perception, of the act of perception; it is a test of sincerity, a test of conviction, the rare poetic quality of truthfulness. They meant to replace by the data of experience the accepted poetry of their time, a display by the poets of right thinking and right sentiment, a dreary waste of lies. That data was and is the core of what "modernism" restored to poetry, the sense of the poet's self among things. So much depends upon the red wheelbarrow. The distinction between a poem that shows confidence in itself and in its materials, and on the other hand a performance, a speech by the poet, is the distinction between

poetry and histrionics. It is a part of the function of poetry to serve as a test of truth. It is possible to say anything in abstract prose, but a great many things one believes or would like to believe or thinks he believes will not substantiate themselves in the concrete materials of the poem. It is not to say that a poet is immune to the "real" world to say that he is not likely to find the moment, the image, in which a political generalization or any other generalization will prove its truth. Denise Levertov begins a fine poem with the words: "The authentic!" and goes on to define

> the real, the new-laid,
> egg whose speckled shell
> the poet fondles and must break
> if he will be nourished

By speaking against literary contrivance, Oppen argues both for the possibility, or necessity, of an immediacy of poetic engagement or intervention, and against the "poetic," that is, against the devices of a passive and acculturated representation. He argues as well for a gaze turned outward, a responsibility of the self to find its realization, its form as thinking subject, in its relation to the visible and invisible things of the world. The understanding that such a realization is at best problematic is part of what informs the silences and ellipses of his lines with their particular resonance, or perhaps I mean content:

> So spoke of the existence of things,
> An unmanageable pantheon
>
> Absolute, but they say
> Arid.
>
> Glassed
> In dreams

And images—

And the pure joy
Of the mineral fact

Tho it is impenetrable

As the world, if it is matter,
Is impenetrable.

Another music, as determined as Zukofsky's to excise unnecessary notes. As in Zukofsky, as Michael Heller has noted, the concern here is not with "the reified objectification of knowledge into a science . . . but with an objectification of human instance, of witnessing." Conscious, too, that bearing witness is at once necessary and, in any final sense, impossible. The form here is that of the possibility of knowing, but not of a knowing, and least of all the known—hence, perhaps, desire. (Oppen's Heidegger must for the moment remain in brackets, as for example his references to the 1929 University of Freiburg speech and his later use of other texts. For his ontological ground, the poet of radical commitment turns to that "thinking toward being" of the right-wing philosopher, even as the philosopher would turn to Hölderlin and other poets for much of the discursive ground of his later work. Can we cite this too as one of the endless "contradictions" that seem more and more to be not only common but constituent features of modernism? Celan and Heidegger, particularly here and on this day, come to mind, but equally Zukofsky and Pound, Cardenal and Pound, and any number of others. Shifting temporal perspective, we might eventually also ask whether it is not from contradiction that all poetry must attempt to speak.)

Returning to the question of "witness," is it this double acknowledgment, of necessity and impossibility, that leads Reznikoff to construct *Testimony* and *Holocaust* by a process of selection and editing and to remain determinedly silent himself?

Rakosi speaks of poet as amanuensis; discussing negation in Melville's "Bartleby," Blanchot writes, "In 'Bartleby,' the enigma comes from 'pure' writing, which can only be that of a copyist (rewriting). . . . Language, perpetuating itself, keeps still." The subject disappears in the name of the subject, and a lexicon of silence is asked to speak. From Reznikoff's *Autobiography: New York:*

> I am afraid
> because of the foolishness
> I have spoken.
> I must diet
> on silence;
> strengthen myself
> with quiet

The great majority of Reznikoff's Manhattan poems do not offer even this glimpse of the first person. They detail, with clarity and (a perhaps deceptive) simplicity, the urban landscape, often that of the poor and the dispossessed. Material once thought unseemly—unpoetic—like a cracked marble washstand or a red wheelbarrow. They are far from the genteel mainstream of American poetry of the time, as well as from the much later narrative of Lowell's New York (or, more accurately, Lowell in New York). Yet in a sense they are, on the surface, also distant from that fragment of " 'A'-12" I first mentioned, where Zukofsky recounts his father's voyage from Russia, his life as a "presser" amid the immigrants of the Lower East Side, a Jew who keeps Sabbath. Sight and directness of presentation have a priority in Reznikoff and Rakosi that cannot be claimed for Zukofsky's poetics, struggling to conjoin sight (I's pronounced eyes), with that upper limit of music, at some near absolute pitch of definition. Each of the poets, in interviews, has recognized a point at which, after the shared sources and sympathies and shared refusals have been noted, the distinctions or differences must be acknowledged. At that point it might be said that the "subject" of the Objectivists will disappear behind the work. If this is ironic, I hope it is an irony that will be appreciated by Carl Rakosi, who is the most determined practitioner of the ironic mode within this group.

On the announcement for this conference, four Objectivists are listed. To end this introduction I would like to add a fifth, Lorine Niedecker, as yet I gather unknown in France, with only a few poems translated—hardly a surprise, since she is still all but unknown in the United States (thereby carrying on another Objectivist tradition). Until recently her work was effectively unobtainable, but there are now two collections of poetry in print and a selection of correspondence with Cid Corman whose role, along with that of Jonathan Williams and James Laughlin, in publishing these poets deserves our recognition and gratitude. A study of Niedecker's life and work by the Canadian scholar Jenny Penberthy is also due soon for publication. Niedecker lived most of her life in rural Wisconsin, often on the edge of poverty. A lifelong friend and correspondent of Zukofsky, she first found the work of the Objectivists in his 1931 issue of *Poetry* magazine. Her work fuses their visual focus, political skepticism and lyricism with the isolate and resistant awareness of Emily Dickinson. Such a joining reveals a current of critical and analytic lyricism running from the origins of American modernism to the present. It is a poetry of extreme concentration and reticence, alert to the minute signs of the natural world and to the costs of time and isolation. They represent as clearly as any of the work under discussion the reasons a certain number, from the impossible community of poets, found among these barely visible writers a crucial "missing link" in the evolution of exploratory modernist practice, that restored a sense of humane and socially progressive thought to a narrative too often tragically lacking in it. From "Traces of Living Things":

"Shelter"

Holed damp
cellar-black beyond
the main atrocities
my sense of property's
adrift

Not burned we sweat—
we sink to water Death
(your hand!—
this was land)
disowns

[*Talk delivered as introduction to the Objectivist Conference at the Fondation Royaumont in Asnières-Sur-Oise, September 29—Ocober 1, 1989. Published in* Sulfur *26, Spring 1990.*]

COUNTER-POETICS AND
CURRENT PRACTICE

One: Origins (Plural)

So this first talk is about origins. I began trying to think about this a little more coherently in the last couple of years, one, because the picture is so messy in my case, so diverse and pluralistic, that it began to interest me in a way, more than a clear-cut picture might—which, I suppose, says something about my own aesthetic. In any case, I started to think about these origins both in terms of the various cultures I tend to refer to, or derive from, in my work, and along with that, my own sense of an identification with something I fairly crudely think of as a counter-poetics. Of course, as soon as you propose a counter-poetics, it immediately becomes official and therefore it isn't a counter-poetics anymore. It's an illusion. But in some ways I have felt identification with a poetry of a certain kind of complexity and resistance—resistance in terms of resistance to meaning in the simplest sense, certainly not resistance to signification in a larger sense. Resistance, let's say, to pre-inscribed meaning. Resistance to the political orders of culture as represented by conventional gestures of narrativity, conventional gestures of emotion, and so on.

Certainly I was always interested in alternatives to what became the canonical if not unitary mainstream of American culture, which could receive various definitions, but you could think of it in one respect as the Frost-Eliot-Auden core of officially accepted Modernist poetry. There was even posited an Age of Auden at one point. I don't know if anyone subscribes to that anymore. This would even be outside the question of quality, because I think of Eliot at least as a very fine poet, whatever my own contempt for his cultural opinions. One bothers to have contempt for them because he is a major poet. One doesn't bother to have contempt for Archibald Macleish's cultural opinions, or other derivative codifiers who actually stood for poetry at a certain point before time gave up on them.

So I was drawn to an alternative tradition that may have its parallels in nineteenth-century American culture, in the figures of Whitman and Dickinson (Dickinson in particular) and Melville. People who stood deliberately and intentionally against the inscribed meanings of the culture (this would be in contrast to poets such as Holmes, Longfellow, Whittier, etc., who were the figures for the poem in the culture of that time). Whitman, Dickinson and Melville—people who tended to stress the reciprocality of form and content, the inseparability of the two, and who thought of the poem as an exploration of a very profound order. In the case of Dickinson, she works within an extraordinarily reduced mode and yet proves that mode as entirely available to her own very complex and gnomic ambitions with the poem. So that it's not a matter of closed and open in some simplistic sense, in the sense that we take Whitman as an open cadential form and Dickinson as closed. They turn out to be identical in one respect, in terms of their ambitions to renew form, and to create a poetics that answers specifically to their needs. More a matter of shared resistance to given literary conventions, to given literary contrivances, to an a priori notion of the subject of the poem. Strikingly, in both instances, at least when they're working at their best, the poem unfolds the subject.

People stand for contradictory things. Every time I mention, for example, the name Ezra Pound, I think of very contradictory things. I think of a person who was in one respect a kind of primary teacher, and in another respect a man who grew increasingly contemptible over time, increasingly blind, who increasingly gave in to his lack of—his ignorance of his own psyche, let's say, and ignorance of history, ongoing history, and for a man who was writing a poem that was to include history, that's a difficult problem.

I remember that at a certain point one of the things that began to give me a sense of a poetics that stood outside what was being offered happened when I was reading Pound in school and came upon one or another of the versions of the *Donna mi pregha* of Guido Cavalcanti that he had translated. This poem began to offer a return for me into the Romance tradition, that notion which Pound takes from Dante of *the good of the intellect,* that notion of desire and of mind together in one fairly complex and informing moment, and the poem as specifically a vehicle for the expression of that good. Also, Dante in *De vulgari eloquentia* talks about a poetry that comes (remember he's talking about a poetry that's demanding and complicated, a poetry that engages all of one's being rather than being something like a decor for culture, something to put next to the cartoons in that weekly magazine). He talks of that language coming from the tongues of our nurses, our wet nurses, and not being a separate literary tongue, not being some form of hieratic discourse, but something that comes from the language we hear around us. This is strikingly parallel to the way Williams talks about it when Williams is asked where he gets his language from and he says "out of the mouths of Polish mothers." At the same time Dante speaks of what we tend to think of as a very contemporary term, *polysemy,* multiple meanings within one sign (he talks about this both in *De vulgari eloquentia* and the letter to Can Grande della Scala). He's addressing the notion of a charged poetic sign, one that comes from the texture of our daily life but acquires a denser semantic function, one that is more easily engendered in the poem.

Pound translated, I think unsuccessfully, the *Donna mi pregha* poem all the way across his life. It's very striking to look back at it now, thinking of someone like Pound, for example, as one of the origins of one aspect of twentieth-century American modernism, and yet you see a poem that even in its final version, published somewhere in the mid-1930s, is steeped in Rossetti, entirely *fin-de-siècle,* elaborately coded with this nineteenth-century style at a time when many American poets who were less strident in their demands to "make it new" were actually much more engaged by a living speech. People like Charles Reznikoff and Williams, and many others, had actually gone further in casting off the poetic artifices of late nineteenth-century style. But it does give a sense of the variable line, and intensification.

One of the fascinating things about Cavalcanti is the degree of philosophical reflection. I don't mean making philosophy, I mean that thing that occurs in poets like Wallace Stevens, where there's a proximity to the philosophical in the poetry. In " 'A'-- 9" Louis Zukofsky takes a rhyme scheme from Cavalcanti and writes a double canzone that folds in a whole range of references, including the Everyman edition of *Das Kapital.* Zukofsky means it in the deeper sense of translation, of bearing across as an instance of the music you would experience in the period of Dante, which is also, roughly, the period of the Troubadours; in other words, Dante considers himself in the Troubadour heritage, and is deriving his music in large measure from there. Zukofsky used to always say: "Don't worry about the sense for now, just listen to the noise, and if you like the noise, come back and figure it out later."

" 'A'-9" is, of course, an extreme of a certain kind of practice, but this gesture is fascinating to me in that it brings in a quality, a character of musicality, that was otherwise unavailable. So whatever else we want to say, it does broaden the boundaries of possibility. Zukofsky was always thinking about this equation of "Lower-limit speech / Upper-limit music," and it put him in a dilemma. In an early essay for his anthology of the Objectivist poets he talked about this, but he also said we have to recognize that the musical sign and the linguistic sign are not the same thing, and that a poem that confuses its modes ultimately, that aspires to music in a way that a lot of *fin-de-siècle* poets did, will end up in the problem Swinburne ends up in. And yet, you can see a Zukofsky in the extremes of his practice, in the extremes of his urgency to arrive at a musicality, in his last poem, *Eighty Flowers,* and others, getting increasingly into real dilemmas of signification.

Pound talks of Cavalcanti somewhere using the term *intentio,* meaning the intention of the form. Robert Duncan picks this up as the form underhand, apprehended from the information of the world, not the form as a given, as a thing imposed on the work, but as something that grows underhand, the intention then of the work that you follow through to its end as you apprehend it: active form. Another parallel, a direct reference to Dante's time, is a poem from Robert Duncan's *Roots and Branches.* It's a translation—no, it's not a translation—it's a kind of overwriting of Dante's sixth sonnet from the second book of the *Rime,* so Duncan calls it "Sonnet 3: From Dante's Sixth Sonnet." It's also a poem to Robin Blaser and Jack Spicer, a celebration of their circle before it broke up in the usual acrimony and retribution.

This same idea of looking at where one steals one's art from and derives from, and so on, led me back to thinking about the time when I was an undergraduate and first trying to come to some definition of a possible art in a place that was extremely unsatisfactory to me for a variety of reasons. I was by instinct and temperament, I suppose, rather than by any lucid notion of what the hell I was doing, extremely unhappy with the dominant poetics of the East Coast and particularly around Cambridge. It was a dominance of New Critical standards of form, a poetics very much indebted to that normative critical standard, so you had a poetics, in my mind at least, instead of being primary and generative, that was actually answering to an authority, to a set of authorities as represented by the New Critics—a relatively reactionary men's club that came to have enormous influence (not all of it awful, some of it awful) on American literary theory and on American critical practice. It seemed to me then and it seems to me now that aesthetically and certainly politically it tended toward a reactionary nostalgia. It was represented, at least in its

Southern incarnation, by Ransom and Tate (Lowell at least was trying to answer to that, to the authority of that, though in a certain way he was, for his own good, too problematic to be able to answer to that mold).

In any case, I felt there was an extremely stultified relationship to form, and a need to answer to people who frankly didn't know what was going on. I had no respect for the turning away from what I thought of as having been begun by H.D., Marianne Moore, Williams and others, by the sort of grand exploration early modernism represented. When Randall Jarrell announces in the late '40s that it's all over and time to mow our lawns and clip our hedges, well, I felt I couldn't have any identification with that.

I remember going in the summer of 1963 (out to work on the harvest in Oregon) and before leaving I stopped at a bookstore, the Grolier, to say good-bye to some people, and noticed on a poster a thing called the *Vancouver Poetry Conference*. There was to be a gathering of all sorts of people, some of whom interested me very much, whom I didn't even realize (in that curious scattershot way you assemble things) were intimately connected, Charles Olson, Robert Creeley, Robert Duncan, Allen Ginsberg, Denise Levertov, and others, were going to be getting together in one place for the first time. What was useful to me at Vancouver was not so much any particular program (I didn't want to turn out to be a second-generation Black Mountaineer or an Official Projectivist, using breath measures and so on). What was interesting to me, actually, was the possibility of a life entirely given over to the poem. A life that was not referential to "the literary," what qualifies as literature, as to the actual exigencies and demands of the poetic vocation.

Take, for example, the fashion world of American Art at present, specifically the East Village (it's fun if you think of it as rock-n-roll, very boring if you think of it as anything more than that), where every two weeks you have a new graffiti artist or a new somebody or other who enters into all the great collections, an instant millionaire, who has paid his or her dues by working in a loft for three weeks. The reference is so entirely to the world of art and to style rather than to the demands of figuration, let's say, or representation (all of those real problems) that the entire gesture is utterly diminished. We get this all across the board in what we think of as the throwaway world of poetry, which is referential to minor accomplishments of style, and to telling little experiences that we've all had together, and to reflecting, in that respect, to engendering that little shiver of recognition and then passing out of one's memory. I remember, also, at Vancouver, actually after I left and got back to the East Coast, receiving a tape from Creeley, and this was very useful. It began to teach me, first, why one reads poetry aloud, because of the kind of access we can get to the poem aloud that is not available in other ways. It was a tape of H.D., Zukofsky, Ginsberg reading *Howl* at Stan Brakhage's house, early Ed Dorn (those very beautiful Dorn poems from *Hands Up*, and so on, that celebrate Midwestern space). Anyway, I was struck by all of these alternatives which at that point had no place in the picture of modern American poetry.

H.D., incidentally, only begins to have a place, recently, partly because the more recent incarnations of American feminism are looking with a lot of intensity at so-called exploratory and experimental writing rather than simply thematic work. The form she comes to inhabit is entirely her own, one that would be hard to call a narrative sequence—I'm thinking of the later poems, that seriality or sequentiality, which is really her own derivation from the earlier work.

After hearing Zukofsky's " 'A'-11," which I think is one of the most beautiful lyrics in the language, I was drawn (perhaps in compensation against the exploration of psyche and self that was going on in those Eastern literary circles from which I felt simply, for whatever reasons, outside of) I was drawn rather strongly to the Objectivists. This is entirely ironic in light of my recent work. I was drawn to poets like Lorine Niedecker, for example, her precisions, again something rather hermetic and difficult. Zukofsky,

Reznikoff, Niedecker, George Oppen, Carl Rakosi—these were all
people outside, I mean *outside,* unpublished and unpublishable,
in whom I found affirmations of sincerity, as Zukofsky would
call it. The Objectivist program is first of all a way of freeing po-
etry from one of the stultifications that occurred very early with
Imagism, where the image became sentimentalized and gave no
place for thought. Instead of its original aim, which is a focus on
the word, it became a place for false poeticizing and sentimental-
ity, and so the Objectivists tried to address this and take some
of the gains that had come from Imagism in order to make it, as
Oppen once said, "a possible mode of thought." Certainly H.D.'s
later work contributes to that possibility.

I began to be fascinated with a focus on process and the pos-
sibility of alternative measures, and the possibility of using the
poem as a place for prohibited content (there's a politics of sexu-
ality and a politics of the political involved here), and as a place
where things can be inscribed, for attending to the grammar of
perception and the problematic limits that our everyday discourse
tends to put on what we are able to say. I think of the poem in
its exploratory aspect as something that can shatter those limits
rather than address those limits and inscribe itself within those
limits.

I moved to San Francisco in 1969, not at all in relation to
poetry. I did want to be away from the Boston area, but I didn't
have any notion of joining up with an already dead San Francisco
Renaissance. At that point, in fact, I didn't really see any infor-
mation coming out of that environment except for some poets I
respected who were still there, among them Robert Duncan. The
high moment beginning in the '50s and ending somewhere in the
'60s of a literary community in San Francisco was gone. But I did
turn to figures like Duncan for an affirmation of the possibility
of questioning the subject, the speaking subject, what it can be.
In Robert's case this questioning comes from a high Romantic
tradition that you can read through Keats and Shelley as well as
through Duncan: the uncertain identity of the speaker when the

speaker seems to be a conduit, in his case, for an inspired vatic vision. So even though my work was from a radically different tradition, this notion of questioning the forms underhand and the identity of the speaker and reader and listener, their interpenetration, was something I respected a great deal along with his own urgency to include within the poem content that had previously been prohibited.

Another figure is Jack Spicer. The counter-logicality, the Edward Lear/Gertrude Stein investigation of the play of loss and error within the poetic sign, his investigation of the perversity of meaning in the poem, the uses of disjuncture and counter-logic. . . . A poetic logic does not necessarily resemble other logics. If you take classical logic, for example, there's a law of the excluded middle where a thing is either A or not-A, but can never be both A and not-A. In a poem you can be perfectly in a logic where a thing is both A and not-A, it can be both raining and not raining, snowing in the tropics—whatever you want. This isn't simply frivolity—it's an announcement of another area of knowing. There's a particular focus and concentration in this area of poetic logic. Spicer has an entire sequence called *After Lorca* where he plays with the kind of discourse with the dead that poets have, and he invents his own Lorca, and Lorca invents him, in the preface, and so on, all of it a play among the dead—something he shares with Rilke. What seems commonly held by these poets is that they tend to be outside, in their lifetimes, outside what becomes defined (very roughly) as the canonical mainstream. This is a poetry that has its particular and sometimes difficult semantic territory, a poetry that is exploratory, heuristic, a poetry that is not simply a reflection of or a description of a prior state of emotion. This is a poem that is not simply there to reinscribe something already experienced, but is actually a mode of experience in and of itself. Making sense as a process, not a reference to a norm, so it always interests me if someone says *this does not make sense,* because I'm not interested in that aspect of making sense, sense not as something prior to the poem, but something that is an occasion for making sense, of finding out what sense is and making sense anew, changing what sense is. And I do mean the political dimension of that, as challenging the sense that a Ronald Reagan may make in a public address, or the sense of a language that speaks of pacification when it means annihilation. I think the poem challenges that appropriation of the language which the discourse of power represents.

I think the poem represents, even the "nonpolitical" poem at its most effective, an undermining of the possibility of the lie, and a reappropriation, a taking-back of the language and the means of signification. A questioning of the relations and identities between the first, second and third person, between the *I* and the *you* and the *it*, or the thing itself, but also in the plural between the *they* and the *we*, and all the things out there. What are the interrelations? It's always a question. Who are we in relation? Who am I? Am I doing the speaking? Are you doing the listening? A refusal, then, of acculturated norms and the commodification of the poem, as something simply there to improve your digestion. A refusal, also, of the reader as a passive consumer. Speaking to a passive audience is much more the Hitlerian form of discourse where the passivity of the audience is assumed, where they are not involved in an active exchange of meaning.

Edmond Jabès always talked about true discourse as a place where the question is possible, even paramount, and that an authoritarian discourse is one where the question is not possible. And that idea of the poem as an objectified entity, complete in itself, realized beyond time's altering flow. Its "timelessness" is more complex. We tend to think so much of the poem as an object (that's partly a New Critical heritage), as an enclosed object. We forget the fact that it is variable within certain limits, and there's nothing we can do about that—which is terrific. And that the poem only occurs, is only there, in the event of the poem, which is in its engagement with the reader. Except in some platonic sense, the poem is not present when the book is closed. What I mean is that the poem is an event, temporally and historically conditioned. And so I am interested in acts of composition that emphasize this without becoming simply buckets into which anyone can drop whatever they want. The poem is not simply an aleatory event.

Two: Lyric Practice (Analytic Lyric?)

I hadn't realized in mentioning Jack Spicer yesterday that a number of people were relatively unfamiliar with Spicer's work, and not familiar with the texts I had referred to, which were a couple of statements on poetics, as always, perverse and joking in a profoundly serious way. And so I thought that as a bridge between yesterday and today I'd begin with a couple of Spicer's letters to Lorca, to the dead Lorca, or else it's the dead Spicer writing to the dead Lorca, as he thought of it, and now since Spicer's dead—he's correct. They speak to a number of things besides Spicer's immediate concerns in the letters to Lorca about how we signify in a poem. They also speak to the conversation that occurs among poets over time, and Spicer created a nexus of a number of figures, including Rimbaud and Lorca and several others, with whom he spoke in conversation about a number of things—in Spicer's case also having to do with sexuality and sexual politics, and so on, and obviously Lorca would be a figure who appealed to him from the agony of the poems in New York, and others.

The book *After Lorca* is a series, the first in the *Collected Books* of Spicer, and I don't think necessarily the most realized, though maybe the most popular. It begins, this sequence of prose letters, with an introduction by Lorca from beyond the grave, complaining a little about Spicer's mistranslations of his work, and so on, and wondering who this guy is. And then there's a sequence of translations of a very personal order—some are fairly straight translations, others are willful mistranslations, and others (at one extreme) have almost no reference to Lorca's work. This in itself is interesting because he's effectively referring to the three different levels of translation that someone like Dryden, for example, talks about when he speaks of imitation, metaphrase and paraphrase. Beginning from the most literal would be *metaphrase*, and then *paraphrase*, and then *imitation* as the furthest from the text, the most creative. Dryden, of course, being of a particularly dry age settles for the middle way. But in any case Spicer is playing with this, with going from the most literal to the most parallel mis-translation, the most poetic—in one sense—translation. The same setup that Aristotle follows, actually.

And so, there are these translations of various poems, often dedicated to people, and then works that are not translations of Lorca, that are simply poems of Spicer's, and then these letters that are interspersed. Let me use them here, since Lorca will be coming up, and since a lot of people didn't know much about Jack Spicer.

Dear Lorca,

When I translate one of your poems and I come across words I do not understand, I always guess at their meanings. I am inevitably right. A really perfect poem (no one yet has writ-ten one) could be perfectly translated by a person who did not know one word of the language it was written in. A really per-fect poem has an infinitely small vocabulary.

It is very difficult. We want to transfer the immediate object, the immediate emotion to the poem—and yet the im-mediate always has hundreds of its own words clinging to it, short-lived and tenacious as barnacles. And it is wrong to scrape them off and substitute others. A poet is a time me-chanic not an embalmer. The words around the immediate shrivel and decay like flesh around the body. No mummy-sheet of tradition can be used to stop the process. Objects, words must be led across time not preserved against it.

I yell "Shit" down a cliff at the ocean. Even in my lifetime the immediacy of that word will fade. It will be dead as "Alas." But if I put the real cliff and the real ocean into the poem, the word "Shit" will ride along with them, travel the time-machine until cliffs and oceans disappear.

Most of my friends like words too well. They set them under the blinding light of the poem and try to extract every possible connotation from each of them, every temporary pun, every direct or indirect connection—as if a word could become an object by mere addition of consequences. Others pick up words from the streets, from their bars, from their offices and display them proudly in their poems as if they were shouting, "See what I have collected from the American language. Look at my butterflies, my stamps, my old shoes!" What does one do with all this crap?

Words are what sticks to the real. We use them to push the real, to drag the real into the poem. They are what we hold on with, nothing else. They are as valuable in themselves as rope with nothing to be tied to.

I repeat—the perfect poem has an infinitely small vocabulary.

Love,
Jack

Spicer himself studied linguistics and actually published at one point a paper in collaboration with a professional linguist, and was very concerned in his own way with the problematics of the sign in the sense that he realized any clown can throw a green elephant or a tree or a leaf into a poem and pretend they have an image when in fact that isn't the way the sign is renewed. Anybody can tell you that they feel sad or they feel happy in the poem and it's not the sign for that. We're in a deeply problematic and paradoxical territory when we deal with signification in the poem. We want to point in a certain way, and yet the sign has a certain amount of slippage, loss, and accretions around it that make the thing not a simple task at all, to renew the sign within the poem, to make it, as Matisse says, in relation to painting, a new sign—the job of the painter. Picasso says the same thing: to bring new signs into painting, so that a tree once again becomes a tree —in a painting.

Here's the opening of another letter, again addressing many of the same concerns about this job of the renewal of language and the renewal through language, Spicer being essentially a lyric poet, and is extremely conscious of the difficulties of the lyric mode, of the danger of the lyrical being overwhelmed by what Charles Olson called "the lyrical interference of the ego," by the petty distortions that we are tempted to indulge in and splat on the page.

> Dear Lorca,
>
>   I would like to make poems out of real objects. The lemon to be a lemon that the reader could cut or squeeze or taste—a real lemon like a newspaper in a collage is a real newspaper. I would like the moon in my poems to be a real moon, one which could be suddenly covered with a cloud that has nothing to do with the poem—a moon utterly independent of images. The imagination pictures the real. I would like to point to the real, disclose it, to make a poem that has no sound in it but the pointing of a finger.

This is a lovely and poignant attempt to do an end run on words, I think. Actually, pertinent to what we are going to discuss to-morrow, in the sense of his reference to the practice of *collage,* and the incorporation of actual materials, well, that's a complication of the sign system of painting and of the representational act, such as people like Breton and others in their talks about the painters of that time were very concerned with.

Implicit in this first book of Spicer's is also a critique of the "deep image" that James Wright and Robert Bly misappropriated from Spanish poetry some twenty-five or thirty years ago, not un-derstanding how an image arises and how impossible it is to take that image and reduce it (how it arises in that basically Moorish-

Gypsy-Spanish culture), how impossible it is to appropriate it as a device for expression. Certainly Spicer is trying to transcend such notions, such fairly glib notions of constructing through image, by finding another level of expression where image may or may not be an event in the poem, but is certainly not something you put into a poem, and then think you've done something. There's enough reference obliquely to that misappropriation that I suspect he had it in mind. So much of Spicer, and other poets, is directed against anything that could be taken as a constructive or creative device around which you could build a poetics. And in this respect one can see a Spicer as having a relationship of critical negativity to the culture as a whole, I suppose, but also to the models of poetic making that became so standard.

There's a very lovely and very strange and somewhat hilarious hysterical book called *Letters: Summer 1926* that came out recently, letters of Pasternak, Rilke and Marina Tsvetayeva, written together over a period of several months in the summer of 1926, in a kind of circle to each other, each one misunderstanding the other and falling in love with each other, and so on. I came across one letter that Pasternak had written to Rilke, which is actually published at the end of *Safe Conduct.* It begins: "If you were alive, this letter I would send today. I have just finished writing *Safe Conduct,* dedicated to your memory"—an interesting rhyme with Spicer's letters to the dead. And this morning I came across Flaubert's mother in a letter to him. The quotation is: "Your mania for sentences has dried up your heart." I immediately started worrying.

In one of Hölderlin's fragments, among the last of his poems before he entered into the thirty-five years of madness, he writes, *Es fesselt / Kein Zeichen,* which Richard Sieburth in his recent edition of Hölderlin's *Hymns and Fragments* translates as: *No sign / Binds.* It struck me as one of the sources of the modern lyric and certainly of German Expressionism—this notion of disintegration of faith in the sign. In Hölderlin's case, he's talking about the metaphysical relationship of the sign, the fact that earth and

heaven no longer connected, that you could no longer converse
with God, that our signs do not translate in the literal ecclesi-
astical sense of *translatio:* the bearing across from one realm to
another. And that equally we cannot read the signs of God in the
world anymore. And it struck me that, in his context, the unravel-
ing of the sign was involved with the unraveling of the subject,
because Hölderlin is about to enter into madness, and many of
the works he will write in his madness he signs with the name
Scardanelli, in whatever kind of schizophrenia he was in, and
dated them in the twentieth century, which in its own curious
way was an extraordinarily prophetic event. Extraordinary in the
sense that he projected this disintegrated subject into the next
century where it would have so many manifestations.

   Hölderlin's work, the late work, makes a fascinating paral-
lel with the anxiety of signification that comes along with mod-
ernism and, also, with contemporary linguistics and philosophy.
The sense of doubt about the relationship between (within a sign,
let's say, the signifier and the signified) the acoustical image and
the concept, which is one way of looking abstractly at the sign.
What is striking is the fact that we can no longer put these two
together, that, as Lacan would put it, there's a bar between these
two things, and is that bar permeable or not? And then the fur-
ther anxiety that has been expressed by a number of poets, phi-
losophers, and simply human beings, about their relationship to
a referent in the world, suddenly understanding that they may or
may not refer to the world, that languages break down when we
live in a world where pacification means annihilation. In the case
of Vietnam, what is reference?

   Obviously, this is a concern that came up most dramatically
and poignantly with the attempt to annihilate the Jews in World
War II, and the attempt by Hitler to appropriate an entire lan-
guage, totalitarian appropriation of language. But it is also some-
thing that we find in modern linguistics as the sign begins to be
analyzed. And it's a thing that poets, I might add, resist tremen-
dously. The Objectivist poets, for example, who determinedly stay

within the possibility of reference. George Oppen keeps affirming and reaffirming throughout his life the possibility of the simple words—house, tree, hill—to mean something. It's an act of faith on Oppen's part. In the German tradition it becomes much more problematic.

You have the question, also, of someone like Wittgenstein, where an entire body of work is built on an anxiety about the fragility of signification. At the simplest level we face the fact that *tree* means tree in English but *tree* doesn't mean tree in French. There is no absolute relation which people in a certain act of faith have clung to as a possibility throughout time. There is a certain arbitrariness outside a given language system, so that the possibility of reference and signification rests on an agreement we make in community, and once community begins to disintegrate that agreement begins to break down. In Wittgenstein you have a philosopher of language who deals across a lifetime with this problem. If someone says, "I am in pain," you wonder what that means. If you take it for granted, fine, but if you begin to think about it, "you" wonder do "they" mean pain in the way "I" mean it, do they mean pain in the sense that their toe hurts, or do they mean they're in metaphysical pain? What's the tone of what they're saying? Are they joking? Facetious? Ironic? Have they just made love and say "I am in pain" ironically in order to say how good they feel, how relaxed they feel, or perhaps to say that they actually do feel pain? If you begin to look at the expression, the thing itself, it begins to have a quality of uncertainty. It's like looking at anything under a microscope, where the whole disappears. If you look at the table under the microscope, instead of the table you see all these parts in motion, and you can't find the object again.

This doubt leads to the lyric voice, the problematics of self-expression, as when (with Hölderlin) the unitary and integral self itself is very much in question, and therefore the unitary voice is in question, and the possibility of controlling the tone and all of those things. The self comes dramatically into question if one is going to face the actual condition of the individual. All of these things in a century of holocaust, or multiple holocausts. We think of one holocaust in one respect, but there's been ten or twenty. Millions of people, a worldwide human event.

What you have, finally, is a real crisis of representation and signification to the point where a philosopher, a social philosopher, like Adorno out of the Frankfurt School, spoke of the impossibility or even the immorality of poetry after the Holocaust, in the *Minima Moralia*—a fascinating mixture of things, by the way, a book that has some of the most stunning insights into American culture, and some of the most stunningly mandarin misreadings of American culture, particularly of popular culture, which he is constantly dismissing and speaking about with a sort of mandarin European intellectual misapprehension. But this is a work that is intermittently one of the most lucid feminist tracts I have ever come across. Adorno and the other members of the Frankfurt School, of course, were articulating a neo-Marxist philosophy, political philosophy, and at the same time they tended to be in their persons very conservative European intellectuals. I was recently talking to a person who had studied under Adorno, a German named Klaus Reichert, and Klaus had been studying under him when Adorno was attacked, to his own horror and disbelief, by Left-extremist students during the 1968 manifestations, and he died not long after that of a heart attack. And I was saying to Klaus that really since that time it was interesting how Adorno and a number of other people had become fashionable in academic circles in America as part of a discourse about the Left, as part of a radical intellectual discourse, and Klaus looked at me in disbelief and said: "Adorno *wasn't* radical."

I think of two poets in particular who are important to this notion of an analytic lyric that I would propose here as a way to address the problematics of the purely private utterance in such a time. One is Edmond Jabès, an Egyptian Jew who was exiled after the 1956 Suez Crisis (the Jews were driven from Egypt). He moved to Paris with his family, and the day after he arrived he went for a walk outside of the house where he was staying, and he saw written on a wall, in English, to add to the strangeness of it, "JEWS GO HOME." At that point Jabès began to think about his own human condition as a Jew, as a person who was exiled into the book, and he began to think about addressing the impossibility of writing after the Holocaust. *The Book of Questions* is his answer, a dispersal of voices. In contrast to Celan, Jabès constructs a theater of the page, with fragments of poetry, prose, questions being asked by imaginary rabbis, all with a thread in a nonnarrative way, an almost implicit story of the Holocaust, a story of a pair of young lovers and death in the concentration camps. But the story is never told, the story exists in the margins, and the book is filled with what one would characterize as silence, silence as a refusal of the authoritarian, as a way of not turning his own structure into an authoritarian discourse. In Jabès' case, if you do not allow for silence—silence being the place where you reply to the question, where you reply to the other—if you do not allow for silence, if you don't allow the space for people to ask, then you are appropriating the discourse and entering, then, yourself, into an authoritarian mode. And so, he creates this strategy of fragments, of unanswered questions, incompletions and fractures, in a structure of loss. But it is also a structure of response to the appropriation of language in his time. The sense of the word within this structure is one with an infinite series of possible regressions behind it with this hope of recovering the meaning of words in a time when words have lost their meaning. He constructs exactly out of what is considered the nondiscursive, the spaces between things, the junctures, the breaks and fragments.

On the other hand, there's a poet like Paul Celan, who constructed a body of work where he addresses, in a radically different way from Jabès, the question of the self in language, the lyric self in language. Where Jabès creates this dispersal of voices across the page, Celan creates this concentration, almost an implosion—because Celan is writing in a language destroyed by fire, the speaker destroyed by fire. His response to the discourse of totalitarianism is to create out of the German Expressionist tradition a body of intensely concentrated lyric poetry that addresses the reconstruction of human speech, I was fascinated and very much moved by the sense of the dispersal of the subject, but also the reaffirmation, the fact that it was nobody's voice and yet it was, also, something—again and again and again. The circumstance of the impossibility of reading the world.

Such figures of the international lyric, the investigatory aspects, the taking over of the lyric concentration on the code itself, on the texture of language, the taking over the condensation of lyric emotion and focusing it then on the mechanics of language—I guess is the way I want to put it—in the case of Jabès and Celan among others as a critique of the discourse of power, to renew the function of poetry. I suppose one reason why I am addressing this is that I'm very concerned with the notion of the lyrical as simply an indulgence. For example, among the so-called Language Poets in San Francisco, this is something that Ron Silliman brings up again and again, his own mistrust of the lyric and his attempt to remain entirely outside anything that might smack of the lyrical. And so I thought, well, here I've been operating in the lyrical for twenty years, so I'd better find out why, why the lyrical seems to me still a possibility, a signifying possibility, and why often it doesn't at all, when I see a certain aspect of lyric practice where it does indeed seem trivial.

This notion of the incorporation of silence is one that I want to hold in brackets as we go along, and the notion of doublings of the subject, dissociations, junctures, and ruptures, and a lyric that operates from an economy of loss. The other thing that I would point to, going back to Spicer, is the other forms of lyric practice such as the Madrid School: Lorca, Hernandez, Aleixandre, etc. These are the great poets of the Spanish Republic. Lorca, of course, is well known here, and everyone throws the *duende* around like it was a ham sandwich. Hernandez, also, is a fascinating poet who's been, again, wretchedly translated, who was a shepherd who came down out of the hills around Madrid. He came into town at the age of seventeen or eighteen and sought out the poets and started spouting extraordinary and very sophisticated and very moving poetry. Someone who was jailed by the fascists, as they all were—jailed or murdered—and who wrote great poems from prison, all of them based in a flamenco culture, a culture of song, which goes back not so much to European roots but to Moorish roots, roots that are marginal to any mainstream European culture. These poets were people who, in terms of the Spanish cultural landscape, were always operating at the margins. With someone like Lorca this is compounded by his homosexuality, which marginalizes the self in its own way.

I would point also to the great Peruvian poet César Vallejo as another instance of this kind of practice. Again, a politically radicalized poet whose experiences are very different from our own, who grows up in Peru, and gets himself into trouble writing crazy poetry, spends a certain amount of time in Lima—and one reason why we can't reproduce this occasion is that this city was founded by the conquistadors through which they channeled all the gold and the slave trade of the New World. The poetry has a history very hard for us to comprehend in its full immediacy, its fullest resonance. Vallejo created a ferocious poetry with a great deal of political resonance.

It's interesting to relate this to the problem of political poetry in the United States, which tends to become doctrinal or an occasion for self-display. You take, let's say, the poets' Nicaragua shuttle and go down for ten days, then you return and become a hero of the Revolution. For those who are interested, to come to the deeper responsibility of the political is every bit as difficult and demanding as coming to the deeper responsibility of the emotional. It's instructive to go to the poets for whom the political is not a "topic."

I don't know, it seems to me that teaching is mostly bibliographical, and saying what has been of interest to you, rather than trying to teach people how to make a poem in some mechanical sense of "clean up your metaphor in line 3." It seems much more instructive and useful to point to the poets with whom you can be in conversation. In that respect, a poet I've translated is Vicente Huidobro, a Chilean poet, whose work began like Vallejo's to some degree, but who went to Paris—was influenced by Reverdy—and then returned to South America where his poetry took on a more singular character. ("Voice," that's another misused word.) Also the great Russian poets of the Revolution, of the time around the Revolution, such as Akhmatova, Mandelstam, Tsvetayeva, and others, who are also investigating at this level the functions of language, and someone like Velimir Khlebnikov writing, partly, sound poetry, which is a way in his case of investigating the structure of language, something that often gets misunderstood as a kind of nonreferential babble or Dadaism, Dada sound poetry, and it's neither of those.

From the French, I guess, in part, one can refer to Apollinaire and the incorporation of immediate information, the information that someone like Frank O'Hara in his own very beautiful way (when he writes a poem while he's talking on the telephone about talking on the telephone while he's writing a poem and spilling his coffee on the typewriter). It isn't an easy thing to do, as the mess that some of the second-generation New York School poets made of all those walking-around-eating-lunch poems demonstrates. It's an active discipline of attention. Apollinaire is one of the sources for that kind of thing, with his incorporation of the immediate and the rupture of the single unitary voice, and the rupture of any unitary mode—tone, subject, and so on.

Three: And the Other Arts

It has always seemed to me terribly unfortunate that most English departments are ignorant of the fact that Pierre Boulez is giving a concert next door, or that a major American painter is showing up to talk about his or her work. You get that curiously enclosed sense of what the field is, and I've always taken a field as a thing where, if it has boundaries, it's in the Heideggerian sense of *peras* (which we get in *periphery*). The field has active boundaries, boundaries that are always shifting.

I was asked to write about a dance I had just collaborated on with Margaret Jenkins and her dance company. We ended up calling the dance *First Figure* (the book was still in proofs) and it became a curious parallel, in space, to what I was working with on the page. And so I was asked to write about this experience for a magazine called *Places*, a quarterly journal of environmental design. The article is called "Figures in Space":

> In writing we confront various manifestations of time. There is the "real time" of writing itself, the slippery succession of nows during which we compose. There's the phenomenological duration of the text, the time of its silent reading or oral delivery. Enfolded in the text is a labyrinth of tenses designating past, present, and projected future action, a metaphoric representation of being in time. In a poem, of course, the various measures lie in stress groupings, and stanzas articulate the smaller and larger periods of the piece and define its particular tempo. If the work is sooner or later accepted as significant, it will alter perceptions of previous works and will continue to acquire its audience into the future. Amid diverse perceptions it will exist across time.

> Space is perhaps initially the page, standing for the silence within which writing is unfolded. Space also designates the interior silences of the text, the junctures between stanzas, lines, words, even letters. Space in this respect is a function of time, marking levels of duration, allowing the text to breathe. One can speak, too, of the undisclosed space in which one works as affecting the character of things: cork-lined room, airplane, prison, terrace above the sea. I know one famous French writer who composed the better part of a book in the métro on his way to work. Its form? Fragments of anecdote, voices rapidly succeeding one another, questions hanging in the air.

In dance, movement articulates space even as it is, in turn, being transformed by it. You and the dancers make a dance in a rehearsal space but you must project it into a variety of possible performance spaces: proscenium theaters, lofts, gymnasiums, parks, et al. In the composition of most dance, unlike most poetry, you have a deadline: the work is announced for such and such a date, the audience you hope will be there, and the work had better be there as well. This fixed time of composition profoundly affects how you work: you must attend to the calendar and ultimately submit to it, even as the work must submit in some sense to the dimensions and conditions of the place of performance. "Real space."

Real space is both a limit and an initiator of movement and sound. It defines the event as surely as temporal periods define the poem. When the particular dance event ends it is gone, there are no pages to turn back, and it has vanished into a space now empty and darkened. This ephemerality, the experience of evanescent durations, is essential to its nature. Performance draws its quite desperate meaning from it.

Initially, of course, in that particular cityscape of New York, surrounded by work, I think the first thing before I was listening to new music, was the presence—even as a young teenage kid somewhat befuddled—of abstract painting, gestural abstraction, action painting. The painters in particular of the first and second generations of the New York School. Painters whose information going out to a larger public was met in great measure with bafflement and ridicule. It's amazing in this respect to think of how rapidly it was commodified and then exported as a kind of American creative freedom, and then within another couple of years it appears on the walls of the banks and corporations of America—standing for what, I don't know.

But at the time those painters were largely outside the public eye, and one faced their work with the bewilderment and embarrassment, even, with which one confronts something entirely new. I remember the first show of new painting I went to—it must have been when I was twelve or thirteen—at the Museum of Modern Art. I think I was in there with my mother, actually. There was a woman trailing behind with her child, and she started explaining, in order to be helpful to the kid, that actually these paintings had all sorts of pictures in them, and you only had to know how to look. She started pointing out sailboats and houses and trees. I remember a mixture of—initially—relief, that if we looked hard enough the figures would emerge, and it would be a painting after all, and then disappointment, that all they'd done was to hide these things in the paint. And then, of course, inadequacy, since I couldn't see the damn boats and trees and buildings at all. I did come away with a real fascination and wonder about this thing that I had no terms for approaching.

Over time my relation to those paintings and to later painting developed into one of reciprocality in relation to my work. I think a lot of what I was drawing from had to do with something that I'll get back to later in relation to dance, this question of gesture and gesturality in the physical, vocalic utterance: When you have the text with the voice itself absent there's an ambiguity just as there's an ambiguity about the spatiality of the page in relation to the space of the physical room. There's that question which gets batted around endlessly, *écriture,* writing and speech and authorial absence, ultimately beyond the bald fact that the author, the small author, is not in the book. Partly a question of a kind of subscription we make to one picture or another. One of the problematics of bringing the French model of absence and *écriture* over into American writing is that American writers have been so eager to presence themselves, in whatever complex and ambiguous ways, at least since the time of Whitman, *in the book.* I think it makes no sense to deny that hopeless urge as being a significant one, or an illusory one.

There is an extraordinary moment in abstract painting, for example, where we have the trace of the gesture in the air, actually

present, and we have physical paint, and we have the thing stand-
ing for itself. This has always thrilled and depressed me, because it
seems so beyond the goals of a possible writing. I've always held a
tremendous envy of painters, being able to bypass some of the cir-
cuitry and physically work with the body of this *thing*. I remember
going to a Jackson Pollock retrospective, and the first thing that
hit you was this overwhelming, wonderful smell of oil. Pollock so
thickly layered his paintings that the paint is probably going to
spend the next three hundred years trying to dry. The whole room
stank of oil. It was like a house being painted. There was nothing
genteel about the event. It did start me thinking usefully outside
the given poetics—New Critical authority and the limits and the
unitary nature of the poem, the poetic object as they posited it,
since I was looking very much for alternative models. I also didn't
want to grow up to be a member of one of those men's clubs that
the New Critics were endlessly posing for—in their beards—look-
ing like they've just been in some terrible tragedy, that this was
serious business—a matter of endless pedagogy and authority. I
guess I was drawn to the romantic image of the painters covered
with their own stuff—still am—and wanted to conceive of a life
outside of that image of the academy. (I don't want this to sound
childishly antiacademic, in the sense that I do respect the work
that gets done there by very interesting people.) I didn't want any
kind of circumscription of the art, an art that had to obey certain
given dictates in order to signify within a particular community.

I referred to the notion of field. I loved the way Pollock's
painting spilled off the canvas and out over its edges. That there
was a certain amount of arbitrariness to lifting the thing away
from its bed of paint and *that* becoming the work. One of the
things that I learned from de Kooning was how to deal with an
emerging work, not in terms of correcting the work—again, in
discussion with people like Creeley, I found that Bob's model of
the one-shot poem, that you either made or you didn't make it,
was simply inadequate to the notion of layering I was involved
with, and the fact that a lot of my work takes a great deal of time

to complete, and yet I was drawn to his sense of staying away from one aspect of revision, which is the normative sense of revising to conform to certain expectations. And so, I turned to de Kooning, who in an interview talked about returning and returning to the first moment of the canvas, and the layering process, the process of accretion and the process of emergence. In other words, you return into the act of the thing until the thing is complete. This seemed a way of evading revision as correction that would allow one to layer the work and to allow it to acquire levels of complexity and disjuncture.

These terms that we deal in are not posited solely as the territory of the poem. If they were solely the territory of the poem, if they did not have a referential value in the world, then the poem itself would be a relatively trivial event. But when we speak of field and durations and successions, and so on, we're speaking of elements of our human ontology, of the actual structures we can see in the cosmos. It was Stockhausen, for example, who started composing—in his middle period, before he went completely cosmic—with the beat as something you would feel initially in your pulse, and that it corresponds with a mathematically verified cosmic pulsing that occurs every 8,000 years or so. An instance, again, of the fact that these things are relational, and are not limited to what we mistakenly think of as the scale of the poem: the starts and stops and the ways of figuring duration and figuring time. The poem "The Circular Gates" is a work (characteristically, I suppose, disjunctive) written in relation to the Vietnam War, and about war in some larger sense, its horrendous contention. I was trying to think back and forth between Vietnam and art, the paradox of trying to enter these pure events that seem to be nonreferential and politically nonspecific. I could almost only make sense by bringing them into a radical disjunction. But for me it was very much a poem against the war. Formally, the central thing was trying to deal with recurrence and sequentiality—seriality, if you will—in relation to what I derive from someone like Stella, rather than a literary, thematic recurrence, though it does thematize itself as it goes along. I wanted to do it in the material nature of those recurrent phrases, so that in an accretive way, even though the work was not in itself continuous and narrative, the central figures of the discourse would preserve themselves.

This is a thing that carries out into my work with dance, where you have the problem of doing something that is naturally complex and difficult to apprehend while difficult movement is going on. One of the things I settled on was designing a pattern of recurrence, since I was giving up narrative sequence and linearity, as one way of making things present to people, perhaps even comprehensible, so that by simply *coming back* the figures of the work would become comprehensible even though they might not have their conventional place in a discourse—noun, verb, object, and so on—that their weight would be cumulative. I had never realized how, oddly enough, there is one rhyme present: war, everything begins to rhyme with war, so that all of these elements of painting and all of these various texts are brought into configuration with what is the undisclosed subject of the piece. And trying to deal with words *beside* any sense of literary consideration, but the way you would deal with them as paint, deliberately ignoring their actual referential nature.

The only other thing I would add, in relation to painting, is that in the last few years I've been working in collaboration with a painter named Irving Petlin in New York, a painter who has evolved outside the stylistic fashions of New York. His roots—he's from Chicago—are in German Expressionism and if not Surrealism, a certain "sur-real" figuration, rather than the more formalist Cubist orientation in New York. Our collaboration took the form of talking about the way figures emerge in a work as significant. One of the things that always fascinated me about Irving's work, as opposed to some of the quick-shot work you see in New York, is the things that come to stand for things, the things that signify, the signs, evolve over time. Someone who was interviewing me recently remarked on the fact that there were certain words and phrases in my work, like *red* and *and so on*, that seem to have an accretive weight through the duration of a book, and Irving has such figures in his paintings. There's an early painting called *The Green Chair*, and it's a painting of a green wooden chair that's been in his studio forever, which he has covered with paint over the years, and it emerges as a sign that's uncertain. And then this green chair starts appearing in all sorts of work of his. At one point, for example, in a recent painting that's in his current show at the Marlborough, this green chair is sitting on a balcony overlooking a landscape vaguely filled with figures from his own childhood, or pre-childhood, the stetl life of his forebears in Poland. So this green chair becomes a vehicle for presencing this painter back in the landscape of memory, so to speak. These things are evolutionary: you don't place something in a poem, it has to have the character of emergence from the work. The figure cannot be a device. One of the problems I referred to in relation to James Wright and the Deep Image is that it's the appropriation of something that is emergent over time in an entire cultural tradition, that you cannot simply pluck from that context and bring over as a compositional mechanism. All you'll end up with is contrivance.

Painting has been allowed much more latitude, in relation to juxtaposition and freedom, maybe because of its material aspect, its commodity aspect, than a much more conservative literary world allows the poem. It keeps retreating from the Anglo-American empirical tradition. I remember a number of times reading in art galleries, for example, where the room would be filled with women with four eyes on one side of their head, or no eyes at all, and thinking that the same audience that was going to have no problem with the permissions that these paintings represented, was going to have all kinds of problems with similar permissions or liberties or deviations performed in the text. Likewise in relation to music—the exploratory nature of compositional processes is still a given, though mass audiences tend to remain in the nineteenth-century repertory, which was built for them. (I don't mean "masses" in any derogatory sense, but the music that was built for the rising middle class and that addressed it specifically.) At least in orthodox literary circles, it becomes once again very dubious if your procedural methodology deviates from accepted models of composition. Why is that? But feeling that sense of the exploratory as being more energetic elsewhere is why I went to music and painting, among many other poets, for models of possibility.

[*Talks given at the Iowa Writers Workshop, University of Iowa, February 1986. First published in* Pavement 7, 1986.]

AUTOBIOGRAPHY, MEMORY AND
MECHANISMS OF CONCEALMENT

Possibly to begin: dinner at Michael Davidson's Berkeley apartment with Robert Duncan in 1971. I mentioned the difficulty I was having writing, that is, inventing, an autobiographical note for my first book with Black Sparrow Press, *Blake's Newton*. A special delivery letter had arrived from the publisher early that morning urging me to finally send the note along with a photograph so that the book could go to press. So the question who I had been or was going to claim to be, alongside a poet's face, apparently mine, on final page of book that same poet had apparently written. Cloned as a chance by-product of the Manhattan Project in the early forties? Born in Tierra del Fuego under still mysterious circumstances to the mistress of the British vice-consul? Dago alto saxophonist from Boston? (Novelists are great at this—they all seem to have worked on lobster boats.) How in fact to fill a space approximately two by three inches—with words—in such a way that at the end that space would appear to a reader perfectly blank, or as the French can't stop themselves from saying, white? or maybe to take the special delivery letter as a message not to publish the book at all, given my inevitable doubts that it and its so-called author had attained anything like "identity." Who in face had written the book? Some sense of a person in his late twenties, 5' 11½", 160 lbs., clean-shaven. Identifying marks would

include barely visible scar over left eyebrow and one on left index
finger caught in bathroom door of hotel apartment (Room 1108)
at age two. Mother had rushed to doctor's office, child in arms,
holding the virtually severed fingertip fully functional if slightly
deformed. Minor atrophy of left calf muscle due to congenital
lower-back condition. I.e., characteristic micro-asymmetries:

> I paced up and down my room from early morning until twi-
> light. The window was open, it was a warm day. The noises of
> the narrow street beat in uninterruptedly. By now I knew every
> trifle in the room from having looked at it in the course of my
> pacing up and down. My eyes had traveled over every wall. I had
> pursued the pattern of the rug to its last convolution, noted ev-
> ery mark of age it bore. My fingers had spanned the table across
> the middle many times. I had already bared my teeth repeatedly
> at the picture of the landlady's dead husband.   (June 25, 1914)

He was assigned exercises by the osteopath and told that he could
expect increasing discomfort over time, confirmed by the twinges
I feel in lower back, buttocks and thighs as I'm writing this fifteen
years later. A third scar toward the center of the forehead result-
ing from the fall while chasing wire-haired terrier through neigh-
bor's enclosed garden down the street from the hotel at age four.
Surprisingly little pain. My own oddly calm assumption that I
was dying, given that I couldn't see through the torrent of blood
pouring from the wound. Pervasive scent of ether, nuns in white
habits and so on. Constant voice in background mysteriously re-
peating, "Is it critical, is it critical?"

On hearing of the problem, Duncan offered to compose the
biographical note himself. I accepted and he immediately wrote
the following:

> I think Michael Palmer was delivered two blocks astray in 1943
> because he was aborted at our address two months before. Now
> he has arrived I think a long way from the Rhinelander Apart-

ments in Greenwich Village with a poetry addressed to occupant to refund the Indians for the Manhattan sell.

The next day I sent it (special delivery, memory tells me, as a return gesture) to John Martin at Black Sparrow with instructions to use it as the biographical note. In fact when the book appeared Robert's note had been placed below the photograph and above it was the following:

> Michael Palmer was born in New York City in 1943. He was educated at Harvard University and now lives and works in San Francisco.

So. So a decision had been made, if not by the writer whose identity was at issue, to reimpose order and offer an outline of the "real" facts. A person had been born, raised, educated certainly, had lived somewhere and moved somewhere else and presumably there were additional "real" facts that could be supplied to responsible parties upon inquiry. The reader was to be relieved of any puzzlement or unease generated by Robert's note. Something responsible *was* going on: the writer came from a place writers come from, had gone to a place writers often go to (his experience could be said to span a continent), and he had the imprimatur of an institution known for its sobriety in literary matters. The "added" note (for so now Robert's must appear, as subsequent to the real in the eye's natural passage down the page) could be effectively contextualized as metaphoric speech which, if somehow "real" in itself, could not be taken as answerable to or standing for the other "real" that in this case was the set of events and circumstances that go to make up a life. The following from Satie's *Memoirs of an Amnesiac* speaks, it seems to me, to similar expectations and assumptions:

(Part 2, "The Day of a Musician")

An artist ought to regulate his life.

Here is the exact time-table of my daily life:

Get up: at 7:18 a.m.; inspired from 10:23 to 11:47. I lunch at 12:11 p.m. and leave the table at 12:14.

A healthy turn on the horse to the end of my grounds: from 1:19 to 2:53. More inspiration: from 3:12 to 4:07.

Various occupations (fencing, reflections, napping, visits, contemplation, dexterity, swimming, etc. . . .): from 4:21 to 6:47.

Dinner is served at 7:16 and ends at 7:20. Then symphonic readings (out loud): from 8:08 to 9:59.

Going to bed takes place regularly at 10:37. Once a week I awake with a start at 3:19 a.m. (Tuesdays).

I sleep with one eye closed; my sleep is deep. My bed is round with a hole to put my head through. Hourly a servant takes my temperature and gives me another.

For a long time I have subscribed to a fashion magazine. I wear a white cap, white socks, and a white vest.

My doctor has always told me to smoke. To this advice he adds: "Smoke, my friend: if it weren't for that, another would be smoking in your place."

So possibly to begin: much of the complexity in both writing autobiography and discussing it derives from the obvious fact that (leaving aside the convention of William Holden's posthumous narrator in *Sunset Boulevard*) you are also continuing to experience a life, spilling coffee, walking around, accumulating lists of things to do next (that *must* be done next), thus anticipating still further experience at least to some degree continuous with, even deriving from, present experience, and thus to a great degree "linear." Ultimately there is a *definition* that occurs as Gregory Bateson argues "by relation," in fact a story, defining that form as a "knot or complex of that species of connectedness which we call *relevance*" where "any A is relevant to any B if both A and B are parts or components of the same 'story.'" The complication being that while the story is being told the story is going on—at least something is going on—possibly the story of the story, though in fact the story is manifestly other than the sequence of events that through selection and organization go to make up the story. Is the "life" then not the story? Are we in an area like that *regressus ad infinitum* Wittgenstein suggest with the question, "If 'red' is the name of a color, then what is the name of the word 'red'?"? Actually we do confront a dilemma not unlike that of language philosophers, forced to discuss language by means of language, which has led the less optimistic advocates to invoke an indeterminacy principle for such operations.

> The schizophrenic young man was thin like many people in such mental states. Moreover he seemed in effect malnourished. As a result of his very sedentary life, almost that of an invalid (which from many points of view he was), he had very poor musculature and was very weak, that weakness being perhaps an important agency of the great fear which his wide-open eyes reflected; fear of nature as well as of his fellow creatures, fear of death as well as in some sense of life. His face and in particular his mouth seemed contorted most of the time by a mixture of sadness and pain, the mouth being moreover quite small and the corners of the lips turned downward.

This is my translation of the opening passage of *Le Schizo et Les Langues*, written in French by an American, Louis Wolfson. Gilles Deleuze compares Wolfson's procedures to those adopted by Raymond Roussel. Wolfson describes himself as both "student of schizophrenic languages," and "schizophrenic student." He writes in French from a necessary rejection of the mother tongue. That is, unable literally to endure the words of his mother without enormous pain, he must learn a variety of other languages (French, German, Hebrew, and Russian) in order to convert English words as rapidly as possible into foreign words of a similar sound as well as meaning. Like Roussel he must search out elaborate homeomorphic equivalents. So the work, his schizophrenic memoir, consists of a complex chain of linguistic displacements, transformations, and concealments. What is there (or what was there is) can only emerge by passing into a medium where as such it is not. In writing as in his life he must hide from himself what is being spoken and spoken of, in order first to hear and then apotropaically to name it himself. And variously he names himself, "le jeune home schizophrénique," "l'aliené," "l'étudiant schizophrénique," "le schizophrène," "le jeune homme malade mentalement," "le psychotique," "le schizo," and so on insistently, as if to establish a single identity among the multiple nominations that substitute for the absent first-person—as if to make sameness out of difference and deny the alienating or differentiating procedure itself. The effort is paradoxically directed toward a return to a single, unitary language, a prelapsarian concordance between word and thing, or language and experience. In opposition to the text itself, it represents a denial of translation, of the multiplicity of dialects among individuals as well as language groups. So in the book he tells of his bewilderment as a child at the notion of Chinese as the language spoken by the greatest number of people when in fact the language is subdivided into a multiplicity of mutually indecipherable dialects.

> Toward evening I walked over to the window and sat down on the low sill. Then, for the first time not moving restlessly about, I happened calmly to glance into the interior of the room and at the ceiling. And finally, finally, unless I were mistaken, this room which I had so violently upset began to stir. The tremor began at the edge of the thinly plastered white ceiling. Little

pieces of plaster broke off and with a distinct thud fell here and there, as if at random, to the floor. I held out my hand and some plaster fell into it too; in my excitement I threw it over my head into the street without troubling to turn around. The cracks in the ceiling made no pattern yet, but it was already possible somehow to imagine one. But I put these games aside when a bluish violet began to mix with the white; it spread straight out from the center of the ceiling, which itself remained white, even radiantly white, where the shabby electric lamp was stuck. Wave after wave of the color—or was it light?—spread out toward the now darkening edges. One no longer paid any attention to the plaster that was falling away as if under the pressure of a skillfully applied tool. Yellow and golden-yellow colors now penetrated the violet from the side. But the ceiling did not really take on these different hues; the colors merely made it somewhat transparent; things striving to break through seemed to be hovering above it, already one could almost see the outlines of a movement there, an arm was thrust out, a silver sword swung to and fro. It was meant for me, there was no doubt of that; a vision intended for my liberation was being prepared.   (June 25, 1914)

It is interesting to compare Wolfson's self-designations with the studied neutrality of those found in *The Education of Henry Adams*, also written in the third-person. As Adams states near the beginning, "life was double," and the self's double is presented as "the child," "the boy," "the boy Henry," "the rather slow boy," "young Adams," "the young man," "the private secretary," "Adams' son" [sic], "the newcomer," "the Assistant Professor," even—when meeting Kipling—"the American," but most often Adams is simply "he," proposed with the muted Brahmin irony that sets the tone of the work. This "other" Adams is cast afloat among the forces of velocity and change the narrator Adams attempts to quantify by analytic observation. "He" is proposed as an ephemeral particle ("His identity, if one could call a bundle of disconnected memories an identity, seemed to remain; but his life was once more broken into separate pieces. . . ."). At the same time the implicit "I" is unitary and reflective, at rest and distanced, the convention of the omniscient narrator (here the irony is also conscious) brought to bear upon the manifestations of self. The sum of the two is the full faculty of memory the "spider-mind" acquires. This memory is synthetic, as Adams notes, and results in a "life" consisting in great part of omissions (the exclusion of Adams' wife from the memoir being the most notorious). Of Adams we learn a great deal (in terms of quantifiable events) but also surprisingly little. "He" functions most often as an absence, since the pronominal shift empties the subject of self or possibly "myself." The studied neutrality is in its own way as violent or extreme in its alienation as Wolfson's, and in rereading *The Education* for this talk I found myself (I find myself) substituting the designations of Wolfson's persona for those of Adams', "le jeune homme schizophrénique," "l'aliené," etc.

> The horrible spells lately, innumerable, almost without interruption.

> Walks, nights, days, incapable of anything but pain.
>   (June 12, 1923)

The confession form occurs when there is an apparent refusal of displacement from the first-person, when the "I" is everywhere present to reveal itself not in the semidarkness of the confessional booth but in the full light the act of reading elicits. I want to look briefly at a couple of books which in somewhat different ways offer themselves as works of this kind, Augustine's *Confessions* and Hedy Lamarr's *Ecstasy and Me*.

What first interests me about Augustine is his concentration on phenomena such as memory, time, and discourse, that is, those elemental mechanisms and conventions that shape the text itself and are most often taken for granted, as if the categories so named were in fact given, in other words, understood and beyond question, wherever "understood" and "beyond question" are, insanely, paired (this could lead to an endless digression on, for example, the language of warfare—Vietnam would serve—or of the financial pages of our daily newspaper).

Augustine begins the *Confessions* with an invocation of God and a meditation on "presence-absence" as God's nature, a "transcendent presence" that will influence the manner of address and prayer. The concealedness and omnipresence of God as Logos, God's being as both active and at rest bring to mind pre-Socratic speculation on the nature of being and the word. Augustine's underlying assumption throughout the work is the inadequacy of words (as opposed to the Word) not only in approaching the sacred but also in attempting to describe human events and human emotions. "Fear," "pleasure," "pity," etc., are concepts supposedly "understood by all" and as such veil those emotions they pretend to represent. In moving to examine the central mechanism of the book, Augustine finds that memory is as illusive as experience. What is remembered? What is a mental image? What is the image of an image? What is memory as distinct from mind? How does one "search one's memory"? What is it to remember forgetfulness?:

> I can mention *forgetfulness* and recognize what the word means, but how can I recognize the thing itself unless I remember it? I am not speaking of the sound of the word but of the thing which it signifies. If I had forgotten the thing itself, I should be utterly unable to recognize what the sound implied. When I remember memory, my memory is present to itself by its own power; but when I remember forgetfulness, two things are present, memory, by which I remember it, and forgetfulness, which is what I remember. Yet what is forgetfulness but the absence of memory? When it is present I cannot remember. Then how can it be present in such a way that I can remember it? . . . etc. (Book X.16)

The anxiety expressed by the self-interrogation is similar to that of both Wittgenstein and Saussure (and of course the *Confessions* were a favorite text of Wittgenstein). Book XI contains a parallel questioning of the nature of time, in particular of duration vs. present time. How does time exist? How do past and future exist if time can only be measured in passing? His conclusion is that they exist by being present through words. The past is present through words grounded in memory; and when we "foresee" the future we are actually seeing present signs of future events. The three times then might be described as: 1) a present of past things, 2) a present of present things, and 3) a present of future things. He concludes, "Some such different times do exist in the mind, but nowhere else that I can see. . . . It is in my own mind then that I measure time. I must not allow my mind to insist that time is something objective." This may derive from Plato's notion of time in the *Timaeus* or a neo-Platonic version of same. Plato states, "For we say of time that it *was* and *shall be,* but on a true reckoning we should only say *is,* reserving *was* and *shall be* for the process of change in time. . . ." Both memory and time, then, are grounded in the present and its language. Events recalled are present acts, are events in language but in a language which by its nature resists the activity of revelation and naming even as it is spoken. The present, the presence of the speaker, both is and is not, and finally Augustine laments, "If only men's minds could be seized and held still." Augustine investigates both the subject-object relationship in discourse and the structural relationships that constitute the linguistic sign in order *to reveal what he is doing,* to confess the nature of his activity. It is also to confess the identity of self as memory, a "storehouse of the images of material things." And finally it is to confess the mediated and mediational character of all speech. Memory has no memory of the Logos and no being of its own. The relationship between signifier and signified must be reconstituted at each moment of the act of telling, in a constant state of uncertainty. From one point of view this is in fact Augustine's confession—that of the concealedness of language, even that of confessional revelation.

In *The Circular Gates* there is a poem entitled "The End of the Ice Age and Its Witnesses":

> Yesterday your fever returned
> It was near the middle of July
>
> and we went to see the red King
> Then I took out the net
>
> together with the red bird
> and put it down
>
> on the bank of the river. Could the
> flat milling stone and a
>
> subsistence on seeds be originally
> an American invention? We
>
> cuddled on the seat of the car
> until she said desperately
>
> I was never unhappier;
> then I told them that we wished to
>
> continue our journey
> because we were not reaching our destination
>
> at all. But the creatures of this island
> were very kind. The sky
>
> was a deep green, without clouds
> since the rain had been falling regularly

onto the lowest branch of a tamarack
where we hung by our knees. Considering

the look of the trees
we were somewhere in Canada

or the Northeast: flat, blue-green needles
0.8 to 1.3 inches long

that yellow in the fall; ovoid cones,
bark thin, scaly and

gray to reddish brown. The soil
is moist and spongy

under the car. E
is white like fog, and A dark,

cycles at some future time
to tell about—

the white tents in the primer
and the kind of flower that trembles easily—

Nothing of the sort is known
or probable on this side of the ocean

nor is there any early record of tents
On a given evening for example

they're playing cards
at the bottom of a swamp or pond; the Tartar

deserts light up; by the stairways
and armchairs of the rocks a

> small world, pale and flat
> "is coming to understand itself"

The poem draws upon a range of sources including Carl Sauer, Amos Tutuola's *The Palm-Wine Drunkard*, various poems and letters of Rimbaud, *Trees of North America* and Hedy Lamarr's *Ecstasy and Me* (a ghostwritten work, I should note, which she denounced due to claimed inaccuracies). The passage from Miss Lamarr's book reads:

> We got sandwiches and drove to a glen which is beautifully surrounded by trees and leads to the MGM backlot.
>
> "You made it big," Marcia said, "You must be very happy." She ate her sandwich with big bites, while I just nibbled at mine. I had no appetite.
>
> "I was never unhappier," I said, for the first time putting it into words.
>
> She was amazed.
>
> I explained what had been happening. I could see she didn't understand. She said plaintively, "I'll never be a big star. I'll always be a nothing. Two hundred dollars a week with overtime will be the limit. 'Marry a rich actor,' my mother tells me. I'm ready but where is he? They just want to get into my pants. After a lay they can't wait to get away. Men are so cruel."
>
> She was right—in a way, men are . . . etc. . . .
>
> She looked at me. "You're so beautiful," she said. "That's why you are a star. And—I hope you're not offended—you're so cold, so untouchable."

"No I'm not," I interrupted. Then gently I held her face in both hands and sympathetically kissed her. Her reaction was strange. She began to cry. I kissed her tears as if she were a child.

"I need love so desperately," she moaned. "And all I can get is sex. Oh, I hate men."

Then she hugged me tightly. "Will you be kind to me and just care a little, please?"

"Yes," I told her, "I will." . . . etc. . . .

We cuddled on the seat of the car until she said desperately, "I need you." Her hand went under my dress and all over me and I let her do what she wanted to and all my frustrations and hate left me. This was always the solution to my ills. When I came back to reality I realized we were both sobbing . . . etc. . . . [They drive back to the studio]

I thought of her often. It's murder for a girl to have too much need.

Dynamite stuff—but what stuff? What are we being told? Obviously that Hedy got it on with a starlet on a lunch break between takes of an MGM musical being directed by Gene Kelly. And the sensational, confessional aspect of the memoir has to do with the fact that: a) there were many many random couplings, b) a fair number of these were with women, and c) there was a lot of heartache. Now many of us qualify on all three counts but might not think to find an audience for these revelations, not a wide audience in any case, wider than say a circle interested in local literary gossip. Augustine, of course, is also involved with confession of sexual activity tied to a dynamic of spiritual struggle and self-understanding, and it is interesting to examine the convoluted intensity of his language in attempting to come to terms with this persistent aspect of his emotional make-up. With Hedy it's revelation because of the identity of the speaker. She is famous, the object of many private fantasies, and has led a public life constructed by studio PR agents and interspersed with sensational headlines. She is a love-goddess. Love-goddesses are: a) radically unobtainable, since they exist only on the screen and in large, guarded retreats in Beverly Hills, and b) never definitely never hardly ever bisexual, even when their attraction is blatantly epicene (the book appears in 1966 and this mythology has certainly evolved since—popular mythologies don't remain stable). So what is she telling? She is telling us that love-goddesses are often disturbingly attainable, regardless of the pedestal constructed to reinforce a stereotype of enthronement and desexualization; and that love-goddesses may be polymorphous perverse. What is she not telling? Anything. Once this is done there is nothing left. The language of her work, as is usually (but not always) the case, derives from soap opera and is a refusal of identity, that is of the layerings that constitute identity or presence. It is a refusal to tell (though I don't know if it's a willing refusal). As is true in most and possibly all styles of autobiography, the "I" functions as the most elaborate of shifters, and this complexity can be used or not, recognized or not. (There are at the very least two ways of hearing Rimbaud's "Je est un autre.") Darwin for example uses the first-person to project a persona of distinct modesty. In a sense it justifies itself by its resistance to self-promotion. The question naturally arises, "How close to that other 'I' doing the writing, a central figure of nineteenth- and twentieth-century science, is this projection?" Given the recent proliferation of works on the Darwin-Wallace controversy, it appears to be a question that will continue to resist resolution. Darwin's autobiographical memoir is not confessional at all. It reveals no intimate facts of his life and actually offers very little autobiographical detail. There is an interesting passage on the quality of his memory that may be meant to account for the shape of the work:

> My memory is extensive, yet hazy: it suffices to make me cautious by vaguely telling me that I have observed or read something opposed to the conclusion which I am drawing, or on the other hand in favour of it; and after a time I can generally recollect where to search for my authority. So poor in one sense is my memory, that I have never been able to remember for more than a few days a single date or a line of poetry.

Interestingly he portrays his memory as of the intuitive, random variety popularly associated with poetic memory, rather than the scientific kind, which (theoretical physics aside) we tend rightly or wrongly to imagine as precise, instant, and comprehensive within a given range of information. But to return for a moment to Hedy and confession. It is interesting that often the more elaborate the claims to confession become, the more intricate the question of concealedness grows—the very claim itself (whether in popular autobiography or Jean-Jacques Rousseau or Michel Leiris) lends a suspect intentionality to the speaking "I" and a teleological motive to the narrative. Often what is told is other than what it seems is being told or what is being claimed to be told. What, for example, is Rousseau revealing when he claims that he used to expose himself to schoolgirls? What is DeQuincy not telling us that the manner of his writing and the gaps within the narrative tell? And I'm still trying to return to Hedy for a moment and the resistance of her language to identity. I think here the opening passage of Laura Riding's *The Telling* may be useful:

> There is something to be told about us for the telling of which we all wait. In our unwilling ignorance we hurry to listen to stories of old human life, new human life, fancied human life, avid of something to while away the time of unanswered curiosity. We know we are explainable, and not explained. Many of the lesser things concerning us have been told, but the greater things have not been told; and nothing can fill their place. Whatever we learn of what is not ourselves, but ours to know,

being of our universal world, will likewise leave the emptiness
an emptiness. Until the missing story of ourselves is told, noth-
ing besides told can suffice us: we shall go on quietly craving it.

Before I am sure what she is saying about telling I am sure that
she is engaging language at an intimate point of resistance and
that this in itself is—telling. So there is a necessity involved which
we evade and to which we return or to which we are returned, in
anticipation of an impossible telling.

I do in fact enjoy the one-dimensionality of pop autobiogra-
phy (maybe it possesses that quality of blankness I was after for
the autobiographical note). In any case it has a specific linguistic
coloration, which in "The End of the Ice Age" I was trying to use
along with other language colors to make a kind of false auto-
biographical collage that might turn out to be quite true. I was
also interested in so to speak eliminating the seams so that one
thing might flow into another, Hedy for example into the vision-
ary mode of Rimbaud into the taletelling of Amos Tutuola, and
so on. (Remembering now, I think in the back of my mind also
was at least the feel of that "voyage of the soul" as a poetic form
found for example in the *Ch'u Tz'u* songs of the third century
BC which themselves developed out of earlier shamanistic chants
and songs and which we acquire through Dante among many
others, kabbalistic literature, and more recently the *voyage imagi-
naire* of French symbolism.) I suppose too I was bringing forward
the mechanisms of displacement that inhere in language, though
for me to say this may well be a kind of first-person deception.
Now I think I was doing that; *then* I think I was writing.

There is for me an interesting parallel with Bob Perelman's
very carefully titled "An Autobiography" which makes use of
Stendhal's *Vie de Henri Brulard*, Shackleton's memoirs, and Mo-
zart's letters, that is three lives in three kinds of writing. The
result is a complex and ironic document. For example near the
beginning, "But rest assured, dear Papa, that these are my very
own sentiments and have not been borrowed from anyone." The

irony there is of course double since the work is in a literal sense
borrowed, yet what it stands for—what it becomes—is not bor-
rowed at all, but is a singular act of aesthetic identity, an act of
disclosure that speaks quite clearly of the intent of the speaker
who is not speaking, or who is speaking only through the speech
of others. Could he even be said to speak by the fact of his con-
cealedness? The work makes explicit the otherness of the "I"
in autobiographical writing, its distance in time and proximity
as an invention. (Dostoyevsky justifies autobiographical writ-
ing as a *deliberate* form of address to this "other" or "brother.")
A further implication and further irony then seems to be that
we as readers or borrowers of these voices are no more distant
from them than their inventors are. The voices are in a sense
as much ours as theirs. The "I felt . . . ," or "I thought . . . ," of
autobiography (like language itself if we follow the Saussurean
model) proceeds by and is perceptible only through difference.
("Difference" here incurs identity, sameness, similarity, rhyme,
as functions of differentiation.) Were there no change of percep-
tual consciousness over time the writer would have no language
to portray experience and there would be no life to tell. And
there would be no memory. Even tribal memory, which is built
upon and reinforces an ideal of stasis, generates change through
transmission, that is, through an energy-order exchange. Philip
Morrison makes the point in "On Broken Symmetries" that in
the physical world you "pay *in energy* for *order.*" Symmetries are
made manifest to varying degrees in the physical world (for ex-
ample, among crystals as well as subatomic particles), but they
are never carried out to perfection. Perfect symmetry could only
occur at absolute zero temperature, with no randomness, but
at true zero the rate of formation would be zero and nothing
would happen. So there is always difference, gradation, varia-
tion by which we perceive. The I-I symmetry of autobiography
manifests varying degrees of brokenness and the work is real-
ized within that fracture. And—as in the physical world—it is
time (finite duration of events; infinite extension of random

possibility) that guarantees those disturbances and variations in which we are immersed.

The question of "real time" in autobiographical writing is as many-sided as the questions of persona and memory. In one obvious respect real time is the moment of the writing ("I felt pain" becomes "I remember I felt pain" becomes "I am remembering that I felt pain" becomes "I am writing remembering feeling pain" becomes what—some approximation of the (William) Jamesian "conscious" perhaps). And once done it is no longer *in* "real time" which may then pass over to the territory of reader as receiver of this more and more complexly encoded representation. Time only *is,* as Plato puts it, but if so, when? A small, golden-winged insect really is crawling across this page, has just fallen off the edge of the writing tablet, is lying upside down on the oak table, legs flailing as I write this but not now as I type it and not now as I speak it to you next Thursday at a time agreed upon. (It's Saturday night and I've just returned from seeing Carla Harryman's play. At the play Barrett Watten gave me a copy of his new book. I open to the first page and read, "Admit that your studies are over. Limit yourself to your memoirs. Identity is only natural. Now become the person in your life. Start writing autobiography.") Or my notebook entry of June 21st:

> The question in my Langton St. talk: if I'm not writing this now am I saying this now—am I at all remembering—etc. . . . And what of what I conceal here (and now). Eg., of what I did today (tomorrow) that I would not like some or all present to know—or if I wanted them to know all of what I did today (yesterday, tomorrow) what is it by that that I actually want them to suppose they know "of me": that I am purified by confession? that I have nothing to hide? that all I or anyone does is of interest? that someone else did it hidden inside by skin?
>
> Various types of nervousness. I think noises can no longer disturb me, though to be sure I am not doing any work now. Of

course, the deeper one digs one's pit, the quieter it becomes, the
less fearful one becomes, the quieter it becomes. (Oct. 6, 1915)

And my own notes again, from May 19th of this year:

Yeats' *The Trembling of the Veil* as in essence a succession of por-
traits and observations, aesthetic and spiritualist theory . . . re-
sulting in an analysis of an attitude of mind within his circle.
All "intimate" events absent and yet a sense of the intimate
presence of the poet (as he wishes to be present).

Equivalent possibly to his notion of the lyric as "abstract and
immediate"? Like Darwin and Adams he makes use of the trope
of self-effacement that is part, paradoxically, of the projection
of self, an approach common enough to autobiographical writ-
ing to be extremely difficult to recall to its sincerity.

Stanley Cavell in *Must We Mean What We Say* speaks of how phi-
losophy has always employed dogmatics against the possibility of
intellectual competition, and confession against dogmatics:

Inaccessible to the dogmatics of philosophical criticism, Witt-
genstein chose confession and recast his dialogue. It contains
what serious confessions must: the full acknowledgment of
temptation ("I want to say . . ."; "I feel like saying . . ."; "Here
the urge is strong . . .") and a willingness to correct and give
them up. . . . (The voice of temptation and the voice of correct-
ness are antagonists in Wittgenstein's dialogue.) In confessing
you do not explain or justify, but describe how it is with you.
And confession, unlike dogma, is not to be believed but tested,
and accepted or rejected.

(I seem to have left "time" behind, but maybe that's the nature
of talking this way.) So a body of work is offered as confessional
from which the *conventional* data of experience are rigorously ex-

cluded. It is interesting with Cavell to think of Wittgenstein's work as a project of self-knowledge and confession devoid of the recollections and information normally associated with such a task. Having noted Wittgenstein's admiration for Augustine, we can also see how their projects are comparable, how both concentrate on discussion of the means of such discussion, leading to elaborate—but in a sense revealed—methods (rituals?) of evasion and ellipsis. (Wittgenstein's acts of displacement, for example, as he discusses the nature of concealment in ordinary language, the gap between saying and meaning.) I am reminded of the hermetic intensity of Roland Barthes' essay in autobiography, *Roland Barthes by Roland Barthes* (translated by Richard Howard), "par lui-même," as the French put it, or "by himself" the pun might read in translation, because it is a singular document of isolated and isolating self-examination, and an explicit recognition of the nature of such enclosed discourse. I can only think of a few texts that so emphasize the radical alterity of the speaker (Kafka's journals have this effect), to the point where definition occurs frequently through Greek-derived neologisms, words constructed "par lui-même," to disclose themselves only by means of a concentrated hermeneutical effort on the part of the reader. Only occasionally does he break the pattern to catalogue that which he feels is "of no importance to anyone," and suddenly he sounds suspiciously like a writer of the so-called New York School:

> *I like*: salad, cinnamon, cheese, pimento, marzipan, the smell of new-cut hay . . . , roses, peonies, lavender, champagne, loosely held political convictions, Glenn Gould, too-cold beer, flat pillows, toast, Havana cigars, Handel, slow walks, pears, white peaches, cherries, colors, watches, all kinds of writing pens, desserts, unrefined salt, realistic novels, the piano, coffee, Pollock, Twombly, all romantic music, Sartre, Brecht, Verne, Fourier, Eisenstein, trains, Medoc wine, having change, *Bouvard et Pecuchet*, walking in sandals on the lanes of southwest France, the

bend of the Adour seen from Dr. L's house, the Marx Brothers, the mountains at seven in the morning leaving Salamanca, etc.

I don't like: white Pomeranians, women in slacks, geraniums, strawberries, the harpsichord, Miro, tautologies, animated cartoons, Arthur Rubinstein, villas, the afternoon, Satie, Bartok, Vivaldi, telephoning, children's choruses, Chopin's concertos, Burgundian branles and Renaissance dances, the organ, Marc-Antoine Charpentier, his trumpets and kettledrums, the politico-sexual, scenes, initiatives, fidelity, spontaneity, evenings with people I don't know, etc.

The work represents a resistance to such permission even as it portrays it. Such remarks are contextualized as trivial (lesser knowledge) and only in that way does Barthes feel free to insert them:

I like, I don't like: this is of no importance to anyone; this, apparently, has no meaning. And yet all this means: *my body is not the same as yours.*

And so the "bodily" is returned to the analytically distanced mode—yet is offered all the same—much as Hedy Lamarr offers herself and a conventionally framed apology at the same moment. It's an erotic tactic we have all one way or another probably been party to, ecstasy—ec-stasis—and me, I didn't know it was loaded.

But we do know it's loaded or hope it is or at least once was or was at least once. I am after all talking, the tongue and jaws moving, the uvula oscillating at a certain rate to determine the pitch. I am after all sitting here silently writing and so on, neither there nor here after all but at a given moment. . . .

In discussing shifters, Emile Benveniste asks:

. . . what then is the reality to which *I* or *You* refers? It is solely a "reality of discourse," and this is a very strange thing. *I* cannot be defined except in terms of "location," not in terms of objects as a nominal sign is. *I* signifies "the person who is uttering the present instance of discourse containing I." This instance is unique by definition and has validity only in its uniqueness. If I perceive two successive instances of discourse containing *I*, uttered in the same voice, nothing guarantees to me that one of them is not a reported discourse, a quotation in which *I* could be imputed to another.

Now this isn't news to poets and isn't even news to Aristotle, Quintillian or Dionysius of Halicarnassus when they speculate on the communication triad in narrative and rhetoric. And poets and writers of fiction have always tended to play with such possibilities of structural ambiguity, to conceal the source (sources) of "voice" among a range of possible identities. This is partly because poets are not—never have been—quite sure who was doing the talking. I am looking now (almost now) at a medieval woodcut of a poet scribe bent over his desk with a small, winged creature whispering into his ear (as Hermes was called The Whisperer in bearing poetic—usually erotic—messages). As Blake tells us in the opening stanzas, a small fairy sat down on his table and dictated *Europe* to him. Or his letter to Thomas Butts on the writing of *Milton*, "I have written this poem from immediate Dictation, twelve or sometimes twenty or thirty lines at a time, without Premeditation & even sometimes against my Will. . . ." Such complications of the plot, among others, *reinforce the notion of poetry (I mean "poetic speech," not just verse)* as hermetic and undisclosed even in its high vatic-prophetic mode, that is, even when as with Blake it is meant as both revealed and revelatory. And it seems fairly obvious that this is the case, that poetry does participate to greater or lesser degree in a dialectic of concealment and revelation, and that the quality of information it can contain derives in great measure from its play within this dynamic. All speech, even "transparent" scientific and logical discourse, participates to some extent. But

what matters here in relation to the subject of this talk is the
insistence of such elements—shifters, tenses, "real time," etc.,
in poetry, poetic speech, particularly its most concentrated
forms. This often results in a radical agrammaticality (by no
means limited to its most obvious current manifestations; a
Shakespeare sonnet could equally serve as a model). Regarding
this, in *The Semiotics of Poetry* Michael Rifaterre observes that
"the arbitrariness of language conventions seems to diminish
as the text becomes more deviant and ungrammatical, rather
than the other way around." Poetry seems often a talking to
self as well as other as well as self as other, a simultaneity that
recognizes the elusive multiplicity of what is called "identity."
It is heuristic, that is, a procedure of discovery within which
identity may appear as negative or in negative. An obvious re-
sult is that autobiographical material locates itself differently
and memory functions differently than in linear narrative. (I'm
not denying that a great deal of poetry is narrative and more
or less discursive.) By foregrounding the inherent complexities
and complex possibilities of discourse, poetic speech often be-
comes paradoxically more direct in its presentation than ap-
parently simpler forms of writing; the evasions, displacements,
recurrences, etc., stand as an immediate part of the message. I
have been describing how autobiographical and confessional
modes (those that name their function as one of disclosure)
tend often to increase concealedness by masking or disregard-
ing certain elements of discourse. By contrast, in proposing a
different relationship to experience, time, memory, as well as
the act of composition, the apparently hidden nature of much
poetic language may inform both recognition and presence.
Put another way, what is taken as *a sign of* openness—conven-
tional narrative order—may stand for concealment, and what
are understood generally as *signs of* withholding or evasion—el-
lipsis, periphrasis, etc.—may from another point of view stand
for disclosure. I want to mention, as a recent instance of what I
am referring, to Lyn Hejinian's *My Life,* where autobiographical

material organizes itself according to a *melos* or melodic procedure. Given the limited usefulness of such categories, it seems to me an amazing transformation of narrative into an extended lyric mode, resulting in an altered relationship to the apparent "data" of personal experience. Time undergoes reversals and returns, and syntax is explicitly equated with "story" such that each sentence "has to be the whole story" within the story of the whole. In the introduction to *Mind and Nature* from which I quoted at the beginning of this talk, Bateson says, "In truth, the right way to begin to think about the pattern which connects is to think of it as *primarily* (whatever that means) a dance of interacting parts and only secondarily pegged down by various sorts of physical limits and by those limits which organisms characteristically impose." In relation to this, I think also of Proust's attempt to transmute not memory but remembering into experience. And a day or two after receiving *My Life*, David Bromige's *My Poetry* arrived—two possessives in one week. I'll finish with the opening section of Rimbaud's *A Season in Hell* as translated by Paul Schmidt:

> Once, if my memory serves me well, my life was a banquet where every heart revealed itself, where every wine flowed.
>
> One evening I took Beauty in my arms—and I thought her bitter—and I insulted her.
>
> I steeled myself against justice.
>
> I fled. O witches, O misery, O hate, my treasure was left in your care. . . .
>
> I have withered within me all human hope. With the silent leap of a sullen beast, I have downed and strangled every joy.
>
> I have called for executioners; I want to perish chewing on their gun butts. I have called for plagues, to suffocate in sand and blood. Unhappiness has been my god. I have lain down in the mud and dried myself off in the crime-infested air. I have played the fool to the point of madness.
>
> And springtime brought me the frightful laugh of an idiot.

Now recently, when I found myself ready to croak! I thought to seek the key to the banquet of old, where I might find an appetite again.

That key is Charity. (This idea proves I was dreaming!)

"You will stay a hyena, etc...." shouts the demon who once crowned me with such pretty poppies. "Seek death with all your desires, and all selfishness, and all the Seven Deadly Sins."

Ah, I've taken too much of that: still, dear Satan, don't look so annoyed, I beg you! And while waiting for a few belated cowardices, since you value in a writer all lack of descriptive or didactic flair, I pass you these few foul pages from the diary of a Damned Soul.

[*Talk given at New Langton Street, 1980. First published in* Hills 8 (1981) *and* Writings/Talks, *edited by Bob Perelman (Southern Illinois University Press, Carbondale and Edwardsville, 1985.*]

ACKNOWLEDGMENTS

Thanks to the many publishers and individuals for permission to reprint the following texts: "I Know a Man" by Robert Creeley from *The Collected Poems of Robert Creeley, 1945–1975* (University of California Press, 2006). Copyright © 2006 by the Estate of Robert Creeley; "Yes, As A Look Springs To Its Face" by Robert Duncan, from *The Opening of the Field* (New Directions, 1973). Copyright © 1960 Robert Duncan; "O Western Wind," "Thus . . . ," and excerpts of "Psalm" and "Of Being Numerous" by George Oppen, from *New Collected Poems* (New Directions, 2002). Copyright © 2002 by Linda Oppen; Excerpt from the letters of George Oppen in *The Selected Letters of George Oppen*, (Duke University Press, 1990); "The Face," and excerpts from the "Danté Etudes" and "A Seventeenth Century Suite in Homage to the Metaphysical Genius in English Poetry" by Robert Duncan, from *Ground Work: Before the War In the Dark* (New Directions, 2006). Copyright © 1984, 1987 by Robert Duncan; "Phloxes in Town," and excerpts from "Poetry-And-Silence" and "Sleep-And-Poetry" by Gennady Aygi in *Child-And-Rose*, trans. by Peter France (New Directions, 2003). Copyright © 2002, 2003 by Gennady Aygi and Peter France; Excerpts from "What I Heard about Iraq" by Eliot Weinberger in *What Happened Here* (New Directions, 2005). Copyright © 2005 by Eliot Weinberger; Excerpt from *The Origins of Totalitarianism* by Hannah Arendt (Schocken Books, 2004); Excerpt from Ron Padgett's translation of Guillaume Apollinaire's "Zone" is used by permission of the translator; "Black Earth" by Osip Mandelstam, from *The Moscow and Voronezh Notebooks*, trans. by Richard and Elizabeth McKane (Bloodaxe Books, 2003). Reprinted with permission from the Publisher; "Arc" by Michael Palmer, from *The Company of Moths* (New Directions, 2005). Copyright © 2005 by Michael Palmer; Excerpt from *On the Genealogy of Morals* by Friedrich Nietzsche, trans. by Walter Kaufmann (Vintage Books, 1989); Excerpt from *Memory for Forgetfulness* by Mahmoud Darwish, trans. by Ibrahim Muhawi (University of California Press, 1995); "Sonnet 3" by Robert Duncan, from *Roots and Branches* (New Directions, 1969). Copyright © 1964 by Robert Duncan; "Rime: 15" by Dante Alighieri, from *Dante's Rime*, trans. by Patrick S. Diehl (Princeton University Press, 1979); Excerpt from "Conversation about Dante" by Osip Mandelstam, trans. by Clarence Brown and Robert Hughes. Copyright © 1971 by the translators; Excerpt from *The Revolution of the Mind: The Life of André Breton* by Mark Polizzotti (Black Widow Press, 2008); Excerpt from *Critical Dictionary* by George Bataille in *Encyclopaedia Acephalica*, trans. by Iain White et al. (Atlas Press, 1996); Fragment of *The Garden of Effort* by Keith Waldrop (Burning Deck Press, 1975); "The Snow Man" by Wallace Stevens, from *The Collected Poems of Wallace Stevens*, copyright © 1954 by Wallace Stevens and renewed 1982 by Holly Stevens. Used by permission of Alfred A. Knopf, a division of Random House, Inc; Excerpt from *Kora in Hell* by William Carlos Williams in *Imaginations* (New Directions, 1970); Excerpt from *Gadamer on Celan* by Hans-Georg Gadamer, trans. by Richard Heinemann and Bruce Krajewski (State University of New York Press, 1997); "These" by William Carlos Williams, from *The Collected Poems of WCW: Volume 1: 1909–1939* (New Directions, 1991). Copyright © 1938 by New Directions; Fragment of Khlebnikov from *Collected Works of Velimir Khlebnikov: Volume III*, trans. by Paul Schmidt (Harvard University Press, 1998); Excerpt from *Confronting Silence* by Toru Takemitsu, trans. by Yoshiko Kakudo and Glenn Glasow (Fallen Leaf Press, 1995); Excerpt from *Pessoa & Co.* by Fernando Pessoa, trans. by Richard Zenith; and excerpt from Zenith's Introduction (Grove/Atlantic, 1999); Excerpt from "The End and the Beginning" in *View with a Grain of Sand*, copyright © 1993 by Wislawa Szymborska, English translation by Stanislaw Baranczak and Clare Cavanaugh copyright © 1995 by Houghton Mifflin Harcourt Publishing Company, reprinted by permission of the publisher; Excerpt from "The Meridian" by Paul Celan in *Collected Prose*, trans. by Rosmarie Waldrop (The Sheep Meadow Press, 1986); Excerpt from "For Paul Celan" by Andrea Zanzotto, trans. by Pierre Joris, from *Paul Celan:*